AF557769

THE SEDUCTIONS OF KARL MARX

THE SEDUCTIONS OF KARL MARX

Murzban Jal

THE SEDUCTIONS OF KARL MARX
Murzban Jal

First Published, 2010

ISBN 978-93-5002-021-0 (Hb)

Published by
AAKAR BOOKS
28 E Pocket IV, Mayur Vihar Phase I, Delhi-110 091
Phone : 011-2279 5505 Telefax : 011-2279 5641
aakarbooks@gmail.com; www.aakarbooks.com

Printed at
Arpit Printographers, Delhi-110 032
E-mail : arpitprinto@yahoo.com

Contents

Preface

The global economic crisis that is driving dialectics into the heads of the world bourgeoisie can be heard in various forms. Despite "the universality of its theatre and intensity of its action", as Marx once famously said, which "will drum dialectics even into the heads of the mushroom-upstarts of the new, holy Prussian-German empire", the bourgeoisie has become half deaf, half theological, half converted into the old religion of the management of capitalism, the other half into the new religion of political theology. The managers and the theologians each have their respective views on the crisis. The managers say that social engineering will get capitalism back on its feet; the theologians say that God has once again got angry. One thing is clear, the managers and theologians march hand-in-hand—from Washington to Islamabad, Kabul and New Delhi. But what both miss out on is the proletariat which is interested in neither management economics, nor in theology.

The twentieth century witnessed the first wave of socialism starting with the Bolshevik Revolution and ending with the Stalinist counter-revolution. Just as the crisis of the twenty-first century is dressed in the gowns of the managers and the theologians, Stalinism (and all its revisionist forms that swore by the name of Marx) too was dressed up. But 1991 witnessed the tearing of the veils and gowns of the Stalinists. Out marched Stalin, and in marched Francis Fukuyama accompanied by Condoleezza Rice and George Bush, not to forget Osama Bin Laden and L.K. Advani. The managers and theologians took centre stage of world history. Marxism, we were told, is dead.

But then the crisis of global capitalism marched into this little theatre of history. And alongside the storm and stress of this crisis was seen marching, a certain Karl Marx. The second wave of socialism has begun. Its theatre is universal, its action intense. Consequently, it is not the epitaph of Marx that needs to be written, but the epitaph of capitalism. And this time it has to be final.

It is difficult to think of everyone who contributed to the making of this book. The name of the nameless proletariat, of course, comes up first. But there are also other names that do come up. I would like to thank first D.P. Chattopadhyaya and Bhuvan Chandel. Javeed Alam read the entire manuscript and for this I am extremely grateful. I would also like to thank A.V. Afonso, Ishwar Singh Dost, Mohinder Kumar, Asghar Ali Engineer, Daniel Raveh, Uday Chouhan, Arvind Ghosh, Pratyush Chandra and Surinder Jodhka. I cannot forget my two brothers Hoshi and Homiyar and my sister-in-law Nandini, as also Satyabhama Kharat and her three children, especially Amar. Last I would like to thank the publisher, K.K. Saxena of Aakar Books and editor Ritu Singh who made it possible for this book to be realized.

Introduction

Perseus wore a magic cap that the monsters he hunted down might not see him. We draw the magic cap over eyes and ears as a make-believe that there are no monsters.

—Karl Marx, *Capital*, Vol. I.

Philosophy, so it was once said, is the beloved quest for wisdom. As Sophia, philosophy danced like the dancing dervishes. But philosophy stopped dancing. It became a type of onanism and castration anxiety.[1] It thus became the sign of a great loss—the biblical 'fall' where humanity lies in ruins. But then philosophy recovered from this trauma and became not a loss, but a surplus, a surplus of joy as well as a surplus emptied in emptiness, and thus a return to onanism, loss and human estrangement.

This work is on the three principles of philosophy—wisdom, loss and surplus-loss. This work simultaneously becomes a study of radical thinking in the dark caves of imperialism, world conquest and territorialization of the earth. Then philosophy becomes a seduction and the original understanding of philosophy as the love of wisdom returns as the emancipated dervish—the desiring seducer. We have thus the fourth understanding of philosophy—the return of wisdom as the dancing dervish.

"In late capitalism", so Theodor Adorno once remarked, "the regression to magical thinking is readily accepted".[2] Right-wing politics is the best representation of this type of 'magical thinking' wherein operates not real history but its very opposite: mythology. Mythology in the age of late capitalism is (to recall

Adorno again) a "bewitchment of history".[3] Marx's materialist conception of history is a study of this bewitched history. Now this being bewitched remains central to Marx's understanding of the capitalist mode of production. Modernity, as capitalist modernity, is living with spectres. In *Capital*, Marx says that what forms the groundwork of commodity production is not so much science and technology, but in fact its very opposite: mythology, theology, mysticism, magic and necromancy.[4] To produce commodities implies the necromantic art of calling the spirits of the dead. Like Faust, we play around with these necromantic forces, and like Hamlet we are haunted by the spirits of the dead. Capital flows are the neurotic recurrence of this principle of death, wherein dwells not reason but madness. "We suffer", as Marx notes, "not only from the living, but from the dead. *Le mort saist le vif* !"[5] *We are seized by the dead!*

So, alongside Marx we go into the deep pits where the dead are buried in order to understand our contemporary life-world. Marx, who discovered the continent of knowledge (to borrow Louis Althusser's excellent expression)[6]—history—was also the one who discovered the art of counter-necromancy—how to go into the deep interiors of human civilization in order to understand ourselves. "Know thyself!" This great Delphic statement sends Marx into the underworld of human reason, what one may call "the dark pit" or "the black hole of alienation (*Entfremdung*)". In fact, the more the forces of production develop under capitalism, the deeper we move in this black hole. Imperialism, whether under the liberal or fascist garb, is the movement into this dark pit. The latest name of this pit is 'globalization'. One has to consciously move away from this metaphysics of capital flows in order that true human reason be rendered possible.

This book portrays Marx differently from many of his portraits. It takes up Georg Lukács's notion of the reification of consciousness and links it with Freud's psychosis, in particular, and mental illness, in general, and then engages Marx's idea of the *estranged mind*. Though it was known since the late 1920s, with the discovery of Marx's *Economic and Philosophic Manuscripts of 1844*, that human estrangement is not only the fundamental problem of modern capitalism but also of the history of class societies—a feature anticipated by Lukács's *History and Class Consciousness* and later used by the Frankfurt School—the relation between estrangement and class struggle had to be further investigated both at the philosophical as well as the empirical levels. Second, one needed to relate human estrangement with two other of Marx's ideas: reification and fetishism, especially in relation with his celebrated chapter in *Capital*: 'The Fetishism of Commodities and the Secret Thereof'. Though the line of thinking known as 'Western Marxism', from Lukács and the Frankfurt School onwards, brought these three categories in the analysis of the distortions of the human mind in late capitalism, the logical order of these three categories was left largely unexplored. This book consequently engages the philosophical mechanisms of alienation-reification-fetishism and relates it with the social and political life-worlds of the twenty-first century.

The book begins with the concrete (sociology and political science) and moves on to the abstract (philosophy). It thus begins with a concrete problem—the problem of the state and the hegemony of the religious right-wing in the period of what now one may call: "late imperialism in crisis". It then argues out for a humanist and subaltern response to the authoritarianism of the bourgeois state that is manufacturing the spectres of political theology. It grounds this idea in India where it analyses the emergence of the religious-right by relating the ideology of the communal-fascists with Lukács's notion of the reification of consciousness. In contrast to the liberal response to communal-fascism, which mentions the need for the separation of religion from the state and the effective control of the liberal state to deal with the religious-right, this work chalks out an alternative form of revolutionary democracy in the form of mobilizing people on the issue of the transcendence of the state itself by differentiating the religion of the religious-right from the popular culture of the subaltern masses.

After dealing with the issue of the estranged mind of the religious-right, the book explores what India meant to Marx. It highlights Marx's almost forgotten idea of the Asiatic mode of production and relates it with global capitalism and the twin issues of the caste system in India and Marx's fundamental idea of class struggle. It argues that Marx left a space where the caste system becomes not only fundamental for scientific analysis but the core issue for the struggle for democracy in India. From this dialectical engagement of caste and modern classes, the book deals with the problem of globalization and how Marxism can philosophically and politically deal with it. It grounds the understanding of global capitalism in Marx's theory of reification where reification is defined as a process where people are dehumanized and inanimate objects are given life. Now it is well known that the theory of reification was not only central to Marx but also to Freud. For both Marxism and psychoanalysis, the inanimate objects that are given life terrorize humanity. The distorted consciousness that emerges in late imperialism is a response to this reification itself. Now in this setting—of humanity being rendered lifeless and conversely capital being given magical life—capital appears as a monster. Globalization is thus portrayed not merely as a prosperous world governed by the sciences and technology but the world of the monster—Monsieur Capital who, along with his unwelcome fiends: the religious-right, the warfare economy and the authoritarian state are raiding the world.

In order to deal with the raid of these spectres, Marx mobilizes critical philosophy, literature and the sciences to deal with them. When it is firmly understood that the religious-right and capital accumulation are monsters that humanity itself has produced and that there is a philosophical inspired method to deal with it, the work takes up the issue of Marx's philosophy, especially the double role of transcending as well as realizing it. This double role of philosophy has not been dealt with even in the space of pure philosophy; forget in the sociological and political applications. Marx's idea of the estranged mind crops up again but now in the philosophical perspective—especially with regard to the question: "What did Hegel in particular and philosophy in general mean to Marx?" Once this question is dealt with and once the aetiology of the estranged mind is outlined, the alternative reform and revolutionizing of consciousness is made possible. Communism, after all, is possible only when this reform and revolution of the mind is performed.

This work, in dealing with political and philosophical sociology, engages the original German terminologies of Marx—*Entfremdung, Aufhebung, Verwirklichung*, etc.—so as to keep the original philosophic flavour alive and not to confuse it with English translations, which are usually contaminated by Anglo-Saxon positivist meanings. This work then engages his entire philosophic repertoire from his early studies on Hegel to the critique of alienation and the capitalist mode of production. Behind this reading of the original structures of Marx's repertoire, one will be able to get a glimpse of the history of Marxism, where the voices of Engels, Gramsci, Lukács, Althusser, the Frankfurt School and Slavoj Žižek will be heard in the background.

This book comprises seven chapters. The first chapter, 'Reification and Communal-Fascism' deals with the political issue of the emergence of the right-wing in India in the times of economic and cultural globalization. It makes a distinction between the traditional and liberal definition of secularism as the separation between religion and the state and Marx's own understanding of revolutionary secularism as the *Aufhebung* (abolition-preservation-supersession) of both religion and the state that itself would be premised on the *Aufhebung* of class domination, private property and human alienation. The principal point of the argument is that the Marxist critique of the Ideological State Apparatus focuses its attention not on the illusions that the religious right creates. Nor is one to be bewitched by the allegedly clashing civilizations: 'Hindu', 'Muslim', 'Christian', etc. On the contrary, Marxist attention turns towards the double sites of capital accumulation in the period of late imperialism and the reification consequently produced. Reification is literally 'thingification' (*Verdinglichung, Versachlichung*), where humanity becomes a sort of 'fetish-thing'. But humanity is also horrified by the conversion into this 'fetish-thing'. Bewitched history involves the play between the animation of the dead object world (commodity-money-capital-state) and de-humanized humanity. In the process, in the horror in becoming a fetish-thing, a new duplicate world of mythological fantasies is created. Neo-conservatism, whether in the forms of the American religious-right, the Hindutvavadis in India, the global Wahabis or the Iranian Shiites are practitioners of the phantasmagorical politics of this fetish-thing. In this sense the liberal prescription of the separation of religion and the state is nothing but the suggestion that two fantasies ought to be separated.

The second chapter, 'Whither India?' deals with the rather thorny issues of class and the Indian caste system under Marx's original identification of an Asiatic mode of production, a forgotten issue that has condemned Marx as a Euro-centric thinker. Nothing could be further from the truth. Now this condemnation of Marx as a Hegelian European fellow traveller was not only the fallacy that Edward Said practised. Indian 'Marxists', like Irfan Habib, have also fallen into this erroneous line of thinking.[7] This chapter brings in the subaltern reading of 'Indian' history first highlighted by the great nineteenth-century reformist Jyotirao Phule, a practice continued and perfected by Babasaheb Ambedkar. This chapter highlights the myths of dominance of the ruling Indian elites and the subaltern inversions of the myths. It argues that Marxism should be involved with the politics of the radical subalterns, rather than waiting for a Messianic 'class' (a Samuel Beckettean 'class' that never comes) to appear on the scene of world history. Even in the age of late imperialism, now called 'globalization', the Asiatic mode of production yet exists, but now in the political economy of being part of the centre-periphery dialectic of global capital accumulation. Just as the way Marx said that "capital is not a thing, but rather a definite social production relation ... which is manifested in a thing ..."[8], so too one states that both class and castes are not 'things' but social processes that appear as things.

The third chapter, 'The Sorcerer and His Apprentice: Globalization and Culture' deals with capitalism as a living organism—a living organism like Frankenstein, which was created by humanity, but now, in a monstrous rage, is devouring the very creator. The latest name of this rage is 'globalization'.

Everyone wants to be globalized—not only the American and European bourgeoisie, but also the whole of Asia, not to forget the former Soviet bloc. But why does everyone want to be a part of this terror? Why do people give consent to these monsters that are devouring them? To explain this, an understanding of the ideological superstructure is required. Culture is not only a material practice. It is also a desiring machine. The estranged mind desires the devouring fetishes.

The fourth chapter, 'The Return of the Emancipated: On Karl Marx's Question: How is the transcendence (*Aufhebung*) and realization (*Verwirklichung*) of Philosophy Possible?' deals with the makings of the epistemic mechanisms of Marx's philosophy. It deals with the pertinent question: how is the philosophy of emancipation possible, considering that by the time he had raised this question (1843-44) he was already holding the view that *philosophy as philosophy* (i.e. the complete history of philosophy) was only the alien mind pretending to be authentic and objective. Yet Marx never argued for either a 'post-philosophy' or a positivist inspired 'scientistic' method. Instead, Marx said that philosophy ought not to be the uninspiring onanism—a false act that mimes a false belief system, a masturbation that represses the joy of libidinal economy—and an act that causes death itself.[9] In this book, the theme of the double binding of the biblical and Platonic themes are bound together as the ground structure of Western Reason. This same ground structure of the duplicated and false act is then related to Freud's notion of "the uncanny" (*das Unheimlich*), where the uncanny is said to be the source of the double feelings of the arousal of dread and then death itself. Philosophy then is said to be the summation of the principles of dread and death. And, as both dread and death it manifests itself as a spectre. Philosophy is then nothing but a spectre and a quest for the ideal ghost. The *Aufhebung* and *Verwirklichung* deal with the chasing of these spectres.

The next chapter, 'Georg Lukács and the Problem of Romantic Aesthetics' deals with the Romantic obsession with aesthetics. For the Romantics, more than any type of 'scientific' knowledge, it is aesthetics that deals with the 'true' and the 'good'. But for the Romantics more than the aesthetics of the 'beautiful' it is the aesthetics of the 'ugly' that forms the leitmotif of their work. Lukács stood at the crossroads of the beautiful and the ugly. But then, he also stood at the crossroads of revolution and the Stalinist counter-revolution. By 1917, Lukács had already transcended Nietzsche, the mystics and Max Weber. *History and Class Consciousness* —a work in left-wing Marxism— was the fruit of this radical rupture. But when this work was attacked by the Communist Party of the Soviet Union, he decided not to tread on the path that he had tread. Thus the question: "How is revolution possible in the age of reification?" was almost entirely forgotten by him—the Frankfurt School would pick up this theme. Lukács became Hamlet, the slain prince of the International Revolution. But Shakespeare's Hamlet at least saw the ghost of his murdered father. He at least heard the words: "The snake that killed thy father, now wears his crown". But Lukács did not hear the words: *the Stalinists that murdered the Revolution now wear the Leninist crown.* So now, if one spots any ghosts one should be able to differentiate the evil spectre that Marx the seducer and exorcist was expelling from the human life-world, from the ghost of the Bolshevik Revolution.

But history (contrary to the evangelic American doctrine of Fukuyama) did not end. And if the imperialists think that victory is of liberal capitalism and the whole world is with great joy embracing the American project, then there would be not only marks of errors attached to this statement, but also blood and madness. The sixth chapter deals with the idea of justice and equality—in a way, part of all world historical revolutions—and the contemporary liberal reification of these ideas. Phantasmagoria implies this 'magical' mode of transfiguration—to transform humanity into 'thinghood'. Psychosis, the dreadful mental illness in the age of late capitalism, is the illusory escape from this thinghood, but an escape not into the essential humanity of the real life-world, but an escape into delusions. The chapter, 'Psychosis and Phantasmagoria: Reading Justice and Equality in the Text of Marx's Suspicion' is a study of the slippages into the worlds of phantasmagoria and psychosis. Now both liberalism and fascism have mastered the macabre art of slipping into psychosis. The chapter argues that the bourgeois idea of equality is a definite step ahead of the feudal understanding of the essential inequality of people. But this bourgeois idea is in fact a *reified equality*, which masks the essential economic inequalities within society. Instead, Marx insists that one ought not to look through the bourgeois spectacles of the judiciary superstructure, but beyond the class world of estranged boundaries and thus look into the worlds of what he himself called *das menschlichen Wesen*, or simply the human essence, a *Wesen* that is radically distinct from the *Wesen* of 'thinghood' and delusions. And so Marx takes us not into the deep interiors of class civilizations, i.e. not into the world of Aristotle (the ideologist of the slave mode of production and the father of Western Reason) but into the *Book of Genesis* itself where the monist God is understood as the transfiguration of the slave owner, the feudal master and the ravaging bourgeois.

The last chapter continues with this line of thinking and proceeds into the deep interiors of Reason. In 'Human Rites: The Death and the Birth of the Subject', historical materialism studies the onto-genesis of class histories where the commodity is understood in its very basic form, in fact its "economic cell-form" itself.[10] The commodity bound to the principle of estrangement is the basis of the transfiguration of ideas. Thus, when the so-called 'civilized' world talks of human rights, they in fact imply the exact opposite—human rites. The deep interiors of Class Reason appear again. Yet it is not so much the Socrates-Plato-Aristotle triumvirate, but the Holy trinity of Adam-Eve-Moses that forms the groundwork of Western Reason. What is called human rights is in actuality bourgeois reason: Human rites, the slaughter and sacrifice of humanity to the gods (money-capital-state). The Holy Trinity of the Father, the Son and the Holy Spirit, which for Marx were capital, land and labour[11] has now become the Holy Trinity of money-capital-state. One needs to exorcise these ghosts in order that authentic humanity may be rendered possible. Marx the revolutionary is thus at the same time Marx the exorcist.

And because of these haunted fetishes, thinking under class

societies gets subject to confusion; Marx—the humanist, exorcist and seducer—becomes a *de facto* necessity. What Marx repeatedly called, *the necessity of communism*, may be reframed as, *the necessity of being seduced*.

REFERENCES

1. Karl Marx and Friedrich Engels, *The German Ideology* (Moscow: Progress Publishers, 1976), pp. 243-4: "Philosophy and the study of the actual world have the same relation to one another as onanism and sexual life". The idealist philosopher, "does not become a man of the world", so Marx continues, but becomes a "bankrupt philosopher without thoughts".
2. Theodor Adorno, 'Thesis against Occultism', in *Telos*, No. 19 (1974).
3. Theodor Adorno, 'The Idea of Natural History', in *Telos*, No. 60 (1984).
4. Karl Marx, *Capital*, Vol. I, trans. Samuel Moore and Edward Aveling (Moscow: Progress Publishers, 1984), pp. 76-7, 80.
5. Ibid, p. 20.
6. Louis Althusser, *Lenin and Philosophy and Other Essays*, trans. Ben Brewtster (London: Monthly Review Press, 1971), pp. 15, 38, 39, 42, 99; *Montesquieu, Rousseau, Marx. Politics and History*, trans Ben Brewster (London: Verso, 1982), pp, 166-7, 186; *The Humanist Controversy and Other Writings*, trans G.M. Goshgarian (London: Verso, 2003), p. 173.
7. Irfan Habib in 'Introduction: Marx's Perception of India' in *Karl Marx on India*, ed. Iqbal Husain (New Delhi: Tulika Books, 2006), p. XXI says that "Marx repeats, giving an identical description for which he quotes *in extenso* from what was probably Hegel's authority…"
8. Karl Marx, *Capital*, Vol. III (Moscow: Progress Publishers, 1986), p. 814.
9. In the *Book of Genesis*, Onan is the son of Judah who is told by the Jewish god to go to his slain brother's wife and "perform the duty of a brother-in-law to her, and raise up offspring for your brother", Onan went to his sister-in-law but ejaculated on the ground, thereby causing god to be angry and thus god slew Onan. See 'Genesis', 38, 7, in *The Holy Bible* (New York: WM. Collins, 1953, p. 34). Onanism is masturbation plus death. And philosophy for Marx is not only a type of onanism, but this act of premature ejaculation implies ignorance as well as death.
10. Karl Marx, *Capital*, Vol. I, p. 19.
11. Karl Marx, *Capital*, Vol. III, p. 814.

CHAPTER 1

Reification and Communal-Fascism

Man has value because he is man, not because he is Jew, Catholic, Protestant, Italian, etc.

—Hegel, *The Philosophy of Right*.

But almost all our leaders continued to think within the narrow steel frame of the existing political, and of course the social structure. They faced every problem—communal or constitutional—with this background and, inevitably, they played into the hands of the British Government, which completely controlled that structure. They could not do otherwise, for their world outlook was reformist and not revolutionary, in spite of occasional experiments with direct action. But the time had gone by when any political or economic or communal problem could be satisfactorily solved by reformist methods. Revolutionary outlook and planning and revolutionary solution were demanded by the situation. But there was no one among the leaders to offer these.

— Jawaharlal Nehru, *An Autobiography*.

The hegemony of the extreme right-wing Rashtriya Swayam-sewak Sangh (RSS) formed in the 1920s in colonial India, and its political wing the Bharatiya Janta Party (BJP), coincides with the coming of globalization in India, if not the heralding of globalization as the official economic state policy of the Indian government. Whilst communalism in the west European sense implies communitarianism or the sociology of the pre-modern *Gemeinschaft* viewed against modern industrialized society (*Gesellschaft*), communalism in India and Asia is seen as what one may call 'estranged communitarianism' or the world view of primordial identities and conflicting religions. The communalists of whatever religious shade share a very specific and concrete ideology. This communal ideology is composed of the following: (*i*) primacy of religion, (*ii*) religious communities defined as homogeneous communities, (*iii*) shared experiences of these religious communities from a given apocalyptic time (for the Hindus with the *Rg Veda* for the Christians with the *Bible* and with the Muslims with the *Koran*), (*iv*) anthropological and political endogamy that views the other with suspicion and hostility, (*v*) the myth of the community as 'national' identity, (*vi*) consent to violence, and (*vii*) the myth of the realization of religious nationhood through religious wars. The communalists have two main enemies: liberalism and Marxism. In contemporary India, communalism manifests itself as communal-fascism and can best be defined as the cultural and political logic of late imperialism in crisis. It is expressed in India as the 'national' conflicts between Hindus, Muslims, Sikhs, etc. In pluralist and multi-cultural India, which is composed of a number of religious, linguistic and cultural identities, communalism implies a direct challenge to secular democracy and the unified Indian nation-state itself. Besides being based on the myth of a racial-religious community, communalism is also based on the psychopathology of the authoritarian and sadomasochistic personality.

In India, whilst the RSS (which borrows its ideology from Nazism) is the representation of communalism-in-hegemony (sometimes called 'majority communalism'), communalism is actually represented by a number of communal parties, the Jamaat-e-Islami and the Tabligi-Jamaat being the main activist fronts for the mobilization of communalism in the Sunni Muslim masses.

The aim of this chapter is to examine the mechanisms of communalism and to find out whether a rigorous aetiology of religious politics is possible. It principally asks: why have the masses been giving consent to the communal politics of the Rashtriya Swayamsewak Sangh over the last decade? How does the communal right-wing have its hegemony over mass consciousness? How is it possible to break the hegemony of the right-wing Ideological Apparatus wielded by the right-wing religious parties? In this sense, how is popular resistance to communalism possible?

Fascism cannot think. Fascism cannot philosophize. Yet fascism has had a philosopher in the name of Martin Heidegger. What is the core structure of fascism? According to the *Thirteenth Enlarged Executive of the Communist International Plenum on 'Fascism, the War Danger, and the Tasks of the Communist Parties'*, fascism is "the open, terrorist dictatorship of the most reactionary, most chauvinist and most imperialist elements of finance capital".[1]

But, one may ask, how is the dictatorship of finance capital able to grip the masses? How does fascism become a mass movement? According to Heidegger's *Introduction to Metaphysics*, there is "an inner truth and greatness" of fascism, this alleged greatness which would be a "spiritual renewal of life in its entirety" as well as a "deliverance of western Dasein", as he would write to his one-time student Herbert Marcuse, "from the dangers of communism".[2] Not only does fascism save the world from communism, it is also said to rescue civilization from mass society and the brutality of technological society.

For Heidegger, fascism is the culmination of the "destiny of Being" (*Geschlichk des Seins*). Being (*Sein*) is not realized in the Hegelian Absolute Idea where freedom and subjectivity rule, but in the fascist politics of blood and soil. Fascism always seeks this primordiality where the metaphysics of Being is mixed with blood and soil. Whilst primordial Being is the metaphysical base of communal-fascism, the nation defined as the 'Race Spirit' is the representor of this primordiality. National fascist memory is said to lie deep in these archaic images. The makings of a 'Hindu nation state', the 'Muslim community state', etc. lie deep in this archaic Being. To understand communalism in India, one will have to understand this politics of the archaic, for communalism is nestled deep down in this metaphysical longing for the relics of an *Ur*-past. The anti-secular and anti-modern politics of the communalists has to be explored in this site of pre-history. When one has defined communalism as the cultural and political logic of late imperialism, one claims that late imperialism and communalism are manifested as the political economy of global capital accumulation and the underdevelopment emerging thereon. The political economy of the abundance and underdevelopment of capital accumulation and the philosophical critique of estrangement (*Entfremdung*) and reification (*Verdinglichung*) are the keys to the understanding of primordial identities.

This chapter lays the groundwork for the inquiry into the mechanisms of consent and resistance to communalism. First, it understands communalism in Marx's critique of reification whereby it relates Marx's concepts of the human essence (*das menschliche Wesen*) and class struggle with the communal question. In this theoretical space it raises the question of the necessity for the creation of a radical social-psychology, understood as the revolutionary will of the popular masses. Second, it inquires into how *communalism-in-hegemony* functions as the cultural and political logic of monopoly capital accumulation in the age of globalization and third, it inquires into the secular resistance to communalism.

Let us begin, not by entering the catastrophic ghettoes of communalism, but by posing the question of secularism. What is secularism, and what is its relevance in the twenty-first century? What is the world view of this *saeculum*, the ideology that proclaims the birth of 'worldliness' and the philosophy of the being-in-the world? What is this 'worldliness' of secularist discourse? Is it a proclamation of a de-ritualized and de-theologized world, a world now to be comprehended as a rational process, where reason supersedes faith? What is this thesis of separation of religion from the state? Is it to be understood within the process of world history or solely as a product of the European Reformation and the Enlightenment? Should one extend this thesis to the separation of religion from civil society also? How then should one conceive of an autonomous civil society that is not to be imprisoned by the fetters of the political state, nor by religion?

Or is this political notion of secularism only one type of rendering of secularism? Are there several types of secularism?

Is secularism, an *overdeterminate* term, hence *complexly structured* and reaching towards newer meanings? Is there a historicity to the question of the secular? Are these different types of the secular tied down to historical modes of production? Is it specific only to the struggle against feudalism and colonialism? Consequently, is it necessary to rework this concept in the age of monopoly-globalized capitalism and the struggle against RSS fascism?

My point is that one cannot uncritically work on the currently dominant political thesis of the mere separation of religion from the state in order to find an answer either to ethnic and religious struggles or to the rise of the global neo-conservative right-wing parties to power. There is a deeper structure to this question. Marx, in *On the Jewish Question*, critiqued this surface method of perceiving religious conflicts. He distinguishes between political emancipation and human emancipation. Secularism of the liberal varieties by and large coincides with the former, not the latter. On the other hand, the growth of right-wing politics coincides with the growth of reification (*Verdinglichung* or *Versachlichung*) of capitalist society. Literally, reification implies "thingification", which is further characterized as a personification of things (or the animation of inanimate objects) and a de-personification of humanity. Both imperialism and communal-fascism are perfections of this de-personified humanity.

This chapter departs from the usual liberal secular studies. It in fact asks how it is possible to radicalize the idea of the secular and how one should simply jump over the liberal variations on the theme of secularism. This great leap forward encounters three themes: (i) the psycho-pathology of everyday life, (ii) surplus-repression as the organization of late capitalism, and (iii) Marx's critique of political economy, which combines labour and desire and thus involves the critique of reification-repression in order to critique the communal question itself. In this theoretical space, it makes a distinction between traditional secularism and radical secularism. It is to these questions that attention must now turn.

Secularism and the Question of Marxism

Many souls dwell within the breast of secularism in India. Whilst secularism is claimed to be indispensable (Javeed Alam), rooted in the process of acquiring rights (Aijaz Ahmad), rational and necessary (Achin Vanaik), faith based (Asghar Ali Engineer), there is also the antithetical view of secularism as a purely European and Christian phenomenon not applicable to India (Ashish Nandy, T.N. Madan, Partha Chatterjee). There is yet another view that secularism is a vacuous term (Jakob De Roover). Politically, it is the left parties who have been most consistent in their views on secularism: anti-secularism is related to imperialism and local reactionary forces.

But what is this secularism that needs to be defended? Etymologically, 'the secular' means 'pertaining to an age or generation', 'lay or civil as against the clerical', 'pertaining to the present world', 'profane', etc. The fundamental tenets of secularism are liberal beliefs, mutual tolerance, cosmopolitanism, non-discrimination and neutrality of state, separation of religion from the state, non-theocratic state, privatization of religion, faith as not above law, non-politicization of religion, multi-culturalism, etc.

Achin Vanaik claims that there are three notions of secularism: (i) as decline of religious institutions, beliefs and practices, (ii) as relative separation or the disengagement of religion, (iii) as growth of rational thought and activity.[3] Aijaz Ahmad relates communalism with the fascist offensive –"the communist must help the liberal centre in reconstructing those premises of Nehruvian social democracy and independent national development which are so much a target of the fascist attack today".[4] Bipan Chandra claims that secularism implies (i) the separation of religion from political, economic, social and cultural aspects of life, where religion is to be treated as a personal matter, (ii) dissociation of the state from religion, (iii) freedom and tolerance of all religions, and (iv) equal opportunities for followers of all religions and no discrimination on grounds of religion.[5] Secularism is shown by all these to be a categorical imperative for the construction of a good society. Most important, it cannot be cast away as a European import.

I shall digress slightly from the question of the secular and go to another epistemic terrain, that of the universal conception of humanity to show that the question of, if not secularism, then humanism is not a purely European phenomenon, but a historical happening occurring at different times in the unfolding of historical modes of production. According to Samir Amin, there are three waves of the ideas of universalizing humanity. The first is in the period dating fifth century B.C. to the seventh century A.D., which comprises the foundations of the great religions, Zoroastrianism, (though Zoroastrianism is said to have been founded around 1200 B.C.) Buddhism, Christianity, and Islam, and with the formulation of the great Confucius and Hellenistic philosophies (Amin should have added the radical Gnostics and the Sufis). The second wave begins with the bourgeois revolutions and the humanist philosophies laid down by the Enlightenment and modernity, which culminates in the French Revolution. The second wave gives birth to the ideas of social contract, the citizen and the free man. The third wave is that of Marxism and the international communist movements, inspired by the philosophy of the Enlightenment and upholding respect for local identities and linguistic and religious minorities.[6]

It is from this nodal point of universalizing humanity that I would argue that the secularist ideals of tolerance, disengagement of religious tyranny, and the espousal of the 'worldliness' of the secular ideal are not to be found solely in European Enlightenment (though the European Enlightenment perfected the science and art of secularism) but also in different societies existing in different forms. Take, for instance, the Iranian concept of the this-worldly material (*gaetya*) world and ancient Indian philosophy's exposition of the *deha-vada*. Materialist and humanist philosophies are found in most societies and so too is found the struggle against religious authoritarianism, just as class struggles are the motor force of all hitherto class societies.

Every society has its specific and concrete idea of the secular. The anti-secularist theme of the secular as a pure European idea and India re-claimed as a pure spiritualist domain is a continuation of the Orientalist type of thinking initiated by William Jones, Friedrich Schlegel and perfected by M.K. Gandhi, A.K. Coomaraswamy and René Guénon. Secularism is not a monopolistic privilege of Western civilization. Secularism, like modernity, democracy, the state and class struggle is constituted within the process of world history. It cannot be debunked as not belonging to Indian civilization. But nor can secularism as liberal politics of the Anglo-Saxon world be viewed as the sole solution to ethnic and religious conflicts. It is from the wresting of the theory and practice of secularism from these positions (and locating it in the dialectics of modes of production) wherein a de-mystification of both Western liberalism and communalism is possible.

The epistemic position of this chapter is the Marxist position. I am arguing the relevance of Marx's philosophy in the debates on secularism and communalism. Consider the Marxist repertoire of dialectical and historical materialism—class struggle, alienation, ideology, revolution and the establishment of classless society. Now, within this perspective of the struggle for socialism, wherein fits the question of secularism? Is it a class compromising reformist ideology, a petty bourgeois false consciousness that dilutes the ideas of the international proletariat revolution? Is it a confusion, a political idealism and a supra-class ideology, deliberately infused in the socialist movement? Or is it an essential aspect of Marxism?

Why, since the last decade, has the issue of proletarian power taken a backseat if not being literally erased from public memory? How and why has the question of Hindu vs. Muslim, mandir vs. masjid, jehadi terrorist vs. innocent nationalist Hindu taken the vantage point in Indian politics? Is there not a forgetfulness of class struggle?

What is the relation between class struggle and the struggle against communalism? Does Marxism conceive of two separate and autonomous sites of operation: (a) class struggle and (b) struggle against communalism? What is the causal relation between these two?

Truth, as Hegel said, exists in the whole.[7] It is from this perspective of dialectical totality, that Marxism differentiates itself from bourgeois philosophies. Marx's conception of class struggle is woven in this very dialectical totality that binds the economic base and the ideological superstructure. The critique of communalism is constituted within this perspective of dialectical totality.

Anti-communal resistance consequently has to operate within this dialectical perspective. Unfortunately, the anti-fascists in India have not grasped this emancipatory aspect of the dialectic and have worked in the antinomy of an economic reductionism on the one hand, and the idealism of liberal secularism (the thesis of the separation of religion from the state) on the other. This antinomy cannot deal with either communalism, in particular, or societal mechanisms, in general. Recall Lenin's statement: the economist treats society in a mechanical and fossilised manner: they thus *cannot pose the political question.*[8] Nicos Poulantzas claimed that there were two effects predicated on economism: (i) lack of mass line and (ii) growing abandonment of internationalism.[9] One has necessarily to transcend this binary of economism and political idealism to reach the kernel of the matter.

The relation between class and ethnicity is not the same as (a reductionist) reality and the (reflected) copy. This relation between class and ethnicity has to be understood in the *historical conjuncture of class struggles*. Class struggle is not to be viewed in the perspective of economic struggles alone (the line of the economists), but also seen in the sites of political and ideological struggles. One cannot claim that one can deal with the economics of class struggle and ethnic and religious struggles will *automatically* disappear. When Marx talked of the economic base *determining* the political and ideological superstructure, he meant a *dialectical binding* forth of the base and superstructure. Ever since the *Economic and Philosophic Manuscripts of 1844*, the question of *determination* was linked to the problematic of *alienation*. Thus determination and alienation were continuously linked to the sites of property relations, class struggle and the production of social consciousness. It is this site of *alienated determination* that would be a clue to the understanding of the hegemony of monopoly capitalism, in general, and communalism, in particular. Analysis will have to shift from the normative realm of liberal secularism to the barracks of historical materialism.

The Communal Question

On the one hand, in India we have the liberal secularists. The theme of *sarva dharma samabhava* or the equality of all faiths, and *dharma nirpekshta* or separation of religion from politics are the leitmotifs of secularism in India. On the other hand, we have the self-appointed religious nationalists, the RSS, the Jamaat-e-Islami, various other groups that form the Hurriyat, various other ethnic groups (and they exist not only in the north east). These religious politicians all share the same code, the abuse of secularism and the manipulation of democracy. Religion, so they say, is the very essence of their identity and social existence. Then how can one separate this very essence, this *dharma*, this God-given faith from social and public life? How can there be a public site, law and the state without this *dharma*? As there can be no morality without this transcendent *dharma*, the state has necessarily to be anchored in religion. And which religion, one may ask? And this is where the clash of the alleged theologians takes place. The alleged religious moralists, in the form of the RSS will answer, religion that is based on the doctrines of *Pitrubhu* (fatherland) and *Punyabhu* (holy land). Consequently, religions that emerge elsewhere are alien religions. Alien religions mean different nations. Thus there would be various nations, the Hindu nation, the Muslim nation, the Christian nation, etc.

Religious essentialism that claims that religion forms the basis of nationhood functions in the paradigm of the *alienation and eternal conflict of the self and other* and the right-wing threat perception of some illusory enemy. It becomes the shared code and motor force of all communalists from V.D. Savarkar and K.B. Hegdewar to Syed Ahmed Khan and M.A. Jinnah. And in multi-cultural and multi-religious India, the plurality of religious-political games means the Balkanization of India besides the establishment of totalitarian fascist rule. The anti-communalists have long since exposed the politics of these religious essentialists as being anti-people and connected to imperialist politics with fascism as their political model. Remember that by 1937-38, when the extreme right-wing shift took place in the politics of the Hindu Mahasabha, the RSS and the Muslim League, fascism was triumphant in Europe. The communalists already had a readymade model of mass mobilization from the European fascists. For all communalists, whether the RSS or the Islamists, what is important is the idea of *estranged communitarianism*. Thus in national politics it is not unity, especially national popular unity, but divisiveness, not the unity of the popular classes but the liquidation of the proletariat, not the dialogue of civilizations, but the clash of civilizations that forms the basis of their ideology. The *other* is hell for all communalists. The mass psychology of communalism necessitates the splitting of the idea of the national popular in religious and ethnic fragments, each fragment viewing the other as the enemy, where the language of war and riots can be expressed. Theodor Adorno in his *Freudian Theory and the Pattern of Fascist Propaganda* claims that besides bizarre and negative recommendations, like putting people into concentration camps, fascist propaganda is little concerned with concrete and tangible issues.[10] It is more concerned with the abolition of democracy through mass support by evoking the techniques of mass hysteria and paranoia. As Bipan Chandra later remarked, the communalists evoke politics without evoking political thought, emphasize political tactics without political programme.[11] Communalism in India, like global fascism, is basically the functioning of this paradigm of alienation combined with the ideology of regressive thinking. The discourses of communal organizations are based principally on this paradigm of alienation with the totem of (fantasized) ethnic blood descent and the taboo of social exogamy being their fetishized leitmotifs. From this fundamental paradigm, different communal organizations and their respective histories and politics can be understood. Empirical studies of these communal organizations have to be concrete empirical studies. Communalism in India cannot be understood only as a study of one organization but as an analysis of actually existing economic and political conditions and the role of actually existing groups in this scenario. The specific issue is that which relates class struggle with the nature of communities in India. From these empirical conditions can be understood the struggle for state power and the politics of abstractions played by the communalists. It is this dialectics of the concrete and the abstract that shall concern us.

In the scientific study of communalism, I propose to claim that there is nothing in itself that can be called 'Hindu communalism' or 'Muslim communalism'. Nor is the communal question a 'Hindu' vs. a 'Muslim' question. On the contrary, it is the social process of reification within the process of class struggle, which expresses itself in the site of religion and manifests itself as the communal holocaust. Thus reification is the essence and the base, whilst religion becomes the mode of appearance and the political form of this reification. One has to spell out the difference between cause and effect. Scientific study will have to study both—the essence and the cause (reification) as well as the historical mode of manifestation.

It is at this nodal point that we pose a set of questions: what is the nature of the advent of the communal right-wing RSS in power? Is it fascism, or only a variation on the theme of liberal type politics? If it is fascism, what is this type of fascist politics? What is the relation between American-led globalized imperialism and the hegemony of religious fundamentalists in West and South Asia? What forces shall form the historical bloc and the national-international popular front against fascism and compradorism?

Let us now proceed to the analysis of the fundamental principles of communalism-in-hegemony and understand how the communal RSS is able to dominate state power. This analysis will uncover the possibilities of laying bare the mechanisms of consent and resistance to communalism as well as locate the precise site of breaking the communal chain at the weakest link. Communalism-in-hegemony in the form of the RSS (from its inception in the 1920s by Hegdewar to the propagation of religious intolerance as the breeding ground of Indian fascism by Praveen Togadia and co.) based its ideology and right-wing pedagogy on the idea of an indigenous and endogamous, static race that lived happily in an illusory Golden Age till it was harassed by a mysterious other. It is the racial damnation of the other that forms the crux of their xenophobic hate propaganda. Their idea of religion is actually a fascist appropriation of religion where they exploit popular Hindu religion for their fascist hate mobilization. It is extremely important to distinguish the politics of the Hindutvavadis from popular Hinduism. The principles of proletarian unity (along with the idea of the national-popular front) will form the parameters of the isolation of the Hindutvavadis from popular Hinduism and the masses in general. It is in this context that one exposes Savarkar's *Hindutva* and M.S. Golwalkar's *We or Our Nation Defined* as the master-texts of the racial view of Indian politics as well as the grounding texts of Indian fascism and communalism-in-hegemony. Incidentally, the genesis of Indian fascism in the above-stated works is also bound with the colonial collaborationist history of the RSS and the Hindu Mahasabha where the anti-colonial struggle and the processes of the bourgeois democratic revolution were continuously sabotaged by them. Sabotaging the anti-colonial unity necessitated the creation of a *hostile other.*

According to Golwalkar, there is a taxonomy of the damnation of the other. For instance, Parsis and Jews are guests, whilst Muslims and Christians are aliens who have to be subdued. (Note the schizophrenic element in the paranoid communal ideologist's claims: Jews are guests, but in this same work he justifies the purging of Jews by Hitler. This schizophrenic doublespeak forms an essential aspect of the RSS along with the general regression of thinking). This is where the paranoia-driven biologistic conception of nationhood as conceived by the RSS is formed. And it clearly distinguishes itself from the democratic conception of nationhood. Rights and citizenship emerge from the latter, the racial ideal is the essence of the former.

If one can talk of the first principles of RSS communalism, it is their idea of the *racial ideal* that needs to be exposed. Anti-communal activists need not concentrate solely on religion (for that is a mere ruse of the RSS) but need to expose their idea of the saga of the (fictitious) Hindu race that has a priori rights to indulge in fascistic politics. The 'Hindu race' is supposed to define Indian nationhood. It is ironical that the Orientalist fiction of the 'Hindu race', which began to define nationalist ideology in the nineteenth century would become the dominant ideology in the twentieth century. Whilst the RSS fascistizes this fiction, they are not the inventors of this term. Left-wing secularists have granted this privileged place of invention to James Mill's *History of British India* where the classifications of 'Hindu' 'Muslim' came into prominence. E.B. Havel, the great 'nationalist' art historian too worked in this fiction, later taken on by A.K. Coomaraswamy. A more Brahminical practice of this ideology is found in Tilak. The secularist Congress too works in this ideological space, only to form a brotherhood of these alienated communities. In the mid-nineteenth century, James Fergusson classified Indian architecture on a denominational basis—'Buddhist', 'Hindu', 'Jaina' and 'Muhammadan'. This estranged communitarianism has seeped so deeply into the national imagination and the political vocabulary of the ruling class that it would corrupt everyday language itself, till different religions start fantasizing that they are different nations.

But the paradigm shift is taken by the RSS with a clear parallel to Hitlerite fascism. Consider Golwalkar's statement: "All those not belonging to the national, i.e., Hindu race, Religion, Culture and Language, naturally fall out of the pale of real 'National' Life."[12] If the idea of Indian nationhood is equated with Hindu race, religion, culture and language, who comprises the nationalist? According to Golwalkar: "Those only are nationalist patriots, who, with the aspirations to glorify the Hindu race and Nation next to their heart, are prompted into activity and strive to achieve that goal. *All others are traitors and enemies to the National cause, or, to take a charitable view, idiots.*"

Consider how the communal argument shifts to the terrain of racial-religiosity with its emphasis on a closed transcendent fatherland, which is surrounded by the *estranged other.* Note also how xenophobia and paranoia govern the functioning of the communal mind: "Ever since that evil day, when Moslems first landed in Hindustan, right up to the present moment, the Hindu Nation has been fighting on to shake off the despoilers."[13] The first shift in the communal paranoia registers an erase of all *traces of the social and the Real*, to produce the phantasmagoria of the 'Race Spirit'. And race is never an innocent category. According to Golwalkar, purity of the race has to be carried out by purging other races, the way fascist Germany purged the Jews. Assimilation of races is simply not possible:

> The foreign races in Hindustan must either adopt the Hindu culture and language, must hold to respect and hold in reverence Hindu religion, must entertain no idea but those of the glorification of the Hindu nation and lose their separate existence to merge in the Hindu race, or may stay in the country, wholly subordinated to the Hindu Nation, claiming nothing , deserving no privileges, far less any preferential treatment—not even citizen's rights.[14]

The very difference between Hindutvavadi racism and any form of democracy is obvious. The claims made by the anti-communalists that Hindutvavadi is an unnoble savagism and a political Talibanization is correct. Race vs. citizenship, totalitarianism vs. democracy, primordialism vs. modernity, mythology vs. history and archaicism vs. futurism are the principal oppositions defining the struggle between Hindutva communalism and secularism. Yet, it is not the victory of secularism but that of the RSS's political wing—the BJP—consolidating political power in New Delhi, whilst unleashing its para-military-like organization, the Bajrang Dal, on the minorities. Why has secularism not been able to counter this?

A Brief Note on Historical Materialism and the Posing of the Question of Communalism

Engels writing to Josef Bloch in 1890 claimed:

> According to the materialist conception of history, the *ultimately* determining element in history is the production and the reproduction of real life. More than this neither Marx nor I have ever asserted. Hence if someone twists this into saying the economic is the *only* determining one, he transforms that proposition into a meaningless, abstract, senseless phrase. The economic situation is the basis, but the various elements of the

> superstructure—political forms of the class struggle and its results, to wit: constitutions established by the victorious class after a successful battle, etc., juridical forms, and even the reflexes of all these actual struggles in the brains of the participants, political, juristic, philosophical theories, religious views and their further development into systems of dogmas—also exercise their influence upon the course of the historical struggles and in many ways preponderate in determining their *form*. There is an interaction of all these elements in which, amid all the endless host of accidents (that is, of things and events whose inner connection is so remote or so impossible of proof that we can regard it as non-existent, as negligible), the economic movement finally asserts itself as necessary. Otherwise the application of the theory to any period of history would be easier than the solution of a simple equation of the first degree.[15]

To place the question of communalism in the repertoire of historical materialism, let us recall Marx's functioning of history, where political discourses are said not to be based on "the so-called general development of the human mind"; on the contrary, said to be rooted (*wurzeln*) in the material conditions of life, the life-world of civil society whose anatomy which is sought in political economy.[16] And this anatomy of civil society rooted in political economy defines the Marxist field of operation. The economic structure becomes "the real basis" (*reale Basis*) on which arise definite forms of social consciousness. The 'mind' that Marx seeks to explore is not an *a priori* free-floating phantasmagorical mind, but a mind that is essentially social, and under this very sociability, which is under *certain circumstances*, a fetishism of the 'mind' takes place. And what is this *fetishism of the mind* built up on the principles of the critique of political economy? Consider Marx's celebrated statement on fetishism: under the homology class domination-commodity production, the products of the human mind appear as "independent beings" endowed with life of their own and entering into relations with one another.[17] It is for this uncanny life-giving force granted to inanimate objects that Marx reserves the term "fetishism", literally a madness that has seized a once sane society. It is in this context that one understands the hegemony of right-wing reactionary forces in Marx's narrative of historical materialism where the mode of production of material life, which is said to condition (*bedingt*) social, political and intellectual processes,[18] is now under the purview of the process of alienation. My intervention in Marxism is to first graft the notions of alienation, reification and fetishism in the sites of the base and the superstructure such that it combines itself with the ideas of class struggle and the balance of social forces, whereby the idea of ideological hegemony is better understood. Second, I would like to claim that the category of determination (*Bestimmung*) is to be understood, not as a determinism but a *definition* that studies how ideological and political superstructures are formed. Determination (*Bestimmung*) is intrinsically related to the notion of formation (*Gestaltung*). In this way, Marx's theorem of *social being determining social consciousness* is understood. Determination (*Bestimmung*) is read as the category that binds the hitherto estranged realms of (alienated capitalist) existence and (reified) consciousness. It is in this terrain of estranged existence in the times of monopoly capitalism that the mapping and analysis of the communal mind takes place.

This mapping of the communal mind is constituted within the real basis: political economy coupled with the theory of alienation. Marxist critique of political economy is now armed with the critique of alienation.

Marxist Philosophy: On the Aetiology of Alienation

Two intertwining episteme guide Marxism as revolutionary theory and practice: the philosophy of dialectical materialism and the science of historical materialism. Alienation and the dialectics of humanism as the philosophy and history as the science become the leitmotifs of revolutionary theory and practice. Whilst historical materialism as the science of Marxism involves the empirical examination of societies, their economies, politics and cultures; Marxist philosophy studies the discursive aetiologies of estrangement and their dialectical supersession. When Marxist philosophy as the critique of alienation is presented, the study of both class societies as well as the conditions of emancipatory histories can be explored. This emancipatory history is necessarily non-alienated history. Consequently, radical historicism is to be constructed in the terrain of classlessness. The young Marx had a term for this classlessness, "the human essence" (*das menschliche Wesen*). In these sites of classlessness and the human essence, the possibilities of real human freedom would emerge.

Consequently, Marxism conceives of a rigorous line of demarcation between the emancipatory and the despotic modes of production. Consciousness that is dominated by the despotic mode of production is analysed within the purview of the critique of alienation. And what is required in this site of reified or false consciousness is not a response to idealized-estranged significations of communal paranoia, but an archaeological uncovering, which lays bare the mode of production of violent and idealized significations.

This scientific act of reading the deep structure Marx gives to the praxis of *umstrüzen*[19] and *umstülpen*[20], understood as a subversion of reified and dehumanized discourses. Earlier, Feuerbach had used the methodology of the transformative or invertive method (*Umkehrungsmethode*) whereby he claimed that onto-theology inverts the subject-predicate, real-imaginary relations. Thus humanity, instead of being conceived as the real-living-sensuous subject, is made the predicate of an imaginary and enslaving object. Marx develops this Feuerbachian method by studying how idealism splits and inverts the existence-essence, real-ideal relations and grants a privileged place to the idealized essence. In this splitting and inversion, the idealized essence is transfigured into a despotic onto-theological regime controlling real human existence. Whilst Feuerbach granted this will to power to religion, the privileging of the inverted and transfigured ideal, Marx gives to commodity production, the modern state and organized religions. The struggle against communalism has to focus on this *inverted ideological ideal* in order to lay bare both its authoritarian character and the way it represses society as a whole.

Eric Fromm, writing in *Psychoanalysis and Religion*, distinguishes authoritarian religions from humanist religions. The former claims that one must exercise "obedience, reverence and worship" to these transcendent laws. Absolute obedience is virtue, disobedience is a cardinal sin. Humanity surrenders itself to these higher forces because of the power exercised. There is no question of ethics. Power is the sole ethical force.

The problem is that these organized religions, whether the Hindutvavadis, the Islamic right-wing, or the American-sponsored Protestant fundamentalists, who are essentially consumerist inspired and communally charged, work in conjunction with monopoly-globalized capital and have infiltrated into every sector of the life-world. Indian communalism works as a conglomeration of these fundamentalists with the RSS at the head of the Indian government. The political recipe written in the cook book of the Indian bourgeoisie is a postmodern kitsch of a comprador economic policy with a foreign policy bent to the fantasies of the American empire. For the first time in independent Indian history, the possibility of the break-up of the nation is foreseen.

What then is to be done? Can the secular disengagement thesis solve the problem?

The Metaphysics of Form and the Problem of Liberal Secularism

Marx writing in the *Theses on Feuerbach* claimed:

> Feuerbach sets out from the fact of religious self-alienation, the duplication of the world into a religious and a secular (*weltliche*) one. His work consists in resolving the religious world into its secular basis (*weltliche Grundlage*). But the fact that the secular basis deserts (*abhebt*) its own sphere and establishes an independent realm in the clouds can only be explained by the self-cleavage and self-contradictions within this secular basis (*weltliche Grundlage*). The latter, therefore, must itself be both understood in its contradictions and revolutionized in practice. Thus, for instance, once the earthly family is discovered to be the secret of the heavenly family the former must itself be annihilated (*vernichtet*) in theory and in practice.[21]

Note Marx's statement: *to annihilate the earthly bourgeois world in order to confront the fantasies of the heavenly family*. I am recalling Marx's fourth *Theses on Feuerbach* as the philosophical groundwork for the understanding of religion and the secular question. Marx's response to the religious question is rigorously distinct from the liberal response. Never did Marx propound a theory of the separation of the religious from the political as the solution to the religious question. Of course, Marx was never an 'anti-secularist' who painted a fantastic identity of the religious and the political.

Secularism (here in this part of the chapter, I mean liberal secularism, or the thesis of the *separation* of religion from the political sphere) in the form of what Marx in *On the Jewish Question* called the political revolution, was "a big step forward".[22] Yet this great leap forward was only "a half-hearted approach", essentially bound to the political economy of private property. Marx's thinking on religion and secularism is not constituted within a formalistic perspective but located within the deep structures of historical materialist thinking. For Marx, the Young Hegelians, most notably Bruno Bauer in *On the Jewish Question* and Feuerbach in the *Theses on Feuerbach*, are the Kantians in the post-Hegelian world. The liberal secularist re-writes the Kantian groundwork of the metaphysics of morality in a world torn by fratricidal strife. The secularist mimes Kant in the parody of the morality of what Engels had once remarked as *impotence in action*.[23] Let us now proceed to the Marxist argument.

The main theme is the rigorous line of demarcation that Marx draws between the political and the human types of emancipation. Political emancipation, the central aspect of secularism, emancipates the state from religion, but not the human from religion. That is why Marx talked of the re-posing of the secular question (*weltliche Frage*). Unlike Bruno Bauer and Feuerbach, like the Young Hegelians in general, Marx does not conceive of ethnic and religious persecutions as purely religious phenomena. For Marx there is nothing called *the primacy of the religious*. If, as in the Feuerbachian dictum, the secret of theology is anthropology, and the idea of God revealed as the ideas of estranged humanity, then it is the anthropological terrain that needs to be interrogated. In this perspective, the fantasies of communal nationalism decoded as the phenomenology of the reified mind are revealed.

Let us look into the fourth thesis from the *Theses on Feuerbach.* First, the secular basis suffers from self-cleavages and self-contradictions and thus establishes itself as an *independent realm* in the clouds. This secular world must consequently be understood in its contradictions and revolutionized in practice. This revolutionary process has to annihilate (*vernichtet*) the contradictory bourgeois world, from which arises the duplicated religious world. Likewise, in *On the Jewish Question*, Marx proceeds towards a genealogy of the secular and the religious. Neither for him are absolute and final concepts. Marx's dialectical framework seeks the cause of the problem. Thus:

> We no longer regard religion as the cause (*Grund*), but only as the manifestation (*Phänomen*) of secular narrowness (*weltichen Beschränktheit*). Therefore we explain the religious limitations of the free citizens by their secular limitations. We do not assert that they must overcome (*aufheben*) their religious narrowness in order to get rid of (*aufzuheben*) their secular restrictions, we assert that they will overcome their religious narrowness once they get rid of (*aufheben*) their secular restrictions.[24]

So Marx proceeds into the critique of the secular world itself. Recall Marx's distinction between civil society and human society[25] and later his claim that civil society is necessarily bourgeois society.[26] The liberal-secular world is not the brave new world to be celebrated. The liberal-secularist prescription of the separation of religion from the state does not engage the real causal mechanisms of religious fundamentalism. At the most, it recalls the formalist categorical imperatives of Immanuel Kant. To recall Isaac Rubin:

> One cannot forget that on the question of the relation between content and form, Marx took the standpoint of Hegel and not of Kant. Kant treated form as something external in relation to the content, and as something which adheres to the content from the outside. From the standpoint of Hegel's philosophy, the content is not something to which form adheres from the outside. Rather, through its development, the content itself gives birth to the form which is already latent in the content. Form necessarily grows from the content.[27]

Just as Kant splits the form from the content, giving primacy to the form, so too the liberal stays at the level of *the primacy of the form*. The parallel with Kant is not only a methodological parallel but a historical one. Kant wrote his *Grundlegung zur Metaphysik der Sitten* (*Groundwork of the Metaphysic of Morals*) in 1785 in the background of the prelude to the French Revolution and the *Declaration of the Rights of Man*, the latter being the paradigmatic essence of liberal-secularism. Though the bourgeois democratic revolution frees society from feudal restrictions and poses questions of 'man' and 'rights', the metaphysics of form will devour the actual social content.

So what are these alleged 'rights of man' that secularism would reclaim? This is where class struggle in the realm of the superstructure takes place. Note the domination of the principle of alienation when the question is posed at the realm of abstraction. Let us recall Marx's *On the Jewish Question:* the rights of 'man' are decoded as nothing but the rights of egoistic man, the alienated 'man' of bourgeois society, the rights of huckstering and trade. If the religious state was built on an arrogant anti-democratic notion of 'the divine right of the king', the secularist state is *founded* on the principle of bourgeois private property and capital accumulation. 'Rights' are the 'rights' of form.

In the *Critique of the Gotha Programme* Marx grounds rights within the economic structure of society and the class struggle thereof. Against the exaltation of the metaphysics of rights, Marx claims, "Rights can never be higher than the economic structure of society and its cultural development thereby".[28] To claim a world of rights without altering the class structure and property relations is pure formalism. The 'ought' is split from the 'is', actuality is hidden in the archives of liberal bourgeois ideology. The arena of operation is shifted from the struggles in the everyday life-world to the formalist terrain of pure superstructuralism. This faulty method lies either in its fixation with the political superstructure or, in the movement from the superstructure to the base. Marx's method is of course not a one-way street from the base to the superstructure, but a multiplicity of dialectics of forces, where the alienated economic base remains *the determining element in the last resort*.

The fundamental problem with liberal secularism is that it lets both religion and the state remain in peaceful existence, albeit in schizoid-dualist form. It neither challenges seriously the existence of religion or the state. It gives them a status quo existence. So what is secularism in the form of the political revolution (of separating religion from the state)? Consider Marx:

> The *political* emancipation from religion is not a religious emancipation that has been carried through completion and is free from contradiction, because political emancipation is not a form of *human* emancipation which has been carried through completion and is free from completion. The limits of political emancipation are evident at once from the fact that the *state* can free itself from a restriction without the human being *really* free from this restriction, that the state can be a *free state* without the human being a *free human.*[29]

And Marx proceeds into the critique of the modern bourgeois state, the state that exists not as a religious state, but as a political state—a "state as state",[30] the state that Marx saw developing in 1843 in North America, the state that exists in its "completely developed form".[31] This state of liberal secular democracy is essentially the state of generalized commodity production and bourgeois property and carries within it the politics of concealment. The politics of the secular will be seen to mime the economics of the bourgeois base. The thesis of separation functions primarily to free the bourgeoisiefied forces of production from all fetters.

Just as there are two realms, as Marx pointed out in the *Theses on Feuerbach,* the realm of the secular and the religious, so too with the secularization process and the political revolution, there are two distinct sites, the site of civil society and the state. Marx claims that the former is earthly life whilst life of the state is heavenly life. So humanity too is split into two conflicting camps: the individualistic being of civil society and the communitarian being of the state, the private person and the public person, the religious person and the citizen. And these very oppositions give rise to the "secular conflict'" (*weltliche Widerstreit*). The liberal-secularist like Bauer, does not see "the conflict between the general interest and the private interest, the schism (*Spaltung*) between the political state and civil society—these secular antitheses (*weltlichen Gegensätze*), (the liberal-secularist like) Bauer allows to persist, whereas he conducts a polemic against their religious expression".[32] So the liberal-secularist remains at the level of expression only, merely at the level of the form of appearance of reality and not reality as such. Because reality is commodified and consequently, estranged reality, their mode of appearance is also estranged-illusory mode of appearance. In this estranged-delusory mode of appearance the communalists are able to race ahead of the secularists in fielding their politics of xenophobic paranoia. The type of reality worked up by the communalists is the epitome of bourgeois mystification, what Marx called reality that exists in "estranged form" (*entfremdeten Form*).[33]

Historical Materialism and the Human Essence

The ruptural principle of the critique of estrangement, whereby one can proceed to the level of the *Real* is found at the double levels of historical materialism and the human essence. The relation between the semiotics of communalism and Marx's demystifying critique is also found at this double site. It is this double site that would be able to articulate the formation of the social composition of the national popular and the anti-communal bloc.

In this section I am highlighting the concept of "the human essence" (*das menschliche Wesen*) that Marx used prolifically in the *Economic and Philosophic Manuscripts of 1844.* This idea of the human essence I shall be using to counter the communalists, both in terms of a formation of what Gramsci called "the intellectual moral bloc"[34] and second, to investigate the formation of communal consciousness. It is important to understand that the human essence is not equivalent to the idea of the "concept of man", "essence of man", "human nature", "man's nature", and the "nature of man". The human essence (*das menschliche Wesen*) is not human nature (*die menschliche Natur*).[35] *Wesen* (essence) is not *Natur* (nature). Nor is the human essence a sort of a-historical, abstract and transcendentally signified 'man'. It may be imperative to use the German original term *das menschliche Wesen*, so as not to get caught in theories of human nature. Unfortunately, a lot of translations, as well as renderings of the concept are incorrect, determined as they were by Anglo-American positivism. Maximilien Rubel's and Tom Bottomore's translation, for instance, identifies the human essence with the "essence of man".[36] Likewise, Louis Althusser's renders the human essence as "the essence of man" which is stated to be a Platonic exemplary "idealized essence", that is cut off from real existence.[37] He claims that the human essence has to be read as the "essence of man" which is equivalent to "the idea of human nature".[38] Norman Geras's rendering of *das menschliche Wesen* is dominated by theories of human nature.[39] Susane Bernhardt's and Norman Levine's translation of Georg Lukács's *The Process of Democratization* too follows the pattern of rendering *das menschliche Wesen* as "the essence of man" and "the real nature of man".[40] Eric Fromm also equates the human essence with the idea of human nature.[41]

In contrast to these hegemonic renderings, I would like to claim that Marx's concept of the human essence develops from a revolutionary rupture from the Feuerbachian as well as the Young Hegelian episteme. This emergence of a new meaning is directly related to the materialist conception of history and the struggle for classless society. In the 1844 Manuscripts it is the fullness of the sensuous human being that signifies the concept of the human essence, whilst a little later he defines it as "the ensemble of social relations".[42] This concept is now directly used in antithesis to reification (*Verdinglichung*) and stands for a de-reified society and the possibilities and necessities of classless society. It must be used as a pivotal category defining the struggle for communist society. I shall now turn to another idea: that of the categories comprising historical materialism and its implication in the studies on communalism.

In the preface to the first German edition of *Capital*, Vol.1, Marx poses the question: How is one to find the core structure of contemporary social reality that is governed by the laws of capital accumulation? Marx claims that one cannot have a microscope, as in the physical sciences. In the study of human society, "the force of abstraction" has to replace the microscope. Marx's principle point is to study the very *cell form* that comprises the make-up of the bourgeois body. The decoding of the deep structure, Marx calls the presentation of the "pure form" of society.[43] The outline of the "pure form" is the revolutionary contribution of Marx.

By the term "pure form" or reality appearing "in its purity", Marx means that social reality now appears in its "completely developed form".[44] Two important concepts emerge: "the human essence" and "the dialectics of productive forces and relations of production". (Both these notions are "pure form" notions, they do not exist by themselves in the real world, but are in states of existence combined with chaotic form notions). It is in the vantage space of the dialectics of productive forces and relations of production, that Marx outlines his discovery: the economic base determines the ideological superstructure. In his 1843 critique of Hegel, Marx claimed that the former is the condition *(die Bedingung),* and the latter the conditioned (*das Bedingte*), the former the determinant (*das Bestimmende*), the latter the determined (*das Bestimmte*).[45] Concentration should not be solely on the former, such that it implies the ineffectiveness of the superstructure. It is this human essence grafted into historical materialism that the false notions of determinism and economic reductionism can be dissolved. Recall Marx in *The Holy Family*, history (i.e. the transcendent form of history) does nothing, it is humanity which does everything.[46]

It is important to note that besides the idea of class struggle as the motor force of history, Marx inscribes a parallel idea of the human essence. The principal dialectical space that Marx works on is that of the alienation of the human essence (*der Entfremdung des menschlichen Wesens*) and the transcendence of this alienation (*die Aufhebung der Entfremdung*), which is also called the appropriation (*Aneigung*) of the human essence.[47] This dialectic serves as the guiding force for the understanding of the origin of stratified societies, as well as their possible termination. Marx's dialectical materialism is essentially human-centric.

Marx's definition of materialism is not to be conceived as the philosophy of inert matter that conceives of reality as existing independent of human will and consciousness. Instead, Marx's materialism as dialectical humanism understands humanity's being-in-the-world as defined by the dialectics of labour. Labour and consciousness form the basis of this episteme. To borrow Gramsci's phrase, the point is to put "the "will" (which, in the last analysis, equals practical or political activity) at the base of philosophy".[48]

I am intentionally raising the fundamental concepts of Marx in relation to communalism. One remembers the Marxist militant Clara Zetkin, who claimed that one of the reasons for the victory of fascism was the inefficiency of the Marxian revolutionary process, for fascism enters the scene with the withdrawal of left-wing communism and revolutionary desire. When there is absence of revolutionary will and action, fascism is victorious. It is in this site of the general erasure that one understands how 'theological' issues, like the opening of the locks of the Babri Masjid by the 'secular' Congress, the infamous Shah Bano case, the 'tragic' emotional 'hurt' of the 'Hindu' sentiments and the battle for Ayodhya, could grip the national imagination. When revolutionary will exists as a lack, not only do the communalists come marching in, but also pitch their tents, castles, temples and mosques on the lifeless landscape of bourgeois politics. So when one wants to put the revolutionary will at the base of Marxist philosophy one has necessarily to draw the line of demarcation between Marx's revolutionary Marxism and post-Marx-Marxism of the Plekhanov-Kautsky-Stalin type of economic determinism, evolutionism and fatalism. Consider Gramsci, who called this type of politics, "impassioned finalism which appears in the role of a substitute for the Predestination and Providence of confessional religions".[49] So what does fatalism claim? That it is not people but the laws of history that are the *causa-sui* of history.

If the Indian Marxists tend to operate at the site of "laws independent of the subject" than *real subjects* in history, the Marxist party work in the masses would only be negligible compared to the communal parties. The illusory and tormented

'Hindu' and 'Muslim' must be more real than the 'laws' of the Indian Marxists. And because these 'laws' claim that the time is not ripe for the revolution, or the revolution is earmarked as the bourgeois-democratic revolution, then what we have is not revolutionary internationalism and the mass struggle against fascism, imperialism and the political economy of under-development, but petty-bourgeois ideologies. So one does not think of the proletariat revolution but one reinvents Nehru. Recall Aijaz Ahmad's quote from the earlier section of this chapter, *the communist must help the Nehruvian liberal social democratic project*. In this case, doesn't one think not of Lenin but Kerensky? Because 'laws' at the time of communal riots ordain liberal-secular peace and not socialism, we have a complete reversal of historical materialism.

It is not historical time, not time (to borrow Engels's phrase) that *breaks open the continuum of history*, but reified time, time embodied in commodity production. Reified time negates concrete time, it posits abstract time. It is read also as neurotic time and the neurotic's compulsion to repeat. But if this reified time becomes the dominant ideology, then this neurotic's reified ideology (as articulated in the Hindutva politics of "*a temple is being attacked*") would find better articulation than secular politics. Historical materialism has necessarily to rupture this reification and all types of bourgeois historiography.

So what does one find? That there is a fundamental difference between the estranged conception of history and actual, concrete history, this difference reflected in the social democratic ideology of teleologism and Marx's historicism. Whilst teleologism functions in terms of "laws independent of humans", surfing the oceans of determinism and inevitabilities; Marx's radical historicism (Gramsci calls this "historicism and humanism") weaves humanity in the dialectics of productive forces and relations of production. Marx's modes of production are not anti-humanist sites, nor is history to be understood as what Althusser remarked in *Lenin and Philosophy* as a "process without a subject".[50] It is necessary to put the subject back into history.

Consider *The Germany Ideology*, where the mode of

production is defined in terms of "real individuals", and thus is stated to be "a definite form of activity of these individuals, a definite form of expressing their life, a definite *mode of life* on their part".[51] This idea of inserting *real individuals* in the site of the economic mode of production is consistent with his earlier philosophical concern of conceiving humanity as the basis. To recall Marx:

> This human (*dieser Mensch*), the member of civil society, is thus the *basis*, the precondition of the political state.[52]

That is why I am claiming that Marxism will have to keep the real, sensuous human, the humanity of the here and the now at the centre of discourse. This humanity of the here and the now will link itself with the levels of "real individuals'" and "human essence". In this way the classical Marxist notion of class struggle as the basis of history is necessarily tied to the ideas of humanity (*On the Jewish Question*), the human essence (*Economic and Philosophic Manuscripts of 1844*) and real individuals (*The German Ideology*). Thus humanity, real individuals, the human essence and class struggle are embodied in historical materialism in a concrete and over-determined manner. It is with this human-centric emphasis of Marxism that the strategies of understanding communalism are possible. (It is important to note that if Marxism does not engage this real human with its real needs then this space is occupied by right-wing forces).

I shall now highlight another important linkage: that of the concepts of alienation and class struggle, such that the chain of concepts is defined as: *the human essence, alienation and class struggle*. Thus the dialectic that Marx explores is the dialectic of the alienation of the human essence that posits the history of class societies; and the transcendence of this alienation, which heralds the struggle for classless societies. The estranged human essence not only grounds the existence of socio-economic classes, but also the caste system, gender discrimination, racism and communalism.

For the estranged human essence is decoded as a reified relation of production, spelt out as a relation mediated by things, and not a humanized relation. It is this terrain of reification or estranged humanity that becomes the focal point in understanding communalism. In contrast to the lumpen army of reification is the proletariat life force comprising class struggle, real individuals and the human essence. Class struggle in the realm of communalism shall begin.

Consent: Ideology and Reification

If social existence determines social consciousness, then historical materialism extends this argument and claims that *alienated existence determines reified consciousness*. This is the first statement used to deconstruct communalism. The second statement claims: "Consciousness must be explained from the conflict existing between the social forces of production and the relations of production".[53] "Consciousness (*das Bewusstsein*)", so Marx had also clarified, "can never be anything else than conscious being (*das bewusste Sein*), and the being of men in their actual life-process".[54]

From these three statements on consciousness I proceed into the critique of communalism. The first aspect of this critique is understanding the nature of mass consciousness that is being subdued by communal propaganda. In order to do this I am distinguishing the mode of production of ideas from the ideological mode of consumption. The various techniques and forms of devices used by the communal RSS have to be analysed within the purview of the Ideological (State) Apparatus. I am bracketing the word 'state' because the RSS does not have full control of the state apparatus. The manner in which it had taken over national educational institutions and defined its communal mythology is through its hegemony over the N.C.E.R.T. (National Council for Educational Research and Training), the U.G.C. (University Grants Commission) and other apex bodies, like the I.C.H.R. (Indian Council of Historical Research). A more fascistic method of mobilization is carried out by the V.H.P. (Vishva Hindu Parishad), a pretentious 'social' and 'cultural' organization, which propagates anti-minority paranoia, whilst its militia, the Bajrang Dal, recruits young males to fight for their mythical cause. The fascistic method of fictitious gender equalization, finds an organization called the Durga Vahini to defend 'Hindu' women from other Indian citizens. Whilst these are active producers of communal propaganda, there is a consequent consumption and internalization of these ideas.

The point is to study the mode of consumption of these ideas. Considering that there is a difference between the Hindutvavadis (with their racial-religious views of right-wing nationalism) and the masses, why do masses give consent to such politics? Why is there an identity formed between the communalists and the masses? How can this identity be broken to create an opposition, in fact an explosive and antagonistic contradiction, which not only negates the hegemony of the communalists, but lifts society at a higher level of existence? (One must recall the dialectics of the negation of the negation and the difficult to translate Hegelian-Marxian term *Aufhebung*, which signifies a "lifting up", which preserves as well as abolishes existence at a higher level of being. This "lifting up", can also be read as a revolutionary "uprising" that recalls the question of mass mobilization by the anti-communal and anti-capitalist popular front).

Let us now look into the question of the *Communal Ideological Apparatus*. At one level politics necessarily works within the Machiavellian logic of conspiracies. Yet ideology does not function solely at this site, where the ruling class conspires in fooling the masses into believing in the ideas of private property and capital accumulation, or the ruling political class befooling the people with the ideas of the mythical Hindu Rashtra. In order to understand the hegemony of communal ideology, it is necessary to understand Marx's concept of ideology and its relation to historical materialism. So was Marx an ideologist, and did he propagate an alternative subaltern ideology? Or is the case that there can be nothing called "Marxist ideology" and such a view is revisionist starting with Eduard Bernstein and the later Soviet bureaucrats? Recall Marx's statement: to set forth the scientific conception of history as *opposed* to the ideological conception.[55]

At least for Marx in *The German Ideology*, ideology is a process of pure idealization, where the *Real* is erased to produce the *Transcendent Imaginary* and the *Symbolic*. The erasure of the *Real* is a necessary condition for the production of ideology. The *Transcendent Imaginary* is not human imagination, definitely not scientific or aesthetic imagination. On the contrary, it is an imaginary that is predicated on the denial of the *Real*, the denial of existence itself.[56] Reality, i.e. as capitalist reality, becomes schizophrenic: sensuous and non-sensuous both at the same time,[57] like the theologian and the mental patient going through the process of "metempsychosis" and "transmigration".[58] The spectre that has *lost its bodily form* that Marx outlined as the genealogy of the commodity is always in a state of perfection in the capitalist system. *Ideology* (like the material base of commodity production) then has to be understood as a process of *disembodiment* where the mind is *split* from the body. Such a view comes close to Freud's reading of psychosis, which implies *a withdrawal from reality.* So when the loss of the *Real* is the signature tune of commodity production and ideology, it is also the same for psychotic illness. *Ideology shares the same space as mental illness*. (It reaches its zenith in fascist ideologies).We now have reification meeting psychosis where ideology and madness are related.

Marx's war of attrition is from outside the space of ideology as the spectre that denies the Real. One cannot operate from the spaces inherited from a mythological past nor an alienated and fetishized present. But to make a claim that ideology in general is false, i.e. denies the *Real*, needs sufficient empirical evidence. It means that the Mauryan state ideology under Asoka, or Sasanian ideology, or Stalinism follows the pattern of the denial of the *Real*. I shall leave this motif for further research. I shall come back to the point of Marx's ideology critique and the question as to why the communalists can, in the period of monopoly capitalism in the age of globalization, dominate over the national imagination.

Consider Marx's materialism:

> The ideas of the ruling class are in every epoch the ruling ideas: i.e., the class which is the ruling *material* force of society is at the same time its ruling *intellectual* force. The class which has the means of material production at its disposal, consequently also controls the means of mental production, so the ideas of those who lack

> the means of mental production are on the whole subject to it.[59]

Now ideology-specterology as the denial of the *Real* is bound up with class struggle. Since *The German Ideology* and *The Communist Manifesto*, the thesis of the dominant ideology woven with the dominant class was born. Ideology as the denial of the *Real* is understood as the hegemony of the material and the intellectual means of production. A change in the hegemonic ideology indicates a change in the hegemonic class positions in the ruling power bloc. Analysis now shifts to the level of class struggle in the realm of ideology.

To understand how the RSS with its political front, the BJP, has managed, suddenly almost, in a sense of a seismic shift to gain political centre-stage since the early 1990s, is to understand the political economy of the project of globalization and liberalization and how it killed the great Indian bourgeois liberal project. It broke the ranks of the ruling class, pushed them towards global capital, who were, until then extremely comfortable with the protectionist state and liberal secular ideology. It saw the dismantling of the welfare system, the crippling of the trade union movement, whilst it let the imperialist multi-national cartels have a free run in the economy. At the same time, voices of the death of socialism and secularism were heard whilst the political elites pushed for an aggressive pro-American foreign policy. On the other hand, the new middle class-caste (the Other Backward Castes or the OBCs) turned towards affirmative action, engineered by Mandal politics, and brought a new political class into power, reflected in the politics of Laloo Prasad Yadav and Mulayam Singh Yadav. The elite of the older power wanted to break the Mandalization of politics. Mandal politics of social democratic egalitarianism had to be broken. Ayodhya and the myth and psychosis of the broken temple were born. But unevenness in the political economy of India saw that complete power could not rest in the hands of the RSS. Multiple power centres emerged and so did the politics of coalitions.

The break-up of the older, secular-inspired power bloc was reflected in the crisis of the ideology of the state. The debate between Hindutvavadi and secularism entered the stage of

Indian politics. And so gripped are the elites and the intellectuals (including the academic secularists) that they could not see the falsity and mystification of this alienated debate (mandir vs. masjid), which demanded equally false solutions. Thus, instead of seeing the ascendancy to power of the RSS as the crisis of the accumulation of global capital and the crisis of the Indian bourgeois state, the secularists saw it merely as violence unleashed by a 'Hindu' majority party, and the solution being a reformed bourgeois liberal state. In order to understand the falsity of this surface debate (liberalism vs. communal-fascism), I am turning to Marx's problematic of alienation and ideology, so as to look into this very mechanism of ideology as false consciousness. Alienation produces false consciousness—this is the theme that runs from Marx's early works to Engels's 1893 letter to Franz Mehring. I would now suggest a humanist reading of Marx's conception of ideology. Take *The German Ideology*, where Marx differentiates ideology from the materialist conception of history.[60]

Just as in the realm of philosophy Marx suggests, do not pay attention to the philosopher's claims, ignore thus the questions of "soul", "God", "Idea", "substance", "Man" etc., instead go to the historical referent itself, so too in confronting communalism do not even attempt to answer the hysteria-induced questions of "Hindu Rashtra", "the hurt sentiments", etc. (for these are the hysterical fantasies of the paranoid communalist), but go to the *Real* itself. And this *Real* is "the existence of living human beings",[61] sensuous beings existing in historical modes of production, actual people, suffering, joyous people involved in real human activity. In contrast, ideology is decoded as the phantasmagoria of the idealization process:

> In direct contrast to German philosophy which descends from heaven to earth, here it is a matter of ascending from earth to heaven. That is to say, not of setting out from what men say, imagine, or conceive, nor from men as narrated, thought of, imagined, conceived, in order to arrive at men in the flesh; but set out from real, active men, and on the basis of their life-process demonstrating the development of the ideological reflexes and

> echoes of this life-process. The phantoms (*Nebet*) formed in the brains of men are also, necessarily sublimates of their material life-process, which is empirically verifiable and bound to material premises. Morality, religion, metaphysics, and all the rest of ideology as well as the forms of consciousness (*Bewusstseinsformen*) corresponding to these, thus no longer retain the semblance of independence. They have no history, no development; but men developing their material production and their material intercourse, alter, along with this their actual world, also their thinking and the products of their thinking. It is not consciousness that determines life, but life that determines consciousness. For the first manner of approach, which confirms to real life, it is the real living individuals themselves, and consciousness is considered solely as *their* consciousness . . . It is self-evident, moreover, that "spectres", "bonds", "the higher being", "concept", "scruple", are merely idealist, speculative, mental expressions, the concepts apparently of the isolated individual, the mere images of very empirical fetters and limitations, within which move the mode of production of life, and the form of intercourse coupled with it.[62]

Deconstructing communal ideology in the perspective of the denial of the *Real*, leads us to Marx's reading of alienation in the *Economic and Philosophic Manuscripts of 1844.* It is in this reading that there can be possibilities of a humanist science of communalism, which serves as a political episteme for mass mobilization. Let us take these human sites for analysis, especially when we have claimed that one does not respond to the trauma, hysteria and other forms of communal blackmail. We proceed now into the sites to be uncovered. Marx claimed that there are four aspects of alienation (it is these four sites that we must encounter), of object, of one's activity and consequently oneself, of society and of one's necessary species being and human powers and potentialities. Now these aspects of alienation are projected in duplicated and distorted form (*projected lack* is what Feuerbach calls it and *censored form* is what Freud claims in the *Interpretation of Dreams*) at the level of the ideological superstructure. Thus what appears, or the *form of deceptive appearance* is a mythical world of imaginary communities, the Golden Age of Lord Rama living in the magnificent temple, till it was destroyed by an invader. And in this deceptive world are engraved the speech-acts of alienated beings of capitalism (who seek their psychotic release). This psychotic realm is where the communally charged individual and social group look for a fascist superman in the fantastic reality (*phantastischen Wirklichkeit*) of heaven, finding, however, only a reflection (*Widerschein*) and mere appearance (*Schein*) of the inhumanity of social reality.[63] Thus what is lacked in the real world is projected into the reified superstructure. This projected and duplicated world Marx claims is "the *fantastic realization* of the human essence (*die phantastischeVerwirklichung des menschlichen Wesens*) since the human essence has not acquired true reality".[64]

That is why, in the critique of fascist-communal ideology and the social psychology of the masses that consume this ideology, I am claiming that the fundamental site for Marx is the study of the alienation of the human essence (the philosophy of Marxism) along with the historical conjuncture of class struggle (the science of Marxism). This alienated human essence is understood as the cell form of class societies that reaches its zenith in late capitalism and becomes the organizational base and motor force of communal fascist politics. This structure of alienation is the dialectical depth structure, whilst paranoia and communal hatred (as the expression of reification) is registered in the form of appearance of communal ideology. It is this double site, which becomes the terrain of the anti-communal revolutionary war of attrition.

Resistance

It is this dialectical process that studies how the hegemony of the communalists is to be broken. As this chapter has noted, the philosophy of alienation questions as to why the human is lost in the marshes and swamps of class exploitation, caste dehumanization, gender oppression, national and religious hatred and the war of nations. It has to be noted that Marx's concept of class struggle is a mass struggle, a struggle that is a concrete struggle and as the notion of the concrete goes, a "unity of diverse elements". To recall Lenin's *What is to be Done?* "all the classes" have to be taken in the struggle for socialism. The struggle against communalism is not only one struggle, but a protracted struggle for real democracy, for the abolition of all classes, for the entire wealth of society that is estranged, to be kept back at the social level. On the other hand, the domination of the communalists shows that something is rotten in the state of the bourgeoisie.

What the communalists do is to borrow all that is decadent from history. What the socialist has to do is to look forward towards a radical future and reclaim all that is great as its rightful heritage. And as the *Economic and Philosophic Manuscripts of 1844* goes, it is the human itself that has to be appropriated. In this way socialist philosophy shall be able to grip the masses. Consider the celebrated passage from Marx:

> Clearly the weapon of criticism cannot replace the criticism of weapons, and material force must be overthrown by material force. But theory also becomes a material force once it has gripped the masses. Theory is capable of gripping the masses when it demonstrates *ad hominem*, and it demonstrates *ad hominem*, as soon as it becomes radical. To be radical is to grasp things by the root. But for the human the root is humanity itself.[65]

It is in this way that the universal concept of humanity is understood by the Marxist dialectic. Consequently, Marxism is able to make a fundamental break from all bourgeois theories. It is in this site that one can clearly view the lines of demarcation between the communal, the liberal and the revolutionary. Whilst communalism is alienated communatarianism with its fascistic politics of religious wars and secularism is about the unity of all religions, Marxism is about the unity and solidarity of people (recall Marx's phrase from *The Holy Family* "the unity of the human essence" which is "humanity's consciousness of its species and its attitude towards its species, for the practical identity of human to human, i.e., for the social or human relation of the human to the human".[66] It is in this emancipatory dialectical space that the authentic dialogue of civilizations is possible and also the space that allows the genuine respect for cultural diversities). Further: if communalism is about the identity of religion and the state, and liberal-secularism talks of the separation of religion from the state, then Marxism is the

Aufhebung of the state and religion (along with the abolishing of exploitation and alienation).

The dialectics of *Aufhebung* is the signature tune of Marxism: the *Aufhebung* of alienation, private property, state and religion. When humanity will rise above these reified situations, basking in the radical historicism of the dialectic that lifts up reality at a higher level of existence, then the solution shall neither be the politics of the bourgeois state, nor the pretentious social character of civil society. Marxism is principally about looking beyond class societies. After all, this is the fundamental idea of the socialist revolution.

It is at this nodal point that the notion of radical secularism manifests itself. By *radical secularism* is meant the unconditional unity of all existence and becomes the necessary condition of the socialist project. It recalls Marx's 1844 appropriation of Feuerbach's concept of species being (*Gattungswesen*), which is the idea of the human species urging towards a classless realm.

This unconditional unity of all peoples of the world is the internationalist project of the radical new world order. Radical secularism is distinct from political secularism (that we critiqued in the earlier part of the chapter). In this radical futurist sense, it appropriates the international Enlightenment project. Just as Marx made a distinction between scientific socialism and other utopian forms of socialism, so too one has to distinguish radical secularism from the politics of liberal-secularism.

In this radical universalizing process it understands the greatness of different civilizations. It demands the upliftment of the languages and literatures of all the people of the world. Consequently, besides the critique of political economy and ideology critique, it is imperative to look into areas of culture whereby the discovery of real humanity is possible.

REFERENCES

1. See *Fascism*, ed. Roger Griffin (Oxford: Oxford University Press, 1995), pp. 262-263.
2. Martin Heidegger, 'Letter to Herbert Marcuse, January 20, 1948', in Herbert Marcuse, *Technology, War and Fascism*, ed. Douglas Kellner (Routledge: London, 1998), p. 265.

3. Achin Vanaik, *Communalism Contested. Religion, Modernity and Secularization* (New Delhi: Vistar, 1997), p. 66.
4. Aijaz Ahmad, *Lineages of the Present. Political Essays* (New Delhi: Tulika, 1996), p. 266.
5. Bipan Chandra, *Ideology and Politics in Modern* India (New Delhi: Har-Anand Publications, 1994), p. 63.
6. Samir Amin, *Capitalism in the Age of Globalization. The Management of Contemporary Society* (Delhi: Madhyam, 1997), pp. 80-90.
7. G.W.F. Hegel, *The Phenomenology of Mind,* trans. J.B. Baille (London: Humanities Press, 1966), p. 81.
8. V.I. Lenin, *The Nascent Trend in Imperialist Economics* (Moscow: Progress Publishers, 1982), p. 11.
9. Nicos Poulantzas, *Fascism and Dictatorship. The Third International and the Problem of Fascism,* trans. Judith White (London: Verso, 1979), pp. 18-19.
10. T.W. Adorno, 'Freudian Theory and the Pattern of Fascist Propaganda' in *The Essential Frankfurt School Reader*, ed. Andrew Arato and Eike Gebhardt (New York: Continuum, 1985), p. 118.
11. Bipan Chandra, *Communalism in Modern India* (New Delhi: Vikas, 1996), p. 350.
12. M.S. Golwalkar, *We, Or Our Nation Defined* (Nagpur, 1947).
13. Ibid.
14. Ibid
15. Friedrich Engels, 'Letter to Josef Bloc, 1890', in *Marx. Engels. Selected Works* (Moscow: Progress Publishers, 1975), p. 682.
16. Karl Marx, 'Preface' in *A Contribution to the Critique of Political Economy* (Moscow: Progress Publishers, 1977), p. 20; 'Zur Kritik der Politischen Ökonomie. Vorwort', in *Marx. Engels. Ausgewählte Schriften* I, (Berlin: Dietz Verlag, 1977), p. 334.
17. Karl Marx, *Capital*, Vol. I trans. Samuel Moore and Edward Eveling, (Moscow: Progress Publishers, 1983), p. 77.
18. Karl Marx, 'Zur Kritik der Politischen Ökonomie. Vorwort', p. 334.
19. Karl Marx, Friedrich Engels, *The German Ideology*, (Moscow: Progress Publishers, 1976), p. 61.
20. Karl Marx, *Capital,* Vol. I, p. 29; *Das Kapital. Kritik der Politischen Ökonomie,* Erster Band, (Berlin: Dietz Verlag, 1981), p. 27.
21. Karl Marx, 'Theses on Feuerbach', in *Marx. Engels. Selected Works* (Moscow: Progress Publishers, 1975), p. 29. The Soviet translation has additional words that Marx himself did not use. I have modified this quotation according to Marx's original. The Tom Bottomore translation is more faithful to Marx. See *Karl Marx, Selected Writings in Sociology and Social Philosophy*, eds. Tom

Bottomore and Rubel, trans. Tom Bottomore (London: Penguin, 1990).
22. Karl Marx, 'On the Jewish Question', in *Marx. Engels. Collected Works*, Vol. 3, (Moscow: Progress Publishers), p. 155.
23. Friedrich Engels, 'Feuerbach and the End of Classical German Philosophy', in *Marx. Engels. Selected Works* (Moscow: Progress Publishers), p. 600.
24. Karl Marx, op. cit, p. 151.
25. Karl Marx, 'Theses on Feuerbach', p. 30.
26. Karl Marx, 'Zur Kritik der Politischen Ökonomie. Vorwort', p. 335.
27. Isaak, Rubin, *Essays on Marx's Theory of Value*, trans. Miloš Samardžija and Fredy Perlman, (Montreal: Black Rose, 1990), p. 117.
28. Karl Marx, 'Critique of the Gotha Programme' in *Marx. Engels. Selected Works* (Moscow: Progress Publishers, 1975), p. 320.
29. Karl Marx, 'On the Jewish Question', p. 152.
30. Ibid, pp. 150, 152.
31. Ibid.
32. Ibid, p. 155.
33. Karl Marx, *Economic and Philosophic Manuscripts of 1844* (Moscow: Progress Publishers, 1982), p. 131.
34. Antonio Gramsci, *Selections from the Prison Notebooks of Antonio Gramsci* (New York: International Publishers, 1987), pp. 332-333.
35. Karl Marx, *Economic and Philosophic Manuscripts of 1844*, p. 133.
36. Bottomore and Rubel render *das menschliche Wesen* as "the essence of man" and "the real nature of man". See *Karl Marx, Selected Writings in Sociology and Social Philosophy*, eds. Bottomore and Rubel, trans. Tom Bottomore (London: Penguin, 1990), p. 83.
37. Louis Althusser, *For Marx*, trans. Ben Brewster (London: Allen Lane, 1969), p. 236.
38. Ibid.
39. Norman Geras, *Marxism and Human Nature. Refutation of a Legend* (London: Verso, 1983).
40. Georg Lukács, *The Process of Democratization*, trans. Susane Bernhardt and Norman Levine (New York: State University of New York, 1991).
41. Eric Fromm and Xirau Ramon, *The Nature of Man* (New York: Macmillan, 1968).
42. Karl Marx, 'Theses on Feuerbach', p. 28.
43. Karl Marx, *Theories of Surplus Value*, Part I, trans. Emile Burns, ed. S. W. Ryazanskaya (Moscow: Progress Publishers, 1975), p. 43.
44. Karl Marx, 'On the Jewish Question', p. 150.

45. Karl Marx, 'Critique of Hegel's Doctrine of State' in *Karl Marx. Early Writings*, trans. Rodney Livingstone and Gregor Benton (New York: Vintage Books, 1975), p. 63.
46. Karl Marx and Friedrich Engels, *The Holy Family or Critique of Critical Criticism* (Moscow: Progress Publishers, 1980), p. 116.
47. Karl Marx, *Economic and Philosophic Manuscripts of 1844*, pp. 109, 130; 'Nationalökonomie und Philosophie', in *Karl Marx. Die Frühschriften*, (Stuttgart: Alfred Kröner Verlag, 1964), pp. 264, 271.
48. Antonio Gramsci, op. cit., p. 345.
49. Ibid, p. 336.
50. Louis Althusser, *Lenin and Philosophy and Other Essays*, trans. Ben Brewster (New York and London: Monthly Review Press, 1971), pp. 121-124.
51. Karl Marx, Friedrich Engels, *The German Ideology*, p. 37.
52. Karl Marx, 'On the Jewish Question', p. 166.
53. Karl Marx, 'Preface', *A Contribution to the Critique of Political Economy*, p. 21.
54. Karl Marx, Friedrich Engels, *The German Ideology*, p. 42.
55. Ibid, p. 22.
56. Karl Marx, *Capital*, Vol. I, p. 45.
57. Ibid, p. 76.
58. Ibid, p. 199.
59. Karl Marx, Friedrich Engels, *The German Ideology*, p. 67.
60. Ibid, pp. 34-37.
61. Ibid, p. 37.
62. Ibid, pp. 42, 51.
63. Karl Marx, 'A Contribution to the Critique of Hegel's Philosophy of Right. Introduction', in *Karl Marx. Early Writings*, trans. Rodney Livingstone and Gregor Benton (New York: Vintage Books, 1975), p. 243.
64. Ibid.
65. Ibid, p. 251.
66. Karl Marx and Friedrich Engels, *The Holy Family or Critique of Critical Criticism*, p. 50.

CHAPTER 2

Whither India?

I am afraid you will make Harijans rise in rebellion against society.
—M.K. Gandhi to Hari Narayan Apte, 1915.

The Mahatma appears not to believe in thinking. He prefers to follow the saints. Like a conservative with reverence for consecrated notions he is afraid that if he once starts thinking, many ideals and institutions to which he clings will be doomed .... In so far as he does think, to me he really appears to be prostituting his intelligence for supporting the archaic social structure of the Hindus. He is the most influential apologist of it and therefore the worst enemy of the Hindus.
— Babasaheb Ambedkar, *Annihilation of Castes*

Caste and the Asiatic Mode of Production

To the question: "Whither the Indian Revolution?" is tied at least two questions: "Whither the Asian Revolution?" and "Whither the World Revolution?" Asia in general and India in particular are hosts to a number of contradictions. On the one hand, Asian civilizations from Egypt, Babylonia, Iran to India, China and the Far East had developed urban civilizations when Western Europe was in the barbaric stage of history. On the other hand, Asia fell under the feudal hammer of what Marx called "Asiatic despotism"—and the "Asiatic mode of production", a mode that was distinct not only from European feudalism but European history itself.

In the 1960s and 1970s, the Indian left turned its attention to the nature of the mode of production in India. Whilst some said that India was semi-feudal, others identified India as the "colonial mode of production", and yet others called India the capitalist mode of production itself.[1] More than Marx's analysis, it was Lenin and Mao who became the theoreticians of the mode of production in India. Little attention was paid to Marx's analysis of the Asiatic mode of production. And it is to this mode of production that attention now turns. Historical analysis will thus have to study the dialectics of class and the pre-capitalist social formations in India keeping in mind Marx's notion of the Asiatic mode of production.

"There have been in Asia, generally from immemorial times," so Marx had once said, "but three departments of government: that of Finance, or the plunder of the interior; that of War, or the plunder of the exterior; and finally, the department of Public Works".[2] Marx should have added one more department—the Department of Caste Stratification—the department that has been from immemorial times the backbone of Indian civilization. Caste—the Indian social system of stratification based on the onto-theology of inequality that realizes itself as the barbaric egotism of village communities, (as we shall see from the following quote of Marx) that worships animals and condemns humanity, that concentrates on some small piece of land oblivious to the outside world—survived Buddhism, survived Islam and would soon collide not only with colonialism, but also with modern industry and modernity itself, and survive that too.

So what do castes and their realization as village communities signify? Would they imply only a division of labour in this 'Indian' type stratification: priests, warriors, merchants and the proletariat; or do castes also signify a peculiar type of racial division that the Indo-Iranian Rg Vedic people introduced? Whatever form—economic and/or racial—caste would serve not only as the foundation of the 'class' system in India, but also of contemporary conservative right-wing movements. And although castes in their existential forms would continuously modify themselves (and though caste discrimination is Constitutionally banned in India), they would cease to be destroyed.

It has generally been said, and Marx thought so too, that

caste would meet its nemesis—industry and the industrial revolution.[3] The latter would become the graveyard that would write the epitaph of the Indian caste system. Industry came and along with it modernity, or at least the Western-capitalist type of societal rationalization, but caste refuses to go. It is the spectre that haunts India—the spectre of the antiquated mode of production that seems so dear, not only for Indian 'civilization', but also for the global accumulation of capital. This chapter, in engaging the cultural politics of Marx, deals with the two types of the politics of emancipation—the theory of class struggle combined with the subaltern-dalit theory of caste hegemony ('subaltern' here does not have to be confused with the postmodern and post-Marxist 'Subaltern Studies' that once became fashionable. By 'subaltern' one means the popular masses). Whilst Marxism deals with class struggle and the struggle for socialism, this chapter actively engages the dialectic of Marx, which is, on the one hand, empirical, and thus concretely engaging the caste system in India; and on the other, it not only allows, but also necessitates the critique of the caste system based on Marx's theory of rights.

As we noted in the previous chapter, for Marxism, the economic structure of society is the "*ultimately* determining element in history", but not the "*only* determining one",[4] and as Marx and Engels had so often stated, there is a tremendous dialectical traffic between the base and the superstructure. History has not to be understood as in the static, building metaphor, where, on a stable economic base there stands a reflected political and ideological superstructure. On the contrary, history is made up of a series of practices: the economic, scientific, political, religious, ideological, etc., all in states of condensation and displacement from one another, wherein these interacting practices in their states of collision "react upon one another" (to borrow Engels's phrase),[5] where one of the practices becomes the structure in dominance whilst the economic becomes the "determining element in the last resort".

There are two distinct sites of the dialectical traffic: (i) between the base and the superstructure , and (ii) between diverse and heterogenous societies which refuse to comply to a unilinear metaphysics of history. Marx did not believe in the monist theory of history (a view popularised by Georgi Plekhanov, the father of Russian Marxism). Marx, in fact, was a pluralist for whom pluralism of histories, and not some abstract type of a *history-as-such* operated in reality. Take this understanding from the *Economic and Philosophic Manuscripts of 1844*, where he did not talk of an abstract economic mode of production, existing by itself but combined with the elements of the superstructure,"religion, family, state, morality, science, art, etc. (which) are particular modes of production, and fall under its general law (i.e. the law of the dominant economic mode of production, my insertion, M.J.)". And if Marx could put religion, family, et al. as particular modes of production, then one can insert caste too within this matrix of modes of production. Not only is caste the clue to the understanding of Hinduism but Indian history itself. According to Marx, the caste-based :

> idyllic village communities, inoffensive though they may appear, had always been the solid foundation of Oriental despotism, that they restrained the human mind within the smallest compass, making it the unresisting tool of superstition, enslaving it beneath traditional rules, depriving it of all grandeur and historical energies. We must not forget that the barbarian egotism which, concentrating on some miserable piece of land, had quietly witnessed the ruin of empires, the perpetuation of unspeakable cruelties, the massacre of the population of large towns, with no other consideration bestowed upon them than on natural events, itself the helpless prey of any aggressor who deigned to notice it at all. We must not forget that this undignified, stagnatory, and vegetative life, that this passive sort of existence evoked on the one part, in contradistinction, wild, aimless, unbounded forces of destruction and rendered murder itself a religious rite in Hindustan. We must not forget that these little communities were contaminated by caste and by slavery, that they subjugated man to external circumstances instead of elevating man to be the sovereign of circumstances, that they transformed a self-developing social state into never changing natural destiny, and thus brought about a brutalizing worship of nature, exhibiting its degradation in the fact that man, the sovereign of nature, fell down

> on his knees in adoration of Hanuman the monkey, and Sabbala, the cow.[6]

How does one understand such a reading? Should one say, following Edward Said, that Marx the great humanist fell prey to the practice of Eurocentric hegemony, just as Eurocentrism had devoured Hegel and Goethe?[7] Or, is Marx's reading an accurate reading of the structures in dominance of Indian society, and these structures are not to be confused with a reading of an 'Indian feudalism', but have to be located in the Asiatic mode of production, the stand that Marx (but not the Marxists) held, and that caste is the deciding factor of this Asiatic mode? That caste is the basis of Indian society is a fact examined by thinkers as diverse as Hibert Risley, John Nesfield, Emile Senart, Max Weber, Louis Dumont, D.D. Kosambi, E.M.S. Namboodripad, M.N. Srinivas and Sharad Patil. That the social process of caste, and all its terrible superstitions and ramifications expressed through the dialectics of *varna-jati* is both the basis and an evil of Indian society was not only recognized by Marx but also the stalwarts of the anti-caste movement, Jyotirao Phule and Babasaheb Ambedkar. The anti-caste revolution remained the leitmotif of their radical politics.

For Phule and Ambedkar, the rebellion against the caste system is of central importance. With them one has a radical re-reading of Indian history, a radicalism that would put them in direct opposition to the Orientalist and Brahmanical phantasmagorical account of India. How both Phule's and Ambedkar's understanding of Hinduism is radically different from the romantic versions of Vivekananda, Sister Nivideta, Gandhi, Ananda Coomaraswamy and Aurobindo is evident in the fact that the former were to tear it down from its roots. Caste had to crumble along with it the superstitious spiritual superstructure created by the Brahmins. The 'nation' that the Brahmanical elites had constructed not only from the middle and late nineteenth century but since time immemorial would be dissolved in its fragments. 'Hindu' history would fall under this subaltern deconstruction, a blow from which Brahmanical Hinduism would never recover. It is in this critique of caste oppression and the radical reading of Indian history that revolutionary Marxism enters the scene of the Indian revolution. Revolutionary Marxism is bent on understanding the process of caste in India and the radical subaltern account of Indian history.

In Phule's account of Indian history, the Brahmins who had paraded the *Sudras, ati-Sudras* and *Mlecchas* (i.e. the lower castes and the Muslims) as the demonized 'other' are themselves deconstructed as the hostile other—the proto-Brahmanical 'other' that came from Iran and destroyed the 'authentic' Indian civilization.[8] Brahmanical history would cease to have the firm and solid foundation that it aspired for. It would be exposed as being neither nationalist nor people-oriented. On the contrary, Phule would reveal the imperialist and inherently tyrannical nature of Brahmanism. The thesis that Phule would create would be the foundation of the anti-Brahmanical movement. It is from this basis that the contemporary subaltern anti-Brahmin movement in India would emerge. Ambedkar would arrive on the scene of Indian history with this Phulean legacy. Though Ambedkar would not fully endorse Phule's historical critique, especially on the 'Aryan' question and the origins of the problem of the subjugation of the subaltern classes in India, differing on the historical analysis of the critique of Brahmanism,[9] both critiques would form an epistemico-politico alliance in the subversion of Hinduism and the caste question.

In the tenth mandala of the *Rg Veda*, the master text of Hinduism, the myth of creation is depicted where the Brahmins are shown emerging from the mouth of god-cum-primeval 'man'—Prajâpati ("The Lord of Beings") later to become Brahmâ, who existed before the creation of the universe—the Râjanya (the later Kshatriyas) from the hands, the Vaiśyas from the thighs and the Sūdras from the legs.[10] The *varna* system is first depicted in this text. It becomes a sort of ideological signifying apparatus to justify later caste stratification and the social-politics of purity, pollution and exclusion. The first question that emerges is: what is *varna* and what is its etymological meaning and how would philology classify the term "*varna*"?[11] The second question relates to the process of *jati* and the historical linguistic analysis of this term. The third question relates to the processes of *varna-jati* with the Marxist idea of class struggles with special analysis of the Asiatic mode of production. For the clue to the analysis of caste stratification a comparative study between the *Rg Veda* and the *Avesta* is necessary in order to know the nature of the tribal and class conflicts, as also to find out why the Iranians did not produce caste but the Indians did. This implies a comparative study in the ideological apparatuses of the Indians and the Iranians.

What one needs is a scientific analysis of the relation between caste in India and class formations, and the location of caste in concrete historical economic modes of production. What seems to be hitherto missing is the disjuncture between the analysis of caste and the Asiatic mode of production. Whilst the question of the Asiatic mode that emerged in the twentieth century was restricted to the question of the hydraulic system and the oriental state, the question of caste seemed to be missing from this framework of analysis. The debate on the Asiatic mode was severely 'restricted' if not curtailed by the Stalinist state capitalist bureaucrats—M.N. Kokin (1906-39) being one victim, presumably killed in Stalin's infamous purge, and second, not sufficiently touched upon by non-Soviet scholars. Karl Wittfogel's *Oriental Despotism. A Study of Total Power* and later Lawrence Krader's analysis turned out to be defective. What has largely happened is the tendency for a moralistic reading of Marx's Asiatic mode of production, claiming that Marx's usage of 'Oriental despotism' was extremely uncharitable towards non-European societies. This moralistic reading would not only devour the once leftist turned renegade Wittfogel, but also Edward Said and the Indian Marxists who championed the term 'Indian feudalism'. Marx was not interested in the mere morality of nations and civilizations, but in an accurate study of the modes of production. There is a fallacy in claiming that Marx was a European fellow traveller of Hegel and Co., a view championed by Said's Foucaultian reading of the West's encounter with the East. Said should have waited for Foucault's *What the Iranians are Dreaming About?*, wherein Foucault praises the politics of Ayatollah Khomeini, the butcher of democracy and the communists, as "political spiritualism".[12]

When Marx talked of the idyllic non-changing system in India, he was referring to the caste system[13]—a system which, according to Ambedkar, is devoid of rationality—a system according to Marx where there are "self-sufficient communities that constantly reproduce themselves in the same form, and when accidentally destroyed, spring up again on the spot and with the same name—this simplicity supplies the key to the secret of the unchangeableness of Asiatic societies, and the never-ceasing changes of dynasty. The structure of the economic elements of society remains untouched by the storm-clouds of the political sky".[14] It is on this site that the critique of the Asiatic mode and Hinduism appear—Marx and Ambedkar now form a concrete alliance. This critique claims that there are multiple monadic Robinson Crusoes based on small property and patriarchal family labour where not only rational cultivation but also the material and spiritual production of wealth is dwarfed; and that social life is fascinated with the totems and taboos of purity and the fetish for endogamy and social exclusion. In this *varna-jati* dominated mode of production there is no possibility of the instrumental rationality of capitalism, leave alone the critical reason of communism. Yet Marx's analysis has not to be confused with Hegel's schematization of civilizations, where the Indians are rated along with the Chinese and the Persians below European civilization.[15] Hegel was Euro-centric, Marx was a humanist and an internationalist: his motto being "nothing human is alien to me" (*Nihil humani a me alienum puto*).[16] *Marx never condemns people and civilizations, he studies modes of production.*

It is to this question of caste that scientific attention must now turn, for it is the decoding of the caste-class question that will understand Indian history as well as define the question of the Indian revolution. Whilst the communists in India have taken the lead in being the vanguard of class struggles and protests against caste oppression, violence against women and minorities, the caste question per se seems to be eluding their radical politics, so as not to be able to fracture the hegemony of the ruling classes in India. Unless this dialectic of caste and class is exposed, even the bourgeois democratic revolution is not possible, leave alone the socialist revolution. The question of caste is the most degenerate structure retarding the democratic process. It is from this site that one can understand the dominant mode of production along with understanding how: (i) patriarchy in India arises, (ii) as also the repression and retardation of an authentic capitalism in India (for capitalism needs free labour as its prerequisite in contrast to the caste-based hereditary unfree labour), and (iii) the emergence of the neo-fascists Hindutvavadi RSS as well as the Islamist Tabligi-Jamaat and the Jamaat-e-Islami. That caste is a living reality and does not die with the growth of capitalism has to be understood. The biggest threat caste poses today is Hindutvavadi fascism of the Sangh Parivar. It ought to be understood that fascism is a far more complex phenomenon than what the Comintern under Stalin's reactionary leadership and Dmitriov understood in the late 1920s and the 1930s. The orthodox definition of fascism, as "the open, terrorist dictatorship of the most reactionary, most chauvinist and most imperialist elements of finance capital", detached capital accumulation from concrete historical conditions. Whilst it is most certainly decaying finance capital that has turned violent, and which propelled the First Imperialist World War and the formation of the anti-communist fascists in Italy, Germany and Spain, what was missing from analysis is the study of the remnants of the German gens (as Marx reminded Engels in 1868 with a quotation from Caesar: "the Germans always settled as kinship groups and not as individuals").[17] This survival of the rural Germanic gens played an extremely counter-revolutionary role in Germany. The same is happening in contemporary India—the caste system is being propelled along with the geo-politics of imperialism to create a conservative neo-fascist political system in India. The ruling political elites, i.e. the Congress, as Ambedkar prophetically summarised in the 1940s, will not go for social reform, but will give the process of social reform to the rank reactionary and fascist Hindu Mahasabha.[18] Nehru, incidentally, had said: "Many a Congressman was a communalist under his national cloak".[19]

The subaltern anti-caste movement claims that India under

the caste system and the totemism of Brahmanism holds on to a sociology of purity, pollution and exclusion making society essentially anti-democratic. The same subaltern critique holds that the idea of the industrial revolution, besides the idea of clock time is absent in Hindu philosophy, thus accounting for the idea of circular history—in fact a history that never happens, even a neurosis of the eternally recurring trauma. Unlike the European Enlightenment ideas of progress and development, as also the Zoroastrian, Judaic, Christian and Islamic idea of spiral history, the Hindu-Brahmin philosophy has no idea of progress. Caste is the social structure whose superstructure is the ideology of anti-progress and the eternal recurrence. The real study of the caste system has to take place, for caste has not disappeared with capitalism but coexists with it.

Why is this so? For one, the growth of capitalism is not according to ideal type logic where some type of neat class system in 'pure form' develops, a purity that is free from caste structures or other disturbing elements. When Marx talks of the "pure form" and says that one has to understand social processes that occur in "most typical form and most free from disturbing influence", he is implying a methodology that is able to pry into the "cell-form" of society.[20] This pure form exists in reality at the level of the cell-form. The cellular pure form is always combined with the *chaotic form*. The dialectics of the abstract and the concrete is the movement from the cellular pure form to the chaotic bodily form.

Raising the question of social formations and modes of production has necessarily to be analysed at the empirical level, which is free from all ideological disturbances. Most certainly one cannot impose the model of the transformation of feudalism to the capitalism of Western Europe on to India. One cannot have what Marx called a "readymade system of logic" that can be randomly applied anywhere.[21] To raise the question of class and caste in India has thus to transcend a priori metaphysical assumptions. Unfortunately, the communist movement had not only the intrusion of upper caste leaders in its ranks, but even the stalwart of the early communist movement was a revisionist, S.A. Dange, who applied a Platonic methodology in the analysis of India, making evident the Brahmanical bias of an alleged leftist, who glorified Vedic society by claiming that the abominable sacrifice, the *Yagna*, was actually a mode of production[22]—to be precise, a primitive communist mode and thus possibly to be celebrated. Second, the dependence on mechanical materialism in contrast to the dialectical materialism of Marx necessitated the domination of the teleological view of history: the idea that history is governed by iron laws independent of human will, where all history is said to follow a predetermined course—from primitive communism to slavery, feudalism, capitalism culminating with some inexorable force in communism. That Marx refused to abide by such metaphysical mechanics is evident not only in the *Grundrisse* and *Capital*, but also in the *Ethnological Notebooks* and his correspondence with the Russian Narodniki revolutionaries:

> The chapter on primitive accumulation does not claim to do more than trace the path by which in Western Europe, the capitalist economic system emerged from the womb of the feudal economic system. It therefore describes the historical process which by divorcing the producers from their means of production converts them into wage workers (proletarians in the modern sense of the word) while it converts the owners of the means of production into capitalists. In that history "all revolutions are epoch-making that act as levers for the capitalist class in course of formation; but, above all, those moments, when great masses of men are forcibly torn from their traditional means of production and of subsistence, suddenly hurled on the labour market. But the basis of this whole development is the expropriation of the peasants. England is so far the only country where this has been carried through completely ... but all the countries of Western Europe are going through the same development".[23]

What, asks Marx, would the analysis of "this historical sketch" have on non-West European countries? It means first, transforming the peasants into proletarians and then being caught in "the whirlpool of the capitalist economy".[24] But Marx warns that it is not possible to transform the historical sketch of the genesis of capitalism in Western Europe into "an historico-philosophic theory of the general path of development prescribed by fate to all nations, ... (One should not use) as one's master key a general historico-philosophical theory, the supreme virtue of which consists in being supra-historical".[25]

So how would Marxism be able to free itself from the metaphysical supra-historical cocoon that it quite often finds itself in, especially in relation to the understanding of India and the caste question? How does one understand the inner dialectics of caste and class so as to shake the very foundations of the political economy of injustice in India?

The idea of a supra-human history had started creeping into the works of Plekhanov and Karl Kautsky, which was reified into an onto-theological doctrine by Stalin and made fashionable by Althusser's "theoretical anti-humanism". That this positivism is estranged reasoning is evident from the early Marx's reading of history and the human essence (*das menschlichen Wesen*). Marx says that the human is the *essence* and *basis* of all activities and situations: "*History* does *nothing*, it "possesses no immense wealth", it "wages *no* battles". It is the *human*, real, living humanity who does all that, who possess all that; "history" is not, as it were, a person apart, using humanity as a means to achieve *its own* aims; history is *nothing but* human activity pursuing its aims".[26]

When Marx had said that the economic base determines an ideological superstructure, he meant that the term determination (*Bestimuung*) connects and binds the sites of the economic base and the ideological superstructure. Determination is not determinism. Determination, as we noted earlier, is related to the idea of formation (*Gestaltung*). It thus relates itself to the living aspect of social formations. What a revisionist interpretation of Marxism did (especially during the Second International and the later Soviet metaphysicians) was to fragment the base-superstructure, thus opening the path of a reductionist and teleological misinterpretation of Marxism. Economism was born in the proletarian movement. Social democracy today is caught in the binary of economic reductionism and political idealism. They cannot pose the caste problem. Why is this so? Whence does economism emerge? It emerges when one tears the mind (the political and ideological superstructure) from the body (the economic base of society).

Just as one cannot have a mind without a body, so too one cannot have a body without the mind. One has to transcend this fossilized and mechanical methodology (that tears the mind from the body) in order to pose the question of class and caste in a scientific manner. Economism neither reveals the mechanism of class nor caste. Economism is vulgar economics whilst Marxism is a critique of political economy. The *Aufhebung* of economism thus becomes an imperative. Just as the international mechanical social democrats split the base from the superstructure, in India we are faced with the splitting of the questions of caste from class struggle. This has been the tragedy of the Indian revolution.

In contrast to economism, we move into the subterranean regions of history with special reference to the debate of the modes of production in India and the questions of *Gemeinschaft* (community) and *Gesellschaft* (society) that first Marx and then German sociology had raised at the end of the nineteenth century. That India even in the twenty-first century is a bewildering combination of communities is a fact. Caste is not a mere pre-capitalist remnant, but a living organic socio-economic structure. These socio-economic structures are also realized as 'communities'. That these 'communities' are compatible with modern class formations is also a fact. How these numerous communities are related to the historical conjuncture of class struggles remains to be seen. For this one has to go to the site of the great revolution in the sciences that Marx had performed. For the first time in history, "the great moving power" (to borrow Engels' phrase) of history was seen in the dialectical clashes between the sites of forces of production, relations of production and the ideological superstructure. It is these ever-mobile clashing sites, which form the motor force of history. In these clashes the economic, political, scientific and ideological sites both condense and displace, creating the seismic shifts that cause the changes in historical modes of production. In the 1859 preface to *A Contribution to the Critique of Political Economy*, Marx highlights the mechanisms of history. The gist of the argument runs thus:

neither legal relations nor political forms can be comprehended whether by themselves or on the basis of a so-called general development of the human mind, but that on the contrary they originate in the material conditions of life, the totality of which Hegel following the example of English and French thinkers of the eighteenth century embraces within the term "civil society"; that the anatomy, however of this civil society is to be found in political economy ... In the social production of life (*Lebens*), people enter into definite relations, which are independent of their will, namely relations of production appropriate to a given stage in the development of their material forces of production. The totality of these relations of production constitutes the economic structure of society; the real foundation, on which arises a legal and political superstructure and to which correspond definite forms of social consciousness. The mode of production of material life conditions the general process of social, political and intellectual life. It is not the consciousness of people that determines their existence, but their social existence that determines their consciousness. At a certain stage of development, the material productive forces come into conflict with the existing relations of production or—this expresses the same thing in legal terms—with the property relations within the framework of which they have operated hitherto. From forms of development of the productive forces these relations turn into their fetters. Then begins an era of social revolution. The changes in the economic foundation lead sooner or later to the transformation of the whole immense superstructure. In studying such transformations it is always necessary to distinguish between the material transformation of the economic conditions of production, which can be determined by the precision of natural science, and the legal, political, religious, artistic or philosophic—in short, ideological forms in which people become conscious of this conflict and fight it out. Just as one does not judge an individual by what he thinks of himself, so one does not judge such a period of transformation by its consciousness, but on the contrary, from the contradictions of material life, from the conflict existing between the social forces of production and the relations of production. No social order is ever destroyed before all the productive forces for which it is sufficient have been developed, and new superior relations of production never replace older ones before the material conditions for their existence have matured within the framework of the old society. Mankind always (*immer*) sets itself only such tasks as it is able to solve, since closer

> examination will always show that the material conditions for its solution are already present or at least in the course of formation. In broad outline, the Asiatic, ancient, feudal and modern bourgeois modes of production may be designated as epochs marking progress in the economic development of society. The bourgeois mode of production is the last antagonistic form of the social process of production—antagonistic not in the sense of individual antagonism but of an antagonism that emanates from the individuals' social condition of existence—but the productive forces developing within bourgeois society create also the material conditions for a solution of this antagonism. The prehistory of human society accordingly closes with this social formation.[27]

Now it is in this unsurpassable terrain of history that the *question of history* itself emerges. The argument to be held is that Marx foresaw multi-linear histories incorporating distinct Asiatic modes of production. History is not a single teleological process emerging from a primitive communism that marches into slavery, feudalism, capitalism and socialism; but world histories emerge from multiple 'primitive communist' sites leading to Greco-Roman slavery on the one hand, and to distinct Germanic mode, African, American and the Indic and Slavic Asiatic modes on the other hand. It is from this Asiatic mode that caste as a hereditary, occupational, hierarchical and endogamous group formation emerged. It is in this Asiatic mode where caste plays the handmaiden to Indian history. The point is to understand the pre-Rg Vedic Indus civilization, what mode of production existed with the Rg Vedic people, the development of Indian society, and what the statement of *varna* fragmentation suggests in the *pursu sukta* in the *Rg Veda.* Irfan Habib suggests that the "original statement for the four *varnas,* is more a description of social classes than of castes: the *rajanyas,* aristocracy, the *brahmanas,* priests, the *vis,* people at large (mainly peasants), and the *sudras,* springing from the *dasyas,* servile communities. There is no hint in Vedic times of either a hereditary division of labour or any form of endogamy. The *varnas* thus initially presaged very little of the caste system that was to grow later."[28] The first questions that emerge are: When do these classes metamorphosize into castes? And what is the relation of *varna* to the hierarchical caste system? How would both *varna* and caste be extinguished? There are two important issues emerging: the historical analysis, that of the Asiatic mode of production and caste (along with the question: "Is India really capitalist, will it ever be?"); and the role of caste in twenty-first century India.

As regards the question of capitalism and caste, it should be emphasized that caste implies the restriction of the individual and the free movement of labour, whilst capitalism necessarily is based on 'free' labour. According to Marx:

> One of the prerequisites of wage labour and one of the historic conditions of capital is free labour and the exchange of free labour against money, in order to reproduce money and to convert it into values, in order to be consumed by money, not as use value for enjoyment, but as use value for money. Another prerequisite is the separation of free labour from the objective conditions of its realisation—from the means and material of labour. This means above all that the worker must be separated from the land, which functions as his natural laboratory. This means the dissolution both of free petty land ownership and of communal landed property, based on the oriental commune.[29]

In this sense India, which had the capitalist market thrust on it by colonialism, has a complex social formation where emerging capitalist social formations are understood as bound to the caste based proprietorship of the Asiatic *Gemeinschaft*. There will not be a fully developed capitalism with a capital/wage labour antagonism, but, as Marx suggests, proprietors or "members of a community, who at the same time work". "The aim of this work", Marx goes on, "is not the *creation of value*—although they may do surplus labour in order to obtain *alien*, i.e., surplus products in exchange—rather, its aim is sustenance of the individual proprietor and of his family, as well as his total community. The positing of the individual as a *worker*, in this nakedness, is itself the work of *history*."[30] This brings to mind Rosa Luxemburg's argument that the capitalist centre necessarily needs non-capitalist peripheries in order to realize the former's surplus value:

> Capital accumulation as the historical process develops in an environment of various pre-capitalist formations, in constant political struggle and reciprocal economic relations. How can one

> capture this process in a bloodless theoretical fiction, which declares this whole context, the struggle and the relations, to be non-existent?....
>
> Capital accumulation can take place in so far as customers can be found beyond capitalists and workers, in which case growing sales in non-capitalist strata and countries are the precondition for accumulation.[31]

And if the non-capitalist periphery is the sine qua non of global capital accumulation, so too the non-capitalist periphery as "the most primitive economic forms are combined with the last word in capitalist technique and culture".[32] Uneven development of capitalism and unequal exchange (albeit in combined form) now necessitates the existence of caste and the pre-capitalist sectors in the global economy. Caste then is not only a pre-capitalist remnant but also an active agent in the global accumulation of capital. Second, the violent imperialist nature of capital accumulation brings in the political compradors like right-wing organizations that are active in recreating primordial identities (whether Hindutvavadi, Tablig or the neo-conservative born-again Christian). In this case the anti-caste democratic revolution will have an entirely different perspective involving the direct struggle against not only the local ruling classes but imperialism as well.

It is from this terrain of the Asiatic mode and capital accumulation in the age of late imperialism that one proceeds into the over-determined character of Marx's idea of mode of production such that one understands how Marxism is necessarily dialectical and anti-reductionist. First, an economic mode of production combines a number of social formations. Second, the elements of the base and superstructure (family, religion and state) are also classified as modes of production, albeit *particular modes of production* which fall under the laws of private property and alienation.[33] Third, the site of relations of production is also complex and multi-layered, involving the following:

1. Historical forms of ownership of means of production, the balance of forces and the conjuncture of class struggles.

2. Type of economy, natural or commodity, caste and class: value, exchange-value, money, capital accumulation and surplus value. Surplus value as "unpaid labour" is the great idealized signifier of commodity production.
3. Alienation (*Entfremdung*), reification (*Verdinglichung*) and fetishism (*Fetishismus*); where alienation implies loss, dread and terror (reminding one of Freud's analysis of *das Unheimlich* ('The Uncanny' or un-homliness), reification is literally 'thingification' or the de-personification of humanity and the personification of the 'thing'. (signifying the character of commodity production), and fetishism is the morbid attachment to the existing-nonexisting-estranged object.
4. "Real individuals"[34].
5. The human essence (*das menschliche Wesen*).[35]

It is from this site that one can view the non-reductionist nature of historical materialism. Those who claim that Marxism has no space for caste and those who claim that Marx reduces everything to 'class' are absolutely mistaken. It is from this site of class-caste in the age of global capital accumulation that the critique of casteism can emerge. The annihilation of caste is not an act that emerges from the writings and enforcements of legal codes. Nor does the annihilation emerge from creating primordial identities and nativism that is to oppose an imaginary phantom of Brahmanism, but the point is to actively engage-disengage real Brahmanism, the Ideological and Repressive State Apparatuses in India (which are yet governed by the *pursa sukta* notion of exclusion and hegemony) and the concrete accumulation of capital. *Otherwise an inversion of Brahmanism will then be an inverted Brahmanism.* Why is one making such a statement? Because there are possibilities of an illusory anti-Brahmanism (disjointed from history and estranged from the concrete mode of production) which functions within the *varna* framework, where an alleged 'subaltern' caste reclaims a 'lost' (or estranged, even 'castrated' in the psychoanalytical sense) *Kshtriya* status. In such a framework, the *varna* framework is retained, even in its estranged-castrated form. The point is to subvert the caste system, but then, as Phule and Ambedkar had reminded us, one has to overthrow the caste-based ideology of Hinduism itself; and as the revolutionary Marxist dialectic goes, one must annihilate capitalism and imperialism itself. The march towards the annihilation of caste has now become a long march.

Entfremdung, Morality and Pre-modern *Différance*

Marx's concept of *Entfremdung* (alienation), which he claimed to be the motor force of the onto-genesis of global class histories and which reaches its full-blown form in the modern capitalist mode of production nestles in a very strange way in Indian history, especially reflected in the Ideological State Apparatus of Hinduism. *Entfremdung* as estrangement and the terrible loss signifies schiziod splintering and manifests itself as the pre-modern *différance* of the *pursu sukta* and the caste laws of Manu. Hinduism for the Indian subalterns is probably the only religion that is based on the onto-theology of inequality; it is the only system in world civilization that has a legal code of exclusion. Its morality is in fact immorality. Its dharma is *varnashrama dharma*, a morality that is based on caste distinctions. Its duty, as Hegel's and Ambedkar's reading goes, is based on the duty of the caste law: the purity of the caste and protection of it from the intermixture of castes and the production of 'inferior blood'.

If one reads the 'morality' of the *Bhagavad Gita*—the master text of the Indian counter-revolution, as Ambedkar called it[36]—as "duty for duty's sake", then it is, in fact, wrong. What it signifies is "duty for the protection of the purity of the castes". One can immediately contrast this caste-based counter revolutionary (im)morality with Kant's *Groundwork of the Metaphysic of Morals* where the idea of "duty for duty's sake" emerges. For Kant, as opposed to Krishna (the great epic hero of India), there is a distinct idea of humanity to be considered as an end-in-itself, thus postulating the idea of goodwill: to be good for the sake of goodness, as well as the concept of the kingdom of ends. For Hinduism (according to the radical subalterns) there is no idea whatsoever of an autonomous individual, thus no idea of goodness as such, and absolute absence of humanity as an end-in-itself. What Marx called the morality of the tribe as herd animal is found in the dharma of the caste law. Ambedkar said, "Hindu society had its morals loosened to a dangerous point".[37] *Différance* is the ontological fragmentation of society into castes. *Gesellschaft* becomes *Gemeinschaft*, morality means enforcing exclusion and meaningless rites. Consider Hegel on the morality of the *Bhagavad Gita:*

> in which the Indian Arjuna's mentality is attached to family ties. To the moral understanding of the European, the sense of this tie is the moral in itself so that the love for one's own family is as such the completion, and morality consists only in the fact that all sentiments connected with this tie, such as respect, obedience, friendship, etc. as well as actions and duties related to family-relationship, have that love as their foundation and as a self-sufficient starting point. We see, however, that it is not this moral sentiment which in the hero causes the reluctance to lead his relatives to the slaughter. We would commit crimes, he says, if we would kill those robbers (Wilkins: tyrants); not in the sense that killing them as relatives (the teachers always included) would be in itself the crime, but the crime would be a *consequence*, namely through extinction of the generations the *sacra gentilitia*, the duty-bound and religious performances of a family would be destroyed. When this happens, lack of godliness affects *the whole tribe*. In that way the *noble* womenfolk—of the tribe the men can first of all be killed, for they alone are engaged in the battle—will be defiled, from which results *varna-sankara*, the mixture of castes (*the spurious brood*). Yet the vanishing of caste distinctions leads to those who are guilty of the extinction of the tribes and the tribe itself to eternal ruin ... for the ancestors drop down from the heavens because in the future they will be devoid of *cakes* and *water*, no more receiving their oblations, for their descendants have not preserved the purity of their tribe ... If the dead do not receive such offerings then they are condemned to the fate of being reborn as impure beasts... .
>
> Here, however, great importance is attached to the conversion of this tie into a superstitious context, into an immoral belief in the dependence of the soul's fate after death on the cake and water-libations of the relatives, that is to say of those who have remained true to the caste-distinction.
>
> The meaning and value of Indian religiosity and the doctrine of duty related to it, can, however, only be understood from the

> caste law—this institution that has made and still makes morality and real cultivated civilization for ever impossible among the Indians.[38]

In contrast to this genealogy of birth and ranking by blood descent (something that fascinated not only Manu and the Brahmins but also Nietzsche and later the Nazis), Kant claimed that:

> Morality consists in the relation of all action to the making of laws whereby alone a kingdom of ends is possible. This making of laws must be found in every rational being himself and must be able to spring from his will. The principle of his will is therefore never to perform an action except on a maxim such as can also be a universal law, and consequently such *that the will can regard itself as at the same time making universal law by means of its maxim...*
>
> Now morality is the only condition under which a rational being can be an end in himself; for only through this is it possible to be a law-making member in a kingdom of ends. Therefore morality, and humanity so far as it is capable of morality, is the only thing which has dignity.[39]

We get an immediate contrast: the morality of the secularized autonomous individual as an end and not as a means, and the tribal onto-theological dharma of the herd—to consider humanity never as an end but always as a means. It is at this juncture that one understands the dilemma of the dharma of the Asiatic mode of production and the dharma of the despot (thus Oriental despotism). If one has to argue for a secularized, modern nation, then one has to discard the caste system, the dharma of the despot and for that, as Ambedkar passionately argued, *one has to abolish Hinduism itself!* But how is this subversion and annihilation possible? Cornelius Castoriadis has argued that reason, individuation, autonomy and democracy emerge from the settings of the Greek *polis* and despite the reactionary sabotaging of Heidegger's "end of philosophy", it remains the central concern of the Greco-Western project.[40] It is this Greco social structure that enabled the emergence of real, secularized philosophy distinct from the mythology of the gods. Now it is not the case that other world systems did not produce *philosophy as philosophy*. That world revolutions are international, de-territorialized and not confined to any restricted space is well known. The thesis of the emergence of real philosophy from Greece is of importance, but one cannot forget that the universal idea of humanity emerged from the ideas of Zarathustra, Buddha, the *Upanishads*, the Hellenistic Greeks, Confucius, early Christianity and Islam; the European Enlightenment; and last and most important, Marxism and the international communist movement.

In the *Introduction to the Lectures on the History of Philosophy*, Hegel had said that there is a sharp line of demarcation lying between the sites of the mythological and the philosophical.[41] To philosophize means to reason with a critical mind. Mythology is the stage of the 'mind' of world history existing in the stage of infancy. Philosophy emerges only with due maturity. For Hegel, the oriental world lies in the realm of the mythological, whilst the occident has the powers of philosophical reflection. Philosophy as such emerges with the Greeks. Whilst Hegel could be critiqued as an example of the Orientalist consciousness that began probably with Herodotus running up to Heidegger and Karl Popper, making an absurd claim that the 'East', as if had no philosophy; the running battle between the mythological and the philosophical is real and does continue even in present times. For the Indian subalterns the Brahmins are mythological, and there is no possibility of reason being drummed into their heads.

Marxism emphasizes the scientific and the reasoning of critical philosophy, and locates the mythological as the 'return of the repressed'. It thus involves a humanist subversion of the same. The mythical is akin to Marx's reading of Hegel's philosophy as the *deranged and estranged mind*—of the world that thinks in a state of self-estrangement and comprehends itself abstractly.[42]

Let us have a look at how caste struggles in India are embodied in myths and counter-myths, each attempting to subvert the other, each attempting hegemony. If the *pursu sukta* embodies a myth of proto-Brahmanical hegemony, there are parallel subaltern myths. It is in this parallel political economy of myth making that the subalterns are able to attempt to destabilize Brahmanical hegemony.

Consider Phule's counter-mythology: If the Brahmins were created from the mouth, from where was the mother of the Brahmins created? Or are the Brahmins motherless? And what about the Europeans? If the Brahmins were created from the mouth, then the mouth becomes a womb for the Brahmins.[43] But, when the mouth turned into the Brahmanical womb menstruates, how did the Brahmanical mouth-womb absolve this pollution?[44] And if creation emanates from the bodily *différance*, then each of these estranged parts are to be affixed with vaginas in order for procreation to take place, and the period of menstruation for Brahma increases.[45]

> It is well known that Savitri was Brahma's wife. Why, then, did he take upon himself the cumbrous responsibility of carrying the foetus in his mouth for nine months, and also of giving birth to it and bringing it up—subsequently? It appears very strange indeed!
>
> Three of his (four) mouths were free from this encumbrance. How then did the impotent Brahma like such childish game of make-believe?
>
> If we call him impotent, then how did he seduce his own daughter—Saraswati (the goddess of wisdom)? That is why he was known as *Brahma the daughter-seducer*! Because of this vile deed he is not worshipped anywhere.
>
> If Brahma, indeed had four mouths, then he ought to have had eight breasts, four navels, four urethras and four anuses.[46]

The libidinal economy reading of the *unheimlich* of Brahmanism destabilizes Brahminical Hinduism. The mythological games of the self-procreating estranged Brahmin are exposed. Hinduism is a game, but not a philosophical "game for nothing" (to borrow Althusser's phrase from a different context).[47] It is a game for something and a nothing, a "religion (that) is at once a religion of sensualist exuberance, and a religion of self-torturing asceticism; a religion of the Lingam, and of the Juggernaut; the religion of the Monk, and of the Bayadere".[48]

So far, it is in this heterogeneity and contradictions that the Hindu system finds pride. When an Indian calls himself a 'Hindu', there is on the one hand, a concreteness involved. Hinduism refers to the system of orthodoxy starting with the

Vedas and the *Upanishads* running up to the *Dharmashastras*. On the other hand, 'Hinduism' refers to a vacuousness. It can mean a romantic universalism—a *Sanatanadharma* (or universal morality)—a line of thought practised by Gandhi. On the other hand, it implies a racial narcissism as exemplified by the extreme-right-wing politics of Savarkar and Golwalkar.

But for the radical subalterns, it is neither the romantic version nor the fascist one that interests them. And if neither transcendent universalism nor neo-conservative racism would do, a paradigm shift in the cultural politics was deemed extremely necessary. For, behind Hinduism, there always stands caste stratification. And it is these left-wing subalterns who claim that not only is the fascist version of 'Hindutvavadi' (first used by Savarkar), but the term 'Hinduism' itself a borrowed term emerging first with the Persians at the times of Achaemenids (549-330 B.C.)— the term is found in the *Avesta*.[49] Later Persio-Arabic writers continued this historical-geographical usage. But when the upper class-caste elites in the middle of the nineteenth century used this term (essentially against the Muslims) the contradictions inherent in it would eventually spill out. The essence of Hinduism—caste—that was to play the role of the phantom of the juggernaut of multiple master-slave games, would now be bursting at the seams. The battle for hegemony and counter-hegemony would also start, whereby the Phule-Ambedkar politics would form a non-negotiable alliance against Hinduism. If caste has to go, so does Hinduism. There can be no Hinduism without caste, just as there could be no morality with Hinduism. Hinduism is slave morality and here the slaves are in a state of rebellion. The subaltern slaves are not enamoured by Nietzsche's master morality, rather Hegel's dialectic between master and slave fascinates them; because in this dialectic it sees the Brahmin's macabre dance taking centre-stage, but also understands that the grand rebellion is waiting in the wings. The slaves want unity, not *différance*. Civil war against this *unheimlich différance* has begun, the only thing is that it appears not to be quite visible. To transform the not-so-visible into the visible is the task of history.

Myths and Counter-myths

If Brahmanical hegemony is veiled in a myth, so too are the counter-myths of the subaltern castes. The Mahars, the lowest ranked of the castes even in the hierarchy of the 'untouchables', have a myth of creation, which depicts their 'fall'. Unlike the biblical myth, which states the fall of entire humanity, the Mahar myth recounts the fall of the Mahars. Like the biblical myth, it has at its epicentre the taboo of eating forbidden food. There were four cow-born brothers, according to this myth, who were asked by the mother how they would treat her after she died. The first three said that they would worship her; the fourth said that he would bear her inside his stomach just as she had borne her children. This fourth child of the cow becomes the exemplaric sinner and the ancestor of the carrion-eating Mahars, for it is he who puts the dead cow in his stomach.[50]

But if there was the myth of the fall there was also the myth of the Mahars as the vanquished tribes, subjugated by the Brahmins. Mahar leaders had used other forms of folklore to stimulate caste pride in the fellow-Mahars: that the Mahars are the original inhabitants of Maharashtra, destroyed and enslaved by the invading Aryans. Kisan Fagoji Bansode, an early Mahar leader, mobilised the Mahars on this issue and in 1890 Gopal Baba Walangkar, a retired Mahar soldier, drew a petition under the banner of *Anarya Doshparikarakham* ('The Non-Aryan Group for the Removal of Wrongs') demanding readmission of the untouchables into the army.[51] Eleanor Zelliot claims that the early claim of a noble pre-Aryan status is passed over for a Kshatriya status.[52] Ambedkar would, late in life (1948) in *The Untouchables*, bring the thesis that the Mahars were former Buddhists who were defeated by the deceiving Brahmins in the fourth century A.D.[53] The heroic image entered the Mahar consciousness. Henceforth, the Mahars would have a heroic leader (Ambedkar himself) and by 1956 (the year of his death) a new ideological discourse, Buddhism.

By independence, the subaltern classes had a new identity, not the unclean untouchables, nor the sinning, guilt-ridden, 'fallen', carrion-eating cow-child, or the innocent Harijan, Gandhi's children of God. The break that Ambedkar would make would instill in the subalterns a different subject position itself. It is the understanding of this new subject position that is of great importance.

Lenin had said that capitalism and imperialism signify multiple subject positions, each non-reducible, and that the rights of oppressed nations (and minorities) for self-determination are of central concern for the world communist movement. The central concern is democracy—the rights of all people for self-determination, not only labour or the proletariat, but *all* people. It is this idea of '*all* people' that has to be understood, the idea that Marx had summed up in his statement—the human essence (*das menschliche Wesen*).

Das menschliche Wesen

Just as caste and the Asiatic mode of production are under-theorized in Marxism, so too is the philosophy of Marx's humanist *das menschliche Wesen.* It was left to Althusser, the guru of structuralism in France, who castigated this radical idea in *For Marx* as an ideological remnant of a bourgeois fiction invented possibly by Ludwig Feuerbach.[54] What was needed, so Althusser suggested, is an "epistemological break" whereby a "scientific Marx" would appear from a young and heady humanist Marx.[55] One must openly speak of a *"theoretical anti-humanism"*.[56]

It seems at one point to be a French philosophical justification of a Slavic Stalinist misunderstanding and murder of Marx. But this misunderstanding will create the earlier philosophies and ideologies that not only Marx, but also Kant, Hegel and Feuerbach had transcended. One has to go through the secularist and humanist revolution of the European Enlightenment. The idea of society, society *as such,* arises with this definite idea of the human, the human *as such.* Yet one must point out that Marx's humanism is not to be confused with the pre-Marxist usage, whether in Rousseau, Voltaire, the French materialists and the utopian socialists. Marx's *das menschliche Wesen* relates itself to the historical origins and mechanisms of *Entfremdung,* private property and commodity production. It thus stands in direct opposition to reification (*Verdinglichung*) or the becoming of the human into a *thing*. For Marx, modern capitalism has reified humanity into a commodity, the grandmaster of this *thingification* game. The human has become a *Ding an Sich*. What now concerns us is how this reified thingification functions in pre-capitalist societies, especially with caste and patriarchal stratification—how humanity not only bows down before Hanuman the monkey, but believes in the legal code of pouring molten lead in the ears of human beings and cutting out their tongues when humanity comes in front of the Holy *Vedas*, and burning widows alive. Hinduism for the Indian subalterns is practical anti-humanism. Anti-humanism in India follows in the brutal fascist form of extermination of people. It is also carried out in innocent 'aesthetic' form. Coomaraswamy, the guru of Indian spiritualism, glorified sati as the "proof of the perfect unity of body and soul ... of devotion beyond the grave", that celebrates the ideal of wifehood that seeks "eternal heaven".[57]

If this is not despotism, then what is it? But Marx does not contrast Oriental despotism with a heroic and rational West, but with a devouring colonialism. Marx contrasts Asiatic despotism thus with European despotism.[58] Both function within the domain of the estranged human essence. Now this idea of the estranged human essence remains a pivotal philosophic germ in Marx's critique of all class societies. History, i.e. history as such, or histories of class societies, are governed by the dialectic of the estranged human essence and the struggle to appropriate this human essence. So we have the alienated human essence and the transcendence (*Aufhebung*) of this estrangement that defines the humanist parameters of Marx's dialectical and historical materialism. This dialectic of estrangement is directly woven within the historical materialism matrix of the forces of production, relations of production and the ideological superstructure dialectic.

That the estrangement of the human essence is directly related with both class exploitation and caste dehumanization is obvious. What the European Enlightenment and the French Revolution did was to uproot feudalism and its ideologies from its roots and instead put 'man' at its epicentre of discourse. What now applies to world history (and not local histories) are the *Rights of 'Man'*, not the morbid rights-rites of purity, pollution and the creation of a terrible fascist superman. For the Brahmin, like Nietzsche and the fascists, man has to be overcome; for Marx and Ambedkar humanity has to be recalled and embraced. The early Mahar leader Walangkar had said that what matters are the "proper rights of humanity"—humanity is *manuski* in Marathi.[59] What India has done is to forget 'man'. Caste is the *forgetfulness of 'man'*. If Phule understood this theoretically, Ambedkar had to practically live through this caste dehumanization—reliving, as if, the entire ages of caste history of his dehumanized people.

Ambedkar was right when he exclaimed that 'man' is not an economic being—that 'man' does not live by bread alone.[60] The idea of labour as the "essence of humanity" (*Wesen des Menschen*),[61] that Marx drew in the *Economic and Philosophic Manuscripts of 1844*, is not to be confused with purely economic labour. Marx instead had the concept of the ontology of labour, which Georg Lukács was later to work on:

> The outstanding achievement of Hegel's *Phänomenologie* and of its final outcome, the dialectic of negativity as the moving and generating principle, is thus first that Hegel conceives the self-creation of man as a process, conceives objectification as loss of the object, as alienation and as transcendence (*Aufhebung*) of this alienation; that he thus grasps the *essence* of *labour* (*Wesen der Arbeit*) and comprehends objective man—true, because real man—as the outcome of man's *own labour*. The *real, active* orientation of man to himself as a species-being, or his manifestation as a real species-being (i.e., as a human being), is only possible if he really brings out his *species-powers*—something which in turn is only possible through the co-operative action of mankind, only as the result of history—and treats these powers as objects: and this, to begin with is only possible in the form of estrangement (*Form der Entfremdung*).[62]

It is important to draw on the Buddhist notion of *Dukha* in Marx's analysis of alienation, reification and fetishism. According to Ambedkar, sorrow emerges from class conflicts.[63] Probably the relation between *Dukha* and Marx's *Entfremdung* has not been studied sufficiently. *Entfremdung* as alienation is not the 'fall', but the entry into the terrible and unhomily class-caste stratified *unheimlich* world. Alienation, reification and fetishism are the notions whereby both caste and class can be both decoded in theory and transcended in praxis. For Marx the transcendence (*Aufhebung*) of *Entfremdung* is of fundamental importance—the strategies of the transcendence of private property, class and caste histories, patriarchy and the construction of communism is bound intrinsically to the transcendence of this *Entfremdung*. For Ambedkar the transcendence of the sociology of *Dukha* is of vital importance. Phule's deconstruction of the devouring estranged Brahmin and Ambedkar's social reformation follows from this deeply philosophical notion of the transcendence of *Entfremdung-Dukha*. Otherwise, an inversion of Brahmanism would be an inverted-Brahmanism; and an inversion of *Entfremdung-Dukha* would imply an inverted estrangement. One does not want the return of the repressed; it has to be transcended once and for all.

Class and caste are not two 'things' whereby comparative analysis and formal alliances can be made on the principle of the 'either/or' formula. Rather, they are to be understood as social processes; and like capital, have to be read as a social relation[64] —and not as the damned thing, but how the social relation is expressed through things.

In contrast to the damnation of humanity as *thinghood*, Marx's notions of species being and the human essence stand as the philosophical keys to the theory and praxis of communism. Both the species being and the human essence signify classlessness. Marx's critique of all class societies is predicated on the philosophical reasoning of these two ideas. When one says: reason with the human essence, one is talking of an internationalist perspective of Marxism (a point that the communist parties in India forgot after Stalin's reactionary "socialism in one country"—which should have been "capitalist restoration in Russia" and the later dismantling of the Communist International under pressure from the Western imperialists). The human essence bent towards classlessness is necessarily an internationalism. Presently, all progressive forces in Asia need to articulate the revolutionary politics of an Asian

Soviets directed against the imperialists and the local reactionaries. The iron cage of the casteist *Gemeinschaft* that Ambedkar had so vehemently criticised,[65] is better subverted in this framework. Ambedkar's criticism of Marxism was a critique of the fatalistic and reductionist pseudo-Marxism that he had to face. Stalinism and other forms of counter-revolutionary politics, like the Brahmin hegemonists, collapse when the internationalist-humanist dialectic enters the scene of a *thinking history*.

One has to make a paradigm shift from the nation-state, with all its reactionary anomalies, like class, caste, patriarchy, etc. in order to find an authentic solution to humanity's problems. To look beyond the nation-state, capitalism and Brahmanism is a challenge to the Indian revolution. But then neither the nation-state, nor capitalism nor the Brahmins will allow this. In this case: *What is to be Done?*

REFERENCES

1. Utsa Patnaik, ed. *Agrarian Relations and Accumulation. The 'Mode of Production' Debate in India* (Bombay: Oxford University Press, 1990).
2. Karl Marx, 'The British Rule in India', in *On Colonialism* (Moscow: Progress Publishers, 1976), p. 37.
3. Karl Marx, in 'The Future Results of the British Rule in India', in Ibid, p. 85 says that "Modern industry, resulting from the railway system, will dissolve the hereditary division of labour, upon which rest the Indian castes, those decisive impediments to Indian progress and power".
4. Friedrich Engels, 'To Josef Bloc. September 21, 1890', in *Marx. Engels. Selected Works*, p. 682.
5. Friedrich Engels, 'To W. Borgius, January 25, 1894', in Ibid, p. 694.
6. Karl Marx, 'The British Rule in India', pp. 40-41.
7. Edward Said, *Orientalism. Western Conceptions of the Orient* (London: Penguin, 1995).
8. Jyotirao Phule, *Slavery*, trans. P.G. Patil (Bombay: The Education Department, Government of Maharashtra, 1991), pp. XXIX-XXXI, 4, 5, 40.
9. Babasaheb Ambedkar, *Who were the Shudras? How they came to be the Fourth Varna in the Indo-Aryan Society.* (Bombay: Thacker & Co., Ltd, 1946).

10. *Sacred Writings. Hinduism. Rg Veda*, trans. Ralf T. F. Griffith (New York: Quality Paperback Books, 1992), p. 603:

    "The Brâhman was his mouth, of both his
    arms was the Râjanya made.
    His thighs became the Vaiśya, from his
    feet the Sūdra was produced."

    It is in this hymn of the primeval man that the hegemony of the Brahmin is constructed. A.L. Basham says that the order of nature in Hinduism is not dependent on the gods, but on the Brahmins who, by "magic of the sacrifice", maintain nature. The Brahmins are more powerful than any god or earthly king and by using the magical ritual could turn the sacrifice against his patrons and destroy them. *The Wonder that was India; A Survey of the History and Culture of the Indian Sub-Continent before the coming of the Muslims* (New Delhi: Rupa & Co., 2001), p. 241.
11. Ambedkar held contrary to Kosambi's 'Marxism and Ancient Indian Culture', in *History and Society: Problems of Interpretation* (Bombay: University of Bombay, 1989), p. 77; Nripendra Kumar Dutt's *Origins and Growth of Caste in* India, Vol. I (London: Kegan Paul, 1931), p. 21 and later Romila Thapar's *A History of India*, Vol. I (New Delhi: Penguin, 1996), p. 38 that *varna* is not "colour" and proceeded to borrow from "my friend Dastur Bode's" interpretation of the *Avesta* to imply an idealist usage of the same (thus making *varna* equivalent to religion and ethics) in *Who were the Shudras?* Why did Ambedkar do so? A probable reason is that he did not want the caste question to be confused with the race one, both of which he had experienced first-hand, the former in India, the latter as a student in the USA. Ambedkar was also against the race-inspired view of early Indian history inspired by the orientalists. In fact, Ambedkar blamed the Brahmins for accepting this racist view because they believe in "the two nation theory" (Ibid., p. 76) and their own imagined 'superiority', where they—the Brahmins the representatives of the Aryan race—rule over the rest of the Hindus, the alleged non-Aryans (Ibid). Max Weber in *The Sociology of Hinduism and Buddhism* (Glencoe, Ill.: The Free Press, 1958) was also against the explanation of the caste system from the race theory—from "race psychology", the "blood", or the "Indian soul" (p. 124). More information can be obtained from the early *Avesta* or the *Gathas* of Zarathustra which has most uncharitable views on the Rg Vedic people whom Zarathustra found to be liars and violent, who were destroying the incipient agricultural and pastoral economies, both as

Gherardo Gnoli in *Zoroaster's Time and Homeland. A Study on the Origins of Mazdaism and Related Problems* (Naples: Istituto Universitario Orientale, 1980), p. 186, claims to exist at the times of the *Gathas*. Gnoli suggests that the struggle was between the *ratheshtra* / *Kshatriyas* and the *vâstryô-fšuyant* / *Vaiseyas* (Ibid). How the Indians produced this strange and perplexing caste system is of great importance. The Iranians also had a three-tier class system; the *âthravan*, *ratheshtra* and *vâstryô-fšuyant*, and Iranian tradition attributed this tripartite division to Yima, though there is no evidence of a caste system evolving from this.

12. Michel Foucault, 'What the Iranians are Dreaming About?' in Janet Afary and Kevin B. Anderson, *Foucault and the Iranian Revolution. Gender and the Seductions of Islamism* (Chicago: University of Chicago Press, 2005).
13. Irfan Habib claims that Marx's idea of the element of the "unchanging" in the Asiatic mode was *unjust*, and that Marx's idea of the village community was "highly idealized". See Irfan Habib, *Essays in Indian History. Towards a Marxist Perception* (New Delhi: Tulika, 1997), pp. 35, 234.
14. Karl Marx, *Capital*, Vol. I, trans. Samuel Moore and Edward Aveling (Moscow: Progress Publishers, 1983), pp. 338-339.
15. G.W.F. Hegel, *Lectures on the Philosophy of World History. Introduction*, trans. H.B. Nisbet from the German edition of Johannes Hoffmeister (Cambridge: Cambridge University Press, 1980), pp. 200-202.
16. Karl Marx, 'Confession', in Eric Fromm, *Marx's Conception of Man* (New York: Fredrick Ungar Publishing Co., 1967), p. 257.
17. Karl Marx, 'To Engels in Manchester, London, March 25, 1868', in *Marx. Engels. Selected Correspondence* (Moscow: Progress Publishers, 1975), pp. 188-190.
18. Babsaheb Ambedkar, *What Congress and Gandhi have done to the Untouchables* (Bombay: Thacker & Co., 1945), 23.
19. Jawaharlal Nehru, *An Autobiography* (New Delhi: Oxford University Press, 2001), p. 136.
20. Karl Marx, *Theories of Surplus Value*, Part I (Moscow: Progress Publishers, 1975), p. 40; *Capital*, Vol. I (Moscow: Progress Publishers, 1983), p 19.
21. Karl Marx, 'To Friedrich Engels in Manchester, Feb. 1, 1858', in *Marx. Engels. Selected Correspondence* (Moscow: Progress Publishers, 1975), p. 95.
22. S.A. Dange, *India from Primitive Communism to Slavery* (Bombay: People's Publishing House, 1949).

23. Karl Marx, 'To the Editorial Board of the *Otechestvenniye Zapiski*, London, Nov., 1877', in *Marx. Engels. Selected Correspondence*, p. 293.
24. Ibid.
25. Ibid, pp. 293-294.
26. Karl Marx and Friedrich Engels, *The Holy Family or Critique of Critical Criticism* (Moscow: Progress Publishers, 1980), p. 116.
27. Karl Marx, 'Preface', *A Contribution to the Critique of Political Economy* (Moscow: Progress Publishers, 1978), pp. 20-22.
28. Irfan Habib, *Essays in Indian History. Towards a Marxist Perception*, p. 165.
29. Karl Marx, *Pre-Capitalist Economic Formations*, trans. Jack Cohen, edited with an introduction by E.J. Hobsbawm (London: Lawrence & Wishart, 1964), p.67. See also Karl Marx, *Grundrisse*, trans. Martin Nicolaus (Middlesex: Penguin, 1974), p. 471.
30. Ibid, pp. 471-472.
31. Rosa Luxemburg, *The Accumulation of Capital* (London: Routledge and Kegan Paul, 1951); Rosa Luxemburg and Nicolai Bukharin *Imperialism and the Accumulation of Capital* , trans. Rudolf Wichmann (London: Allen Lane, The Penguin Press, 1972), pp. 61-62, 77.
32. Leon Trotsky, 'The Death Agony of Capitalism and the Tasks of the Fourth International', in *The Founding Conference of the Fourth International* (New York, 1939), p. 40.
33. Karl Marx, *Economic and Philosophic Manuscripts of 1844* (Moscow: Progress Publishers, 1984), p. 91.
34. Karl Marx and Friedrich Engels, *The German Ideology* (Moscow: Progress Publishers, 1976), pp. 36-37.
35. Karl Marx, *Economic and Philosophic Manuscripts of 1844*, pp. 89, 92, 94-98, 101, 120, 127, 131-134, 136, 140, 143, 145 .
36. Babasaheb Ambedkar, *Buddhist Revolution and Counter-Revolution in Ancient India* (Delhi: B.R. Publishing House, 1996), pp. 155-182.
37. Babasaheb Ambedkar, *Ranade, Gandhi and Jinnah* (Bombay: Thacker & Co., Ltd, 1943), p. 30.
38. G.W.F. Hegel, *On the Episode of the Mahabharata known by the Name Bhagavad-Gita by Wilhelm von Humboldt*, ed. and trans, Herbert Herring (New Delhi: Indian Council of Philosophical Research, 1995), pp. 17, 19, 51.
39. Immanuel Kant, *Groundwork of the Metaphysics of Morals*, trans. H.J. Patton (London: Hutchinson University Library, 1966), pp. 96-97.
40. Cornelius Castoriadis, *Philosophy, Politics and Autonomy*, ed. David Ames Curtis (Oxford: Oxford University Press, 1991).

41. G.W.F. Hegel, *Introduction to the Lectures on the History of Philosophy*, trans. T.M. Knox (Oxford: Clarendon Press, 1985), pp. 17-19, 159.
42. Karl Marx, *Economic and Philosophic Manuscripts of 1844* (Moscow: Progress Publishers, 1982), p. 129; Karl Marx, 'Nationalökonomie und Philosophie (1844)', in *Karl Marx. Die Frühschriften* (Stuttgart: Alfred Kröner Verlag, 1964), p. 253.
43. Jyotirao Phule, op. cit., p. 2.
44. Ibid, pp. 2-3.
45. Ibid, p. 3.
46. Ibid.
47. Louis Althusser, *Lenin and Philosophy and Other Essays*, trans. Ben Brewster (London: Allen Lane, 1975), p. 55.
48. Karl Marx, 'The British Rule in India', pp. 35-6.
49. B.T. Anklesaria, ed., *Pahlavi Vendidad* (Mumbai: The K. R. Cama Oriental Institute, 2002), pp. 12-13 depicts the land of the 'Hindus' thus:

    The Fifteenth of–lands *and* places, I created *the*–
    best, I Who (am) Ohrmazd, *was that* which *was the* Hapt-Hindukân;—
    [Its being Hapt-Hindukân is that *it* has seven chiefs.
    Why do I say this, that *is* seven rivers? For,
    That *is* evident in the Avesta:
    (Av.) 'From *the* Eastern river towards *the* Western river.'
    There is *one* who thus says: "Every clime has
    One"]—
    Thereupon, 'Ganâ-Mînûy', full *of* death, counter-created,
    In opposition to it, (the) abnormal mensuration,—(*it* is very oppressive), and (the) abnormal heat,—(*it* is more then patmân).
50. See Eleanor Zelliot, *From Untouchable to Dalit. Essays on the Ambedkar Movement* (New Delhi: Manohar, 2005), p. 54.
51. Ibid, p. 57
52. Ibid.
53. Ibid, pp. 59, 72.
54. Louis Althusser, *For Marx*, trans. Ben Brewster (London: Allen Lane, 1969), pp. 51-86, 222-223, 227-231, 236-237.
55. Ibid, pp. 13, 28, 32-34, 32 n., 37-39, 47, 168, 185, 192 n., 244, 249, 257.
56. Ibid, p. 229.
57. See Ambedkar's criticism of Coomaraswamy in 'Castes in India', in *Dr. Babasaheb Ambedkar. Writings and Speeches*, Vol. I (Bombay: Education Department, Government of Maharashtra, 1989), p. 13.

58. Karl Marx, op. cit., p. 14
59. Eleanor Zelliot, op. cit., p. 57.
60. B.R. Ambedkar, 'Buddha or Karl Marx', in *Dr. Babasaheb Ambedkar. Writings and Speeches,* Vol. 3 (Bombay: Education Department, Government of Maharashtra, 1987), pp. 461-462.
61. Karl Marx, *Economic and Philosophic Manuscripts of 1844,* p. 132; Karl Marx, 'Nationalökonomie und Philosophie (1844)', in *Karl Marx. Die Frühschriften* , p. 269.
62. Ibid.
63. B.R. Ambedkar, op. cit., pp. 444-445.
64. Karl Marx, *Capital,* Vol. III (Moscow: Progress Publishers, 1986), pp. 814-815.
65. B.R. Ambedkar, 'Untouchables and the Children of India's Ghettos', in *Dr. Babasaheb Ambedkar. Writings and Speeches*, Vol. 5 (Bombay: Education Department, Government of Maharashtra, 1989), p. 62.

CHAPTER 3

The Sorcerer and His Apprentice
Globalization and Culture

The proletariat can thus exist world-historically, just as communism, its activity can only have a "world-historical" existence. World-historical existence of individuals, i.e., existence of individuals which is directly linked up with world history.

—Karl Marx and Friedrich Engels, *The German Ideology.*

The Story of Monsieur Capital

The history of capitalism along with the histories of liberalism and fascism is best understood as the story of a certain Monsieur Capital who, one day, it seems very suddenly and without announcement, marched into the globe. Whilst Moses held the apparently sinful Eve responsible for the 'fall', Marx pointed his accusatory finger at Monsieur Capital. Though Monsieur Capital as baby, infant and adolescent seemed to be a rather innocent fellow, on growing up he discovered America, rounded up the Cape and roused up the then young bourgeoisie.[1] Yet in the beginning he did not seem to be such an awful fellow, though the mission to conquer the entire globe was his chief aim.

Monsieur Capital claimed to be a decent person. Stories of his battle against the feudal lords deck history books. Once upon a time, he told them to keep their theology to themselves. Instead of the story of the divine right of the kings, he talked of the world market, of modern industry and the constant revolutionizing of the instruments of production. Not only did he revolutionize the sciences, but also the very structure of society was changed dramatically. Now this world market that Monsieur Capital created attracted his friends, the bourgeoisie, from all corners of the globe. Even today, Monsieur Capital in his advanced age is constantly running all over the world, seeking to "nestle everywhere, settle everywhere, establish connexions everywhere".[2] There can be no barriers to stop his macabre dance and awful marchpast—not even the Great Wall of China can stop him.[3] He strongly believes in his proselytizing mission. He intends to convert everyone into a bourgeois.[4] Like the ancient God of Judaism and Christianity, he "creates a world after its own image".[5] He destroys the "idiocy of rural life", makes the country dependent on the towns, the semi-barbarian and the barbarian countries dependent on the civilized ones.[6] He then seeks to establish the empire of one nation with one government, one frontier, one code of laws and one-customs-tariff.[7] The empire has now come. Kabul and Baghdad, Abu Gharib and Guantanamo Bay are mirrors of this empire. The 'borderless' world based on free trade is realized in the panoptic prison of the empire.

This present chapter is based on the critique of late imperialism in permanent crisis, parading under the rather innocent mask called 'globalization'. For answers to questions of globalization and cultures, it looks into the history of Monsieur Capital. Though globalization involves the over-accumulation of capital and the abundance of commodities and though it appears through the technological signifiers of the Internet, satellite television and digital technology, it involves a very different type of technological reason based on the imperialist will to economic power. The picture of the global village that it draws seems to be a rather innocent one—for this village is devoid of the noble savage. On the contrary, the savage ruling this village is more violent and of a more discriminatory type than the traditional Hindu village with its apartheid-type laws of exclusion, purity and pollution.

Globalization is a political economy and an ideology, a project well constructed in the depths of the centre of global capital accumulation and in the heartlands of finance capital. But globalization is also about the psychotic who has escaped from the psychoanalytic couch of liberal democracy and is roaming all round the world for its daily prey. The story of globalization is also the story of the noble knights who in days gone by slew dragons. In this case, Cervantes's *Don Quixote* becomes the exemplary economic philosophy for globalization. But the horse that Don Quixote is riding is a wild horse, more untamed and unruly than the horses of his feudal companions and the raider horsemen from the *Rg Veda.*

Whilst culture (as the culture industry) is understood as the dominant ideology of the ruling classes, this chapter understands culture also as the will of the popular masses. In this popular willing it asks the question: will globalization brought in by Monsieur Capital's dream of one nation, one government, one code of laws and one customs-tariff bring in homogeneity of cultures; or would the combined and uneven law of capital accumulation bring in neither a homogeneity nor a heterogeneity but a combined and unevenness of cultures, determined in every resort by the international class struggle? To the question that globalization is an inherently new mode of production free from contradictions and now built on post-material production, this chapter analyses globalization's post-material simulacrum in the double sites of Marx's ontology of the commodity as the alien and hostile *thing* and Freud's psychosis. Globalization will thus be seen in this spectral-commodified psychosis determined by the dictatorship of finance capital. There are five themes, which this chapter's inquiry into the metamorphosis of the combined and the uneven character of capitalism, looks into:

1. The philosophico-political discourse, which poses the question: how is theoretical and practical humanism possible? This site gives rise to another site—the internationalism of the radical subalterns. This world of internationalism is the world of classlessness: the world of the dictatorship of the radical subalterns.
2. The culture industry of global capital accumulation renders two anti-humanist operations: (a) rendering unnecessary the process of thinking, and (b) the transfiguration of pain and suffering into pleasure.

3. Contrary to the sociology of the manipulation of transfigured pleasure, we pose the question of globalization in the terrain of the discourses of Hegel-Marx-Freud. The dominant ideology of transfigured pleasure of the global culture industry is seen in this Freudo-Marxist discourse of the phenomenology of the transfigured mind.
4. Just as Friedrich Nietzsche had said that "God is dead", so too we say "capitalism and the nation state are dead"; and just as Nietzsche had asked: "What are these churches and temples nothing but graves of God?", so we too say: "What is this state of the state if not the death of capitalism and the nation state?"
5. There is no going back into history. We briefly stand at the memorial of God, Capital and the State and bid them a just adieu.

This chapter is thus based on a triple critique: (i) the critique of the ontology of the commodity conceived as the 'alien thing' that is invested with magical and necromantic powers—and with these invested powers is made to rule the globe, (ii) globalization as the culmination of this class history, and (iii) the politics of monopoly and hegemony of these very class histories. All these three sites that form the basics of globalization of capital flows are questioned in the black hole of alienation (*Entfremdung*). This strange and uncanny world of alienation becomes the basis for the world of globalization.

Many a time the rise of capitalism is contrasted with feudalism's stifling authoritarian decay and the world of globalization is contrasted with the old world of caste superstitions and communal conflicts. What is usually hidden is capitalism's violent methods of colonial appropriation of surplus, both in the days of the primitive accumulation of capital as well as in contemporary times of transferring surplus from the lands of the Third and Fourth World peripheries to the centre of capital accumulation. One also forgets that capitalism and caste can live happily together. One is also amnesic about capitalism's compromise with feudalism and the large borrowings that it does from feudalism's ideological bank.

In our post-ideological times, since the early 1990s, when the people of India had to bear the brunt of the anti-people's policies of the World Bank and the International Monetary Fund now functioning as the policemen of the American state which the Indian state readily succumbed to (besides the enslavement to the American imperialist foreign policy), so too people had to bear the brunt of the even more authoritarian Indian state that renounced the welfare state and accepted communal-fascism and the purging of minorities as its official ideology. For India, globalization means scientific development as well as casteism and the domination of Brahmins and the upper castes, the hype of the Internet but along with it the depression of wages, satellite television but also the regular suicide of peasants, the creation of a civil society and with it the semi-fascist state regularly bending to the will of the American empire. Globalization is a matrix of innumerable contradictions where great wealth and even greater poverty meet, where technology and theology live now in sublime harmony and where freedom is happy with its own unfreedom. The dominant discourse of globalization is the free flow of finance capital that is accompanied by the psychotic rightward shift in the cultural politics of India.

Globalization as the political economy of multi-national capital is marked by a number of dominant features. They are the reorganization of world capitalism after the Second Imperialist World War based on the Bretton Woods agreement and the World Bank and the International Monetary Fund as its instruments, the monetarist onslaught on Keynesian capitalism, the trade union movement and the welfare state by Reagan and Thatcher in the 1970s along with the setting of what Jimmy Carter's National Security Advisor Zbigniew Brezinski called "the Afghan trap" and the formation of the global Wahabi terror network by William Casey, the director of the CIA, under Ronald Reagan, the collapse of the Soviet model of state capitalism and the monopoly of the Anglo-Saxon model of capitalism.

Globalization very often is manifested in ethical, neutral and amoral terms and appears as the free flow of capital, commodities and information based on 'post-material' production—a production of the simulacrum where the political economy of the sign (to borrow Jean Baudrillard's term) decentres the political economy of capitalism. This value-neutral, post-ideological political culture of globalization suspends all analysis of the monopoly of imperialism. Contrary to the celebration of the neo-Platonists and the postmodernists, Samir Amin claims that globalization is marked by five monopolist features, namely: (i) technological monopoly, (ii) financial control of worldwide financial markets, (iii) monopolistic access to the planet's natural resources, (iv) media and communication monopolies, and (v) monopolies of weapons of mass destruction.[8]

Now this discourse of monopolism sharply differentiates itself from the postmodern discourses of value-neutrality and the idealizing cultural politics of globalized capitalism. It exposes the value-neutrality of globalization's cultural politics as the deep-seated political anxiety of petty bourgeois narcissism—a neutering that psychoanalysis calls "the castration anxiety"—which is both the basis of the cultural politics of the middle classes as well as the dominant feature of mental illness in the age of late capitalism. The organic intellectuals of global capitalism seek not to talk of the political economy of globalization. They seek a 'culture' that is in the safe abode of a mystical 'post-politics'. Why and how is capitalism in the age of globalization able to necessarily appear in this fetishized 'post-political' form? Because, as Marx says, the very moment that capitalism is born, cultural politics appears in estranged and fetishized forms. According to Marx, this estrangement, this *Entfremdung*, forms the basis of the capitalist mode of production. *Entfremdung* is the parent, whilst capitalism is its beloved child. So what does the contemporary scene of globalization look like? What do we now see? We see capitalism marching with its unbearable estranged parents as well as its equally unbearable 'post-political' children.

In *Capital*, Marx claims that Monsieur Capital as the master of estrangement appears in disembodied form where body and mind are totally split and unable to coordinate their fragmented selves. Now this estranged and disembodied Monsieur Capital, who is deceptive, is perpetually in disguise. He continuously "changes its features, its hair and many things besides".[9] Now both this *thing* as well as the *changing of this thing* will fascinate Marx, as it would intrigue Freud a little later. This *thing* will turn out to be the instrumental reason of the Frankfurt School and the phallus signifier of Lacan. And presto! Monsieur Capital now with his changed features, hair and the thing-in-itself would appear in a "form different from its physical form".[10] So, in case one decides to embrace this uncertain Monsieur Capital, one would have to be very careful.

Martin Heidegger (known for his extremely sordid support of the Nazis) had asked the very pertinent imperialist question: how is "the complete Europeanization of the world and all mankind" (*vollständige Europäisierung der Erde und des Menschen*) possible? To be in control of the entire world, is many a time said to be the project of Western Reason (in both its secularized and philosophical forms emerging with the Greeks as well as with the onto-theological domination of the world in the Judeo-Christianity tradition by Lord God, the first monopolist and globalized capitalist). Horkheimer and Adorno's *Dialectic of Enlightenment* is a text that draws the genealogy of fascism from Homer to the Nazis as inherent in the Western telos. But this control of the globe—this terrible will to power—can also be said to be emerging with class civilization, and does not have to be confused with the monopoly of Western Reason. What Western civilization has done is to monopolize this will to imperialist power with the help of Monsieur Capital and Madame Rent. So Monsieur and Madame are the causes and the grounds of the imperialism of the will to global power, whilst Western Reason is only its effect. To remain on this "real ground of history"[11]—to borrow Marx's phrase—is the most important thing to do. It is on this real ground, and neither in the Hegelian 'Idea' nor in psychosis, that one will one find the solution. Yet, both the 'Idea' as well as psychosis as the phantasmagorical superstructure intervene in history in constant companionship of Monsieur Capital. This companionship of the 'Idea', psychosis and Monsieur Capital would have a devastating effect on the entire globe.

By the close of the twentieth century, Monsieur Capital had turned both liberal and fascist. He fought two brutal World Wars, he tempted the ex-priest Jusif Jugashvili (or Josef Stalin, as history would know him), annihilated the Bolsheviks and then tamed the Soviets and the Chinese. The more he grew, the more he produced, true to the obedience of Lord God's word, which told sinning men to "Be fruitful and multiply, and fill the earth".[12] The earth is now overfilled by Monsieur Capital's own creations. An epidemic has broken—the epidemic of overproduction.[13] "Society suddenly finds itself", so Marx said, contrary to Lord God's will, "put back into a state of momentary barbarism; it appears as if a famine, a universal war of devastation has cut off the supply of every means of subsistence; industry and commerce seem to be destroyed; and why? Because there is too much civilization, too much means of subsistence, too much industry, too much commerce".[14] We are living in the epoch of surplus civilization, waiting to become barbarians once again.

But along with this now completely deranged Monsieur Capital, who desires complete conquest of the globe, also arrives the proletariat as the democratic multitude that has renounced all nations and all national superstitions.[15] The democratic multitude inhabits the entire globe. Monsieur Capital is creating anti-immigrant laws in North America and Western Europe against this democratic multitude. But the multitude refuses to leave. The entire globe is its scene of action. If Monsieur Capital thinks that globalization of the entire world is its sole and monopolistic privileged project, then he could quite possibly be mistaken. Globalization is a scene of conflict and more deadly than that of Ohrmazd and Ahriman. And this global proletariat agrees with the Marxist proposition: communism has to be a global phenomenon. It cannot take place in one country.

The project of globalization is now stolen from the capitalists. The international proletariat becomes the modern-day Prometheus who steals the fire of internationalism from the bourgeoisie and distributes it amongst the masses.

Hysterical Blindness

"Truth", so Hegel had once remarked, "is a process", and this process, as we noted earlier, is to be found in the whole.[16] The question now is how to grip these holistic processes. And since contemporary social sciences are either preoccupied with abstract definitions, or with purely formal analysis, one must transcend the realm of abstractions and move directly from myth to reality.

Globalization, we are told by its votaries, is a new state of affairs, a novelty that firstly recognizes that socialism and ideology (implying Marxism) are dead, and that development —according to the law of the market—is the order of the day. It is also said that a new borderless world is created where there is an unhindered free flow of capital and commodities. This free flow of capital in this new borderless world, we are assured, will remove all inequalities and poverty.

'The Death of Distance', 'Weightless World', the 'Connected World', the 'Digital Economy', 'Knowledge-Based Economy' and 'Virtual Organizations' decorate the picture of globalization.[17] We now are in the brave new world of post-ideology, a surreal world where the entire picture of the earlier world of manufacturing and agricultural economies has been erased. And if it has not been erased, then, so we are told again, let us erase it. We must embrace these new technologies where there exists only the 'simulacrum' that has totally erased its material referent. Marxism is dead, the welfare state dies with Marxism, and with these multiple deaths also dies the entire project of modernity. If postmodernity was born in the 1960s in Western universities as an academic and ideological discourse to counter Marxism, then at the same time Keynesian economics and the welfare state were transcended for monetarism and the anti-worker policies of the Reagan-Thatcher administrations. Not only was the project of the welfare state abandoned and trade unions coming under the fire of neo-conservative politics, but imperialism—which was already proving to be utterly inhuman and racist—was under William Casey, the director of the CIA in the times of Reagan, manufacturing a political Islam to fight the Soviets. When one is told to ride the horse of global reason then one ought to know that this economics of monetarism, the political culture of postmodernity and the ideology of clashing civilizations would form the *basis* of the leitmotif of globalization. And along with this lethal triumvirate would appear the political discourse of imperialism in the form of the 'empire'. The 'empire of capital' would be realized in this newly founded project of the (American) empire. Yet this newly founded project is based on old precedents. The American project to be the policeman and philosopher king of global capitalism took off from where the Nazis (and earlier the Czarist state) left off. One recalls Ernst Bloc (one-time member of the famed Heidelberg Circle and colleague of Max Weber, Rickert, Dilthey, Simmel and the young Georg Lukács), who said that fascism was not defeated in 1945; it merely shifted its headquarters from Berlin to Washington DC.

So, how to accept this deal of globalization now becomes a problem. The deal, as almost all capitalist deals go, is a package deal. And with "an immense accumulation of commodities"[18] also arrives the empire, and with the empire, the philosopher kings and warriors. If ancient Indian philosophy had (in great regard for ideology and war) given the Brahmin ideologists and the warriors the place of God's head and arms, then one ought to understand that the legs would also have to be fitted in. And this empire in search of its new legs will want to form "one nation, with one government, one code of laws, one national class-interest, one frontier and one customs-tariff".[19]

It is tempting to proceed into the cultural and technological realms of globalization (Internet, satellite television) and see them as primary causes (besides being fixated with what the empire talks of as the surreal 'knowledge society'), than seeing the actual currents of global capital accumulation that give rise to these cultural (many a time fictitious) discourses. Technics is, to borrow Marcuse's term, "but a partial factor" of technology.[20] And technics "can promote authoritarianism as well as liberty, scarcity as well as abundance, the extension as well as the abolition of toil".[21] What the capitalist mode of production has done is to use technics for its own use of creating abundance as well as scarcity. Globalization is the technical management of this abundance and scarcity. Technics is the instrumental reason for the imperialist will to economic power and for the construction of a totally administered society.

What technological reason, as administered reason, does is to drive out the idea of critical reason and to bury the idea of *das menschliche Wesen*. Technological reason is built on the notion of a rationalized-reified life-world. And on this body of the rationalized-reified world is planted the deranged mind of the psychotic. Modern technics necessarily loses its philosophical foundations of the human essence. According to Marcuse (following Husserl), "the humanistic structure of Reason collapses with the release of science from this philosophical foundation".[22] Technology and science have themselves become ideologies and replaced theology (as well as synthesized with it) as the dominant ideology. The technicians of globalization are the priests of modern capitalism. According to Habermas (quoting Marcuse):

> The very concept of technical reason is perhaps ideological. Not only the application of technology but technology itself is domination (of nature and men)—methodical, scientific, calculated, calculating control. Specific purposes and interests of domination are not foisted upon technology "subsequently" and from the outside; they enter the very construction of the technical apparatus. Technology is always a historical-social *project*: in it is projected what a society and its ruling interests intend to do with men and things. Such a "purpose" of domination is "substantive" and to this extent belongs to the very form of technical reason.[23]

So when Monsieur Capital displays his wares, even the commodity called 'science and technology', then it has to be considered with great care. For they are contaminated by the anti-humanism of bourgeois reason. Bourgeois ideology has attacked even 'pure science'. But this in no way depreciates the idea of scientific reason. What one has to re-think is the notion of the reification of the sciences; as also to think what Marx meant a *new science* that is built on the principles of a "human natural science" (*die menschliche Naturwissenschaften*) which is the "natural science of humanity" (*die natürliche Wissenschaft vom Menschen*).[24]

Capital does not produce merely surplus value. As the "perineal pumping machine of surplus-labour",[25] it also produces fantasies. Capital-flows are always accompanied by psychotic-flows. When Freud defined psychosis as "the withdrawal from a piece of reality",[26] this realm of mental illness fits in with Marx's outlining of commodity production (and along with it the foundation of the history of class societies as well as modern capitalism). In this ontological grounding, Marx says that existence as a "material thing" is actively repressed by literally being put "out of sight".[27] (We shall continue with this theme of the blinding of reality in the next chapter). Now this putting out of sight "material existence" is both "hysterical blindness"[28] as well as psychosis. So when we are welcomed in the brave new world of capitalist globalization, we have to be both blind as well as mad, with a blindness and a madness which involves a *fetishism and a regression of thinking.* The current complex of ideologies of globalization (whether in the form of the American political economy of overproduction, or the Third and Fourth worlds of under-consumption, thus whether it involves Fukuyama's liberalism, Huntington's proscribed violence, or Hindutvavadi, the Evangelic right-wing and Wahabi fundamentalism) involves a regression of thinking—best identified by an extremely ideological theme of the 'end of ideology'.

Thus when it is said that globalization deals with a weightless-borderless virtual economy, then one ought not to forget that monetarism (with the death of the welfare state) and the brutality of capital accumulation would now appear in full-blown form. And marching with capital marches the ideologies of the crusading God of the neo-conservative American administration seeking to kill the terrorists in the lands of the 'axis of evil', the Allah of the Wahabi conservatives, who has become furious with the infidels and the recently constructed Lord Rama of the extreme right-wing fascists in India who intend to destroy modernity, secularism, democracy, the communists and minorities. The postmodern onto-theologians say that humanism is an error, that secularism and the entire project of the Enlightenment is a creation of atheism. Atheism, (along with the humanist and secularist projects of the Enlightenment) we are told, destroys our cultural roots. The crisis exists because *we are breaking the covenant with God*, a theme of contemporary Iranian Shiite Heideggerean ideology,[29] a theme that is shared by the Iranian imams, the global Wahabi movement, and their American adversaries. Globalization necessarily involves *the forgetfulness of humanity*. Anti-modernity, anti-secularism and anti-humanism form the core of the dominant ideology of globalization. If postmodernity is said to be the cultural logic of late capitalism,[30] then globalization can be said to be the logic of the political economy of late imperialism in permanent crisis. To detach globalization from the crisis of capitalism (and its anti-humanist ideologies) is an error. Just as Horkheimer and Poulantzas had said that one cannot talk of fascism without talking of capitalism and imperialism,[31] so too one says that one cannot talk of globalization without talking of the permanent crisis of capital accumulation and its ideologies emanating thereon.

There is a critique of globalization appearing in a supposedly 'subaltern' form that even surpasses the critique of Western Reason that was articulated by Horkheimer and Adorno in the *Dialectic of Enlightenment*. This conservative, or what Wilhelm Reich called *pseudo-radical*[32] critique had its precedents in the neo-romanticists of the nineteenth and twentieth centuries—Ruskin, Coomaraswamy, Gandhi, etc. Now these same neo-romantic themes appear in the philosophies of Michel Foucault who amazingly hailed the ideology of the Shiite imams and the theological butchers of the communists in the late 1970s as "spiritual politics".[33] One does not fight the Anglo-Saxon imperialists with Third World capitalist nationalism. One cannot fight *Entfremdung* with *Entfremdung*, private property with private property.

Thus one does not have to fight for an independent 'India', 'Pakistan', 'Bangladesh', 'Israel', etc. each of whose contours were drawn with colonial ink seeped in people's blood. On the contrary, one has to think beyond capitalism, colonialism and the nation-state, and to rethink the rights of all people to self-determination. This right to self-determination has to then imagine a Popular Front for the Liberation of Asia—a front that is essentially stateless and classless, a classlessness that actively discovers the human essence by *positively* involving a transcendence (*Aufhebung*) of private property and human estrangement (*die Aufhebung der Entfremdung*), as also positively involving the appropriation of the human essence (*die Aneignung des menshlichen Wesens*).[34] Communism is the "complete return (*Ruckkehr*) of man to himself as a social (i.e., human) being—a return accomplished consciously and embracing the entire wealth of previous development".[35] One must learn how to embrace the human essence and this entire wealth of previous development. Only then will we able to solve, what Marx calls *the riddle of history.*[36]

The Anatomy of Monsieur Capital

In order to study the very peculiar and contradictory world of globalization—one that claims to be free and open, but which is a prison-house of stored dead people, we need to study the anatomy of Monsieur Capital. To turn to the culture of globalization, one must turn to its culture industry, which itself turns to the study of Monsieur Capital himself. According to Marx, the globe that the bourgeoisie has occupied is like the evil sorcerer who, with his diabolic spells has conjured up terrible spirits from the netherworld, which he cannot contain.[37] One must remember the crucial difference in the ideas of the globe (and globalization/internationalism) of the bourgeoisie and Marx's view of world history and communism. Whilst the former in its anti-humanist zeal deals with alien objects,[38] is obsessed with dead labour, mysticism, necromancy and the conjuring of spirits from the netherworld, the communists refuse to deal with estranged objects, nor with its specterology. In contrast to the Stalinist, social democratic, fascist and the Gandhian nationalist response to global capitalism, Marxism does not give consent to the utopian pre-capitalist critique of capitalism. Marx celebrates the world as the theatre of operation; he embraces "the actual existence of people in their *world-historic* instead of local, being", and affirms the "universal development of productive forces" and "the *universal* intercourse between people", which "produces all nations simultaneously", "and finally puts *world-historical*, empirically universal individuals in place of local ones".[39] The discourse of the 'local' that the American academic subalterns and the French postmodernists would celebrate (alongside the right-wing Shiv Sena in Maharashtra) since the 1960s, is considered by Marx as the culture of under-consumption. It creates *privation* and the generalization of want, and with it the restoration of the "old filthy business" of class histories will begin once again.[40]

So one thing is very clear: the response to globalization cannot be any type of localization or nationalism. One does not have to fight imperialism on its own territory of the nation-state. Likewise, Marx did not think that much would come from feudal, patriarchal, idyllic relations, except feudalism, patriarchy and idiocity.[41] Instead, modern industry and technological reason have to be embraced, but neither in the terms of bourgeois science, nor in the structures of the capitalist mode of production. That is why we pointed out the Frankfurt School's reading of the difference in the 'science' of the bourgeoisie and a post-capitalist science. Science thus does not have to be seen as an objective process, but what Marcuse called a 'project', hence linked to the dominant class and its ideology.[42]

But then, Monsieur Capital and Madame Rent enter modernity and teach (not merely the feudals but also) technological reason a lesson or two with even more brutal specteroly than the one the witch-hunting feudals in Europe did by doing "their ghost walking as social characters",[43] then one realizes how, from the naked, shameless brutality of feudalism[44] would emerge the capitalist sorcerer wearing the mask of "false appearance and illusion", speaking henceforth only "half-truths and unsolved contradictions".[45]

Thus when Monsieur Capital claimed that as ghost and as a mere thing it had inherent right to perform its awful marchpast all over the globe, then at least Marx would be highly offended by this transfiguration of privileges and might for right. Now Marx, the atheist and humanist, was not going to believe Monsieur Capital and his monstrous false appearance and illusion. Marx decided to strip Monsieur Capital and see what he really had to offer, besides free trade and the garble of liberty, equality and fraternity. Marx says that he does not see liberty, equality and fraternity; instead, he saw infantry, artillery and cavalry. Monsieur Capital insists that he can offer real equality. So Marx decides to go to "the bottom of this equality".[46] Now viewing the bottom of Monsieur Capital was always going to be difficult. So Marx decides to study philosophy and science, besides jurisprudence, to avoid legal troubles. But besides these disciplines, Marx also studies theology, necromancy and the black arts knowing that Monsieur Capital deals with magic and necromancy[47] . To avoid both legal troubles as well as to catch Monsieur Capital napping Marx goes to the graveyard of humanity, for Marx knows for sure that Monsieur Capital was born there and resided there as well. Marx takes his telescope and microscope in order to study that which is both the largest as well as the smallest of the capitalist mode of production. As a scientist, he wants to study not only the bottom of Monsieur Capital but also its cell form.[48] So he also takes a spade in order to dig the graves of Monsieur Capital and his bourgeois companions. He wants to study their essences. He wants to know what the "common something"[49] is between different bourgeois corpses. He finds "total abstraction"[50] from the humane and material characteristics of real humanity. They are useless and "do not contain an atom of use-value",[51] Marx exclaims after careful microscopic examination. He digs further and finds some "residue"[52] left from these capitalized corpses. He shrieks at what he, atheist and humanist, finds—"ghostly objectivity" (*gespenstige Gegenständlichkeit*).[53] These ghosts have now escaped from the graves and now "appear as independent beings (*selbständige Gestalten*)", so Marx warns us, "endowed with life and entering into relation both with one another and the human race".[54] We are bewitched! The feudal theologians claimed that they had burnt all the witches, but there is nothing left but the spectre of this capitalist *gespenstige Gegenständlichkeit* everywhere. The spectre is haunting the world—the spectre of global capitalism. Monsieur Capital and Madame Rent shall knock at every door. None shall be spared. What then is to be done, when this enlightened Monsieur is dressed up in "false appearance",[55] and where "the intermediate steps of the process vanish in the result and leave no trace behind"[56] ? How should one deal with Monsieur Capital, who is the ghost and deceiver as well as the murderer, who wipes off all traces of his deadly act?

In the graveyard of capitalism Marx hunts down the bourgeois spectres. He sees them hanging from forbidden trees. He screams at them to leave immediately and not to haunt humanity. Well learnt in the ancient necromantic art of exorcism, Marx compels them to leave. The spectres shriek back at Marx. They throw the holy book of capital accumulation at him. He picks up the good book and begins to read it. It says how the world is divided in the regions of the good capitalist world and confused regions of the periphery. God has told all people of the confused periphery to reform and privatize. He also tells the good capitalist how to convert the entire world into the good religion of the eternal capitalist mode of production. Those who resist are deemed evil and struck by the temptations of Satan. Their lands are declared to be the 'axis of evil' inhabited by terrorists, who need to be blown off from the face of the earth. The knights of the round table are ordered to destroy evil once and for all.

But there is also something written in illegible ink, and extremely difficult to analyse. So Marx exercises his art in philology. He takes out his microscope and begins careful investigation of this illegible ancient script. Suddenly he breaks out in laughter. The illegible verse is the tenth mandala of the *Rg Veda.*

> The Brâhman was his mouth, of both his
> arms was the Râjayana made.
> His thighs became the Vaiśya, from his
> feet the Sūdra was produced.[57]

Marx's laughter signifies why the poor Sancho of the Third World marched with the deluded Don Quixote. On this topic of consent, political legitimacy and the culture industry of globalization, Bertolt Brecht said it in a slightly different way:

Two robbers were plundering the province of Hesse
Many a peasant's neck they broke
One was as thin as a hungry wolf
And the other as fat as the pope.

But what made their bodies so different?
It's because they were servant and master.
The master swigged the cream of the milk, so then
The servant got his milk already sour.

The peasants caught the robbers
And when they hung by *one* rope
One hung there thin as a hungry wolf
And one as fat as the pope.

The peasants stood there crossing themselves
And staring at the two
They saw that the fat man was a robber
But why was the thin man too?[58]

Epitaph

The secret lies in the simple fact—if money comes into the world with "blood-stain on one cheek", then "capital comes dripping from head to foot, from every pore, with blood and dirt".[59] And neither simulacrum, nor knowledge society can wipe out these stains.

It is as simple as that.

REFERENCES

1. Karl Marx and Friedrich Engels, 'The Manifesto of the Communist Party', in *Marx. Engels. Selected Works* (Moscow: Progress Publishers, 1975), p. 36.
2. Ibid, p. 38.
3. Ibid, p. 39.
4. Ibid.
5. Ibid, p. 39; Karl Marx, *Capital*, Vol. I (Moscow: Progress Publishers, 1983), p. 19.
6. Karl Marx and Friedrich Engels, 'The Manifesto of the Communist Party', p. 39.
7. Ibid, pp. 39-40.
8. Samir Amin, *Capitalism in the Age of Globalization. The Management of Contemporary Society* (New Delhi: Madhyam Books, 1997), pp. 4-5.

9. Karl Marx, *Capital*, Vol. I, p. 58.
10. Ibid.
11. Karl Marx and Friedrich Engels, *The German Ideology* (Moscow: Progress Publishers, 1976), p. 61.
12. 'The First Book of Moses commonly called Genesis', in *The Holy Bible* (New York: Wm Collins, 1952), p. 7: 9.1.
13. Karl Marx and Friedrich Engels, 'The Manifesto of the Communist Party', p. 40.
14. Ibid.
15. Ibid, p. 51.
16. G.W.F. Hegel, in his *Phenomenology of the Mind*, trans. J. Baille (London: George Allen & Unwin Ltd., 1966), p. 81, says that: "The truth is the whole". And to this whole scientific analysis must proceed.
17. Ursula Huws, 'Material World: The Myth of the Weightless Economy', in *Global Capitalism Versus Democracy. Socialist Register.* ed. Leo Panitch and Colin Leys (London: Merlin Press, 1999), p. 29.
18. Karl Marx, *Capital*, Vol. I, p. 43.
19. Karl Marx and Friedrich Engels, 'The Manifesto of the Communist Party', pp. 39-40.
20. Herbert Marcuse, 'Some Implications of Modern Technology', in *The Essential Frankfurt School Reader*, eds. Andrew Arato and Eike Gebhardt (New York: Continuum, 1985), p. 138.
21. Ibid, p. 139.
22. Herbert Marcuse, 'Science and Phenomenology' in *The Essential Frankfurt School Reader*, p. 476.
23. Jürgen Habermas, 'Science and Technology as Ideology' in *Toward a Rational Society: Student Protest, Science and Politics*, trans. Jeremy J. Shapiro (London: Heinemann, 1971), p. 82.
24. Karl Marx, *Economic and Philosophic Manuscripts of 1844* (Moscow: Progress Publishers, 1982), p. 99.
25. Karl Marx, *Capital*, Vol. III (Moscow: Progress Publishers, 1986), p. 822.
26. Sigmund Freud, 'Neurosis and Psychosis' and 'Loss of Reality in Neurosis and Psychosis', in *The Penguin Freud Library*, Vol. 10, *On Psychopathology* (London: Penguin Press, 1993).
27. Karl Marx, *Capital*, Vol. I, p. 45.
28. Sigmund Freud, 'The Psychoanalytic View of Psychogenic Disturbance of Vision', in *The Penguin Freud Library*, Vol. 10, *On Psychopathology* (London: Penguin Press, 1993), p. 108.
29. Riza Davari-Ardakani, *Inqilab-i Islami va Vaz'-I Kununi' Alam [The Islamic Revolution and the Current Conditions of the World*] (Tehran:

Markaz-e Farhangi-I' Alame Tabatabai, 1982), *Falsafih Chist?* [*What is Philosophy?*] (Tehran: Anjuman-i Islami-I Hikmat va Falsafih-i Iran, 1980). See Farzin Vahadat, 'Post-revolutionary Islamic Discourses on Modernity in Iran: Expansion and Contraction of Human Subjectivity', in *International Journal of Middle East Studies,* Vol. 35, Nov. 2003, No. 4.

30. Frederic Jameson, *Postmodernism, or, The Cultural Logic of Late Capitalism* (London: Verso, 1991).
31. Max Horkheimer in 'The Jews and Europe' says that, "whoever is not willing to talk of capitalism should also keep quiet about fascism". See Max Horkheimer, 'The Jews and Europe', in *Critical, Theory and Society. A Reader*, eds. Stephen Bronner and Douglas Kellner (London: Routledge, 1989), p. 78; Nicos Poulantzas, *Fascism and Dictatorship. The Third International and the Problem of Fascism,* trans. Judith White (London: Verso, 1979), p. 17.
32. Wilhelm Reich, *The Mass Psychology of Fascism*, trans. Vincent R. Carfango (New York: Farrar, Strauss & Giroux, 1970), p. XIV.
33. Michel Foucault, 'What are the Iranians Dreaming of?', in Janet Afary and Kevin B. Anderson, *Foucault and the Iranian Revolution: Gender and the Seductions of Islamism* (Chicago: University of Chicago Press, 2005).
34. Karl Marx, *Economic and Philosophic Manuscripts of 1844,* pp. 90, 94, 109.
35. Ibid, p. 90.
36. Ibid.
37. Karl Marx and Friedrich Engels, 'The Manifesto of the Communist Party', p. 37.
38. Karl Marx, *Economic and Philosophic Manuscripts of 1844,* pp. 63, 68, 70, 136.
39. Karl Marx and Friedrich Engels, *The German Ideology,* pp. 54-57.
40. Ibid, p. 54.
41. Karl Marx and Friedrich Engels, 'The Manifesto of the Communist Party', p. 38.
42. Herbert Marcuse, 'Industrialization and Capitalism in the Work of Max Weber', in *Negations. Essays in Critical Theory,* trans. Jeremy J. Shapiro (London: Allen Lane, The Penguin Press, 1968), p. 224.
43. Karl Marx, *Capital,* Vol. III, p. 830.
44. Karl Marx and Friedrich Engels, 'The Manifesto of the Communist Party', p. 38.
45. Karl Marx, *Capital,* Vol. III, p. 830.
46. Karl Marx, *Capital,* Vol. I, p. 66.
47. Ibid, p. 80.

48. Ibid, p. 19.
49. Ibid, p. 45.
50. Ibid.
51. Ibid.
52. Ibid, p. 46.
53. Karl Marx, *Das Kapital. Kritik der politischen Ökonomie*, Erster Band (Berlin: Dietz Verlag, 1981), p. 52.
54. Karl Marx, *Capital*, Vol. I, p. 77; *Das Kapital. Kritik der politischen Ökonomie*, Erster Band, p. 86.
55. Karl Marx, *Capital*, Vol. I, p. 95.
56. Ibid.
57. *The Rig Veda*, trans. Ralph T. H. Griffith (New York: Quality Paperback Book Club, 1992), p. 603.
58. Bertolt Brecht, 'The Robber and His Servant', in *Bertolt Brecht. Poems. 1910-1956* (London: Eyre Methuen Ltd., 1976), p. 244.
59. Karl Marx, *Capital*, Vol. I, pp. 711-2.

CHAPTER 4

The Return of the Emancipated

AN ESSAY CONCERNING KARL MARX'S QUESTION: HOW IS THE TRANSCENDENCE AND REALIZATION OF PHILOSOPHY POSSIBLE?

Ah, I have studied philosophy,
Medicine, jurisprudence too,
And for my sorrows theology,
Over and over, through and through.

—Goethe, *Faust*. Part One.

Reason has always existed, but not always in reasonable form.

—Karl Marx. 'To Arnold Ruge, 1843'.

Not only in its answers,
even in its questions there was a mystification.

—Karl Marx and Friedrich Engels, *The German Ideology*.

Philosophy, which once seemed obsolete, lives on because the moment to realize it was missed.

—T.W. Adorno, *Negative Dialectics*.

Introduction

Marx's question on the critique of the Hegelian dialectic in particular and the history of philosophy in general, which is summed up in his statement on the transcendence and realization of philosophy (*Aufhebung und Verwirklichung der Philosophie*) is probably the most important question in his philosophy, unfortunately not sufficiently analysed. Unfortunately, because the neglect of critical Marxism led to the most spurious studies in Hegel and Marx. This neglect played a pivotal part in the ideological struggles (following Lenin's death) which culminated in the counter-revolutionary coup against the Bolsheviks led by the Stalinist oligarchy in the late 1920s and the inability of either the left-opposition led by Trotsky or other revolutionary groups to deal with the Stalin question (especially the restoration of capitalism in Soviet Union by the Stalinists), and the rise of fascism in Germany. The fall of the Soviet bloc was a mere necessary end result of a falsification of Marxism by a state-capitalist bureaucracy.

The Second International had stressed the primacy of the political in the revolutionary desire to overthrow international capitalism. However, the question of the primacy of Marxist philosophy as the dialectical unity of theory and praxis was largely put on the backburner. In the fury of the First Imperialist World War, Lenin was studiously involved in the studies of Hegel. In these notebooks, known to history as the *Philosophical Notebooks,* Lenin insisted on the knowledge of Hegel (in fact the complete *Science of Logic*) without which it was impossible to understand Marx's *Capital*, especially the first chapter. Consequently, Lenin mourned that even after half a century after Marx, the Marxists have not understood Marx. Alas, how true were to be these words!

Prelude to the Return of the Emancipated

Philosophy is essentially political. Political because it deals with the question: *What is 'man'?* The three Kantian questions: "What can I know?", "What ought I to do?", "What may I hope for?", followed by a fourth one "What is 'man'?" deals with this very philosophical question that is essentially political.

The twentieth century saw four unsurpassable horrors: the two imperialist World Wars, the rise of Stalinism, Nazism, and the formation of the American 'empire'. Whilst Stalinism and fascism are (at least officially) dead and buried, the empire (which ought to have been dead and buried) is alive and doing a spectral marchpast over the entire globe. In this context one asks: What relevance does Marxism have in the twenty-first century? And how can it deal with the very philosophical question that is essentially political: "What is 'man'?"

It is quite often said that philosophy in the telos of Western Reason emerged with the Greeks and philosophical reasoning from the Greek *polis.* Philosophy as philosophy emerged not only with the inquiry of the Being of beings understood as the destiny of Being, but also with the questions of democracy and liberty, as also the question: What is 'man'? Even two thousand five hundred years after this question, we ponder: "What is 'man'?" Marx had raised two questions with regard to 'man': "What are *Gattungswesen* (species being) and *das menschliche Wesen* (the human essence)?" It is with these questions that we pose the most important question of our times: "What is socialism and how is it possible?"

Though philosophy emerged in the telos of Western Reason with Anaximander and Thales that provided a setting for the rise of Socrates, Plato, Aristotle and the Sophists; there remained at the background of the politics of 'man', the telos of the 'Idea', which moved from the *Book of Moses*—the Judaic, Christian and Islamic account of creation—to Hegel. Now Marx, the modern Sophist and Cynic, had nothing to do with the 'Idea' except that he had everything to do with it, just as Freud had nothing to do with psychosis and yet had everything to do with it. The movement towards the 'Idea' would be a movement towards the history of philosophy along with the question: "What is 'man'?" And in this 'Idea' is posed not only the perfection of Western culture and civilization but its very imperfection. In this 'Idea' we have both reason and psychosis. The formation of the empire under the rather innocent name of globalization is the perfection of this 'Idea' as psychosis. It also implies the death of 'man'. And in this perfection and imperfection we pose the question: "What is Marxist philosophy and what relevance does it have for the twenty-first century?" With this in mind we begin the Marxist interrogation of philosophy.

This chapter inquires into Marx's question of the *Aufhebung der Philosophie* based on the following sites:

1. The Being question. Herein is situated the forgetfulness

and the remembrance of Being. The recurrence of Being is the return of the neurotic trauma facing global class societies. Philosophy is then considered as the eternal recurrence of the neurotic self-same. 'Being' as both 'Matter' and the 'Idea' are games played by philosophy's neurosis. Yet one must understand that this neurosis is rooted in actual reality. Marx does not think that philosophy's neurosis can be wished away. In *Capital* he recalls the question of Being. There are three sites—'Being', 'being' and 'beings'. Now 'beings' (i.e. 'men' who are essentially political) are alienated and thus we have a positing of 'being' and 'Being'. Both 'being' and 'Being' are reifications, these awful 'things' that are given life. Now these animated 'things' with these alchemical magically bestowed powers are represented in philosophy as the story of 'being' and 'Being'. The story of 'Being' is the story of the double forgetfulness of 'man' and the politics of 'man'.

In *Capital*, 'being' is reified society, reified relations between things; whilst 'Being' is the 'essence', 'substance' and 'groundwork' of 'being'. Now 'being' is a 'thing', whilst 'Being' (the Being of beings) implies the total loss, not only of all human characteristics, but also the loss of all materiality and concreteness. To borrow Marx's phrase again: *existence as material things (sinnlichen Beschaffenheiten) are put out of sight (ausgelöscht)*.[1] The story of philosophy is the consequent putting out of sight sensuousness. Philosophy is the story of blindness.

2. Disembodiment and metamorphosis. There are a number of binaries governing the history of philosophy: Matter/Idea, body/soul, necessity/freedom, etc., and despite each philosopher attempting to give solutions, it turns out that this is only the self-same problem returning again. The neurotic has returned. Plato's fundamental philosophical statement: to leave the cave of darkness and shadows, and embrace the world of light, is forgotten. We have returned to the cave, in fact descending deeper and deeper into this dark cave of eternal darkness.

When Marx said that "existence as material things (*sinnlichen Beschaffenheiten*) are put out of sight (*ausgelöscht*)", he meant that not only did philosophy (and theology, especially

Christianity) but also class civilization as its fundamental *point of departure*, implies this blindness. Why is this so? It is because class civilization in the production of commodities, necessarily *sheds its character of materiality* (use values) to posit this ideal character of value and exchange value. Both class societies and philosophy shed this materiality. This process of disembodiment and metamorphosis forms the essential characteristics of both class societies and philosophy. Marx calls these processes fetishized, irrational, magical and necromantic processes.[2] Philosophy is this exemplary forgetfulness of the *sinnlichen Beschaffenheiten*. The *Aufhebung* of philosophy is necessarily the war against this amnesia.

3. Alienation-reification-fetishism. This triad forms the cell form and the backbone of the epistemic mechanisms of the blindness of philosophy. To explore this cell form is a categorical imperative.

4. The question of 'man' that is essential political. The remembrance of this story is the narrating of the story of the desiring human essence (*das menchliche Wesen*).

In this chapter Marxist philosophy is submitted to a double-fold reasoning: the genealogy of estrangement and the hermeneutics of translations, where philosophy's 'Being', 'Consciousness', 'Truth', 'Essence', 'the Essence of Truth', etc. are translated into the question of 'man' that is essentially political. If Ludwig Feuerbach thought that the truth of theology is anthropology, then for Marx the truth of philosophy is 'man', who is essentially political.

Now to the well-known site of understanding philosophy as class struggle, we explore another site—the site of estrangement. In understanding philosophy being registered in the dual sites of class struggle and estrangement, Karl Marx the philosopher of practical reason (also the registrar of unpractical reason) registered not only a different type of a 'turn' in the history of philosophy, but a very radical subversion. Philosophy since this subversion ceased to be read in the texts of understanding (*Verstand*) and reason (*Vernunft*)—as, for instance, the way Kant and Hegel read philosophy—but was inscribed in the dual flows: capital flows and psychosis. And it is in these sites that Marx raised the question: *"How is philosophy to be real and praxical, and thus how is one to transcend and realize philosophy?"*

Marx's historical materialist inscription: the economic base determines (*bestimmte*) the ideological superstructure, redrafted as the reified economic base determines the philosophical superstructure brought forth the notion of the philosophical mind as the estranged mind. Now this philosophical-estranged mind is notified within the flows of being and consciousness—capital accumulation + psychosis. So what is so fundamental that happened in these flows? That the philosopher Aristotle (the greatest mind of antiquity, as Marx thought him to be)[3] was seen as riding on the horse of reason and barbarism both at the same time, and thus necessarily accompanied by his student, the schizoid Alexander "the great", who is apparently also at the same time "the accursed" (*guzastag*).[4] Greatness and curses move hand in hand. It is this ironical position that not only philosophy but also the history of humanity is caught up in. Great civilizations are almost always accompanied by great barbarisms. One recalls Walter Benjamin: "There is no cultural document that is not at the same time a record of barbarism."[5]

Thus the ancient Heraclitean dictum: *everything flows* is transformed into the dictum: everything great flows in an accursed manner. We have this dual type of flows determining history—capital flows and psychosis that would interest this Marxist reading of philosophy. Now this is a very peculiar type of reading that Marx suggests. To read philosophy in the dual estranged flows of (i) capital flows, and (ii) psychotic flows is to read philosophy in the text of imagined madness. For, when the young Marx suggested that one ought to read philosophy as the speech act of the estranged human essence,[6] he implied that this text had to be translated into the (psychoanalytic) text of repression. Philosophy not only represses, it also says exactly the opposite of what it represses. And to grasp the importance of philosophy is to grasp this very important point in the history of human repression.

There are two important points that Louis Althusser raised in *Lenin and Philosophy*: to understand philosophy as a lost path, as a *Holzweg*, and to understand Marxism as a different practice of philosophy that records these false paths.[7] Now one may ask: how is one to read philosophy as the story of human repression? Is this not taking matters a little too far? Is this combination: repression-philosophy, or even estrangement-philosophy (the classical young Marx repertoire) taking things on to the routes of a messianic utopianism that no one would want to traverse? Why should wisdom, the privileged vantage position of philosophy, be aligned with madness? How far can one go? To which different realm must one go in order to free oneself from this imagined madness?

There are three important points emerging from the above observation on philosophy as the lost path (*Holzweg*): (i) To understand the aetiology of philosophy as estrangement-repression, (ii) to locate the 'origins' of this estrangement-repression, (iii) to study the 'origins' of philosophy, and (iv) to seek the 'origins' of class civilizations. It is with these points that Marx the adventurer sought to walk the paths of philosophy. But his walk was not to be a lonely one, for the German dialecticians, the Scottish political economists and the French socialists accompanied him. And knowing that the French were to be around insurrection could not be far behind.

Now Marx, who insists on reading history as the history of class struggles and the history of philosophy as desiring human estrangement, claims that there are a number of layers constituted within the history of philosophy and (to borrow an idea of Marx's reading of Hegel) one has to discover the rational element that lies hidden behind the mystical shell of philosophical reasoning.[8] One has to be an archaeologist in order to understand philosophy. For to philosophize means for Marx (besides the recording of class struggle in the field of theory),[9] a rather peculiar act in which one is living a human estrangement (*Entfremdung*) and the history of violent and explosive distortions, as well as transgressing these estrangements and distortions. If one could, at least for temporal epistemic purposes, define Marxism, then one could call it the genealogy of estrangement and its critical-dialectical transcendence (*Aufhebung*). The history of philosophy is read in the continuously shifting sites of *Entfremdung* and anti-*Entfremdung*. To register this class struggle in the realm of theory and praxis is the leitmotif of Marx's philosophical repertoire. And to signal the 'end of *Entfremdung*' is Marx's chief aim. Wisdom is born only when estrangement dies. In this very modern regime of this 'end', can the deaths of madness and the birth of authenticity and the desiring human essence be rendered possible? It is at this site that one poses and re-poses the question of Marx's philosophy. The special relevance of this question can be re-posed as: *"What relevance does Marxist philosophy have for the twenty-first century?"*

Now one knows that the question: 'What is Marxist philosophy?' is a question that cannot be posed and solved once and for all times. It is a spectre that has risen again and which haunts not only bourgeois Europe but also the whole world; and that, despite the 'end of history and ideology' as also the 'death of Marxism' sung by the global bourgeoisie (after the death of Stalinist social engineering), history, ideology and Marxism have emerged posthumously from their graves to haunt the world again. We earlier lived in the realms of reality. Now we are condemned to live the lives with spectres. Why is this so? Because we did not bury the dead properly. Also because Stalin, the ex-priest, refused to let go of the fetishes of the past, in fact, insisted that all the spectres of the past (led by the commodity and the authoritarian state) were to be incorporated into the present. Maybe the rites that we were to perform were not the proper rites. We thought that we should let the dead bury the dead, but now the dead have emerged from the graves and have gripped the living. "We suffer not only from the living, but from the dead. *Le mort saist le vif!*"[10]

And so the truth of Lenin's words rings out again: the Marxists have not understood Marx! Why is this so? Because the Marxists did not read Hegel—hence they could not understand the aetiology of idealism and the history of global specterology. If they could not understand this, then how was one to exorcise the spectres of estrangement and imagined madness?

For Marx the adventurer, to philosophize means walking on paths that have hitherto not been walked on. On these unwalked paths Marx arrives at the crossroads—the paths of idealism (Hegel) and philosophical anthropology (Feuerbach). It is on these crossroads that Marx, along with two friends, Scottish political economy and French socialism, writes the obituary of the spectres. But for that, Hegel has to be understood in particular, and the history of philosophy in general. There is a concrete observation that Marx makes on the very first moments on entering the *Holzweg* of philosophy: that reality appears as object form *(der Form des Objekts)*[11] and where alien objects litter the paths of philosophy.[12] The history of philosophy is dominated by the "alien world of objects".[13] So the form of philosophical reasoning is reasoning in "estranged form" (*entfremdete Form*)[14] where this "form of estrangement" (*der Form der Entfremdung*)[15] has beneath it an "estranged essence" (*fremden Wesen*).[16] Now the question: "What is wrong with philosophy?" added to the question: "What is wrong with class civilizations?" is answered rather simply—that both are governed by an "*alien* reality" (*fremde Wirlklichkeit*).[17] We live thus in occupied territory.

Let us move now to the concrete Marxist question: what did Marx mean when he said that the economic base *determines* the ideological superstructure? How do the concepts of alienation, reification and fetishism enter the scene of Marxist philosophy such that historical materialism redrafts the base-superstructure problematic as: *the alienated political economy determines the reified mind?* How then does one understand the category of determination (*Bestimmung*) as *estranged determination*?

It is with this variation on a theme of historical materialism whereby we focus our attention on the neglected theme of the problematic of philosophy that the young Marx had raised in his 1843-44 critique of Hegel. In this essay, Marx mentions a revolution in philosophy with special reference to the issues of the reification of philosophical consciousness and the transcendence (*Aufhebung*) and realization (*Verwirklichung*) of philosophy. It is in this dialectical setting of transcendence and realization that one attempts to understand the nature of Marx's revolution. Marx relates the history of philosophy (especially the fundamental structural changes taking place as in the shifts from the Greek philosophers to Christian medievalism to the Enlightenment and the Renaissance, culminating in the philosophies of modernity and the international communist movement) not only with the history of class struggles but also to the question of human estrangement. What then is this uncanny relation between alienation and philosophy and can one prove such a relation? What does this relation imply?

The question on the nature of Marx's great revolution in thought remains unanswered. If philosophy is written in the text of repression and imagined madness, then in what manner would Marxism reveal itself as an alleged therapist model? Is Marxism a 'science', an 'ideology', or 'philosophy'? Or is it involved in the postmodern world of free-floating 'posties' that refuses to be defined? Or, in contrast to the postmodern discourse, does Marxism in its radical engagement-disengagement of the bourgeois life-world, actually pose the question of a revolutionary mass philosophy—*of a theory that has become radical because it has been able to grip the masses*?[18] And how is this "gripping of the masses" possible?

The chapter is divided into the following parts: (i) 'Dialectical Materialism and the problem of the Reified Mind' that highlights Marx's idea of the "estranged mind" and the conception of philosophy as "the alienation of the human essence", (ii) 'The Birth of the Spectre' that relates philosophy with the psychoanalytic conception of the uncanny (*das Unheimlich*) or the feeling of the arousal of dread and terror, followed by the outlining of Marx's idea of Hegelian philosophy as inverted consciousness and the consequent inversion of this reification, and (iii) 'Subverting the Spectropoetics of Philosophy' that shows how Marx subverts the shadowy spectral ideological world that has, from time immemorial, been haunting humanity.

Dialectical Materialism and the Problem of the Estranged Mind

In the *Manifesto of the Communist Party* Marx, along with his revolutionary compatriot Engels, said that communism "abolishes eternal truths, it abolishes all religion, and all morality instead of constituting them on a new basis, it therefore acts in contradiction to all past experiences".[19] And since then Marxism is understood as the discontinuation of traditional thinking involving a radical rupture (*das radikalste Brechen*)[20] with traditional ideologies and philosophies. It then became not only what Louis Althusser called a "different practice of philosophy",[21] but also a different theory and praxis of philosophy constituted in a new continent of knowledge.[22]

So what is this new continent of knowledge? Marx answers: it is the unknown continent in which the even more unknown "estranged mind" (*entfremdete Geist*)[23] has immigrated. Now one knows that Marx had reserved this term 'estranged mind' for Hegel, the master deceiver and truth teller. But for Marx, Hegel is merely a symptom of an even bigger estranged mind in this big game of the history of philosophy. Marx then asks: What should one do with this estranged mind that has immigrated into a far-off continent? Marx answers: to make philosophy confess (even in the safe abode of the far off continent) that it is:

> nothing else but religion rendered into thought and expounded by thought, i.e., another form and manner of existence of the estrangement of the human essence (*eine andere Form und Daseinweise der Entfremdung des menschlichen Wesens*); hence equally to be condemned.[24]

Now Marx, the alleged registrar of unpractical reason, says that there are some types of reservations constituted within the continent of the estranged mind, and that is the reservations which have hidden the true people of this continent, the people of "*true materialism*" and "*real science*" whereby flow freely the "social relationship(s) of "human to human"" (*gesellshaftliche Verhältnis des Menschen zum Menschen*).[25]

And in these reservations of the colonized continent, Marx openly declares the conscious negation of philosophy (*Negation der Philosophie*), of "philosophy as philosophy".[26] In fact, Marx is all out for the indigenous people of *real and true humanity.*

Yet one must point out, Marxism in its now well thought-out 'just war' on philosophy's cruel conquest of the continent, is not a positivism, which collapses all knowledge into a sort of imaginary and exemplary 'scientistically' defined natural scientific system. Marx thinks this to be an abuse of the natural sciences by the technological rationalists and the positivists—a collapse of knowledge, which, like the German idealist philosopher Schelling produces a mystical philosophy of identity, and to borrow Hegel's phrase, lives in a "dark night where all cows are black". Nor is Marxism a sort of a Heideggerean "end of philosophy". That philosophy remains essential for Marx, but not as traditional philosophy running from Anaximander, Thales and Plato to Hegel, but as a 'new' philosophy (a philosophy that confesses to its imagined madness), is evident from his statement that for the emancipation of humanity, the head of this emancipation is philosophy, whilst the heart is the democratic multitude, the proletariat—and thus philosophy finds its material weapons in the multitude, just as the multitude finds its intellectual weapons in philosophy.[27]

The Birth of the Spectre

We move into the realm of the ideological superstructure in order to understand Marx's reading of the history of philosophy in the unexplained continent of the estranged mind and the reservations of true materialism and real science. In these locations one asks: "What is the speciality of Marx's theory of philosophy, and how should one reveal the aetiology of repression, estrangement and class struggle?" What is the nature of causality between the economic base and the ideological superstructure, and how does one relate philosophy with the political economies of estrangement and class struggle? We know that since Lukács and Bakhtin, the notion of mechanical causality was purged out from revolutionary Marxism, yet this uncanny mind refuses to leave the scene of history. Why is this so? One may answer that it is because the notion of *expressive-fetishized causality* is hidden so that one cannot understand how an ideological-fantastic superstructure emerges from an economic base. Does this not remind one of magic and alchemy—to grow the tree of philosophy from the soil of economics?

Now, in order to explicate Marx's alchemical and phantasmagorical reading of philosophy we move initially in its margins—a document on revolutionary political praxis and a sketch on madness—in order to move into its core. We take thus two texts, the *Manifesto of the Communist Party* and E.T.A. Hoffmann's *The Sandman* in order to understand how the nature of the estranged mind immigrated to an unfortunate continent that it would mercilessly decimate; and then we proceed into Marx's understanding of Hegel.

In the *Manifesto of the Communist Party*, Marx had pointed out that the motor force of hitherto existing history is the history of class struggles. That class struggles are directly related to the problem of alienation, reification and fetishism, was, on the one hand, accepted by thinkers like Georg Lukács, Raya Dunayevskaya, Theodor Adorno, Isaac Rubin, Roman Rosdolsky, Erich Fromm, Herbert Marcuse, Jürgen Habermas, Fredric Jameson, Jacques Derrida, Slavoj Žižek, etc. and on the other hand, ignored by the Stalinist dominated communist parties, or attacked, as was the case with Althusser. That it is linked to the idea of reification, especially with the reification of consciousness, is evident from the opening sentence of the *Manifesto* itself: "A spectre is haunting Europe—the spectre of communism" (*Ein Gespenst geht um in Europa—das Gespenst des Kommunismus*).[28] And what does it mean? That the holy capitalist empire comprising the Pope and the tsar, Metternich and Guizot, French radicals and German police-spies have declared that the anti-Christ, now in the form of communist revolutionaries, are to destroy all that is holy and eternal—private property, the family system and the state. Marx takes on the challenge of the holy capitalist empire—he seeks to tear down the spectre hurled on to the revolutionaries by saying that the communists should openly declare themselves to the world by publishing their views and thus able to "meet this nursery tale of the Spectre of Communism with a Manifesto of the party itself".[29]

Now this question of "nursery tales" is not a question of children's innocent comic books. It is well-known that at that time these tales stood for stories of terror that aroused fear. In the times of Marx and Freud too, children's stories were those that brought in the feeling of dread. Freud immortalized his observations in *das Unheimlich* ('The Uncanny').[30] To understand Marx's idea of the *estranged mind*, let us move to the question of the uncanny in psychoanalysis. Freud here mentions the story of E.T.A. Hoffmann's, *The Sandman*. In this story, Hoffmann tells us about Nathaniel who is haunted by the trauma of a certain fictious "sandman", whose footsteps he allegedly hears every night.[31] As regards the question: "Who is the sandman?" —he is told by his nurse that he is a wicked man who sprinkles sand in the eyes of children who do not sleep at night, and then flees to the moon, where he gives the eyes to his children who live in a nest. Nathaniel does not understand the metaphorical level of the story and associates both the steps that he hears at night, as well as this newfound fear of losing his eyes, with some unforeseen event in reality. This fear grows and the fictitious 'sandman' repeatedly appears in his imagination, initially in the form of a certain repulsive advocate called Coppelius, (the transfiguration of the father image) whom he associates with an alchemist who helps his father in some strange experiments, which apparently kills his father; and later with a strange dealer of barometers, Coppola, who sells all sorts of glasses which Nathaniel mistakes for damaged eyes. ("Coppo", so Freud claims following Beate Rank, means, "eye-socket").[32] Each time this image of the sandman occurs, Nathaniel is struck by mental illness, only to recover, helped by the beautiful Clara. Later Nathaniel goes to university and forgets his beloved Clara only to fall in love with an automaton, a life-sized doll called Olympia who is made by his professor, Splanzani and helped by a watchmaker, the nasty Coppola (a recurrence of the image of the sandman) who sets up her eyes. (Note the process of reification working here. For reification as "thingification", *Verdinglichung* or *Versachlichung* implies, *life given to lifeless objects, and also a maddening love for this object*, a theory that would interest Marx as well as Freud.) Now, due to an argument on the question of ownership of Olympia, and the consequent tussle by the two people who had made this doll, Olympia breaks into pieces in front of her shocked lover. The beloved lifeless object is broken! The eyes come out from the eye sockets! Nathaniel goes insane again, only to recover. One fine day, when he is with the now reconciled Clara on the top of a tall tower, he sees a mysterious object moving below. He takes out his pocket-telescope given to him by Coppola, and he imagines that he sees the horrible image of the sandman in the form of the repulsive Coppelius. He is struck by madness again and tries to throw Clara down, only to fling himself to death. So what is the moral of this story? That the estranged mind with its borrowed vision leads to death.

That this narrative of reification and horror is important for Freud is well-known. That it ought to be important for Marx should also be obvious, since there is the theme of blindness, psychosis, violence and death running throughout the history of class societies. But for Marx, there is something more than the Freudian motif of individual mental illness, namely, the theme of the *reification of consciousness* and the consequent enslavement of the subject, the theme that is manifested as the *problem of ideology*—'ideology' implying not only 'political ideology' and the principle of domination but also the ontology of fetishism that erases the 'Real'. In *The German Ideology* Marx says that ideology is haunted with the history of ghosts (*Gespenstergeschichte*).[33] Henceforth ideology aligns itself with philosophy and becomes 'ideology-philosophy' that speaks the language of the repressed unconscious. Now what happens is that philosophy, the rather 'innocent' wisdom searching enterprise, is aligned with the not-so-innocent discipline of ideology. In fact, no philosophy has ever been innocent, and no philosopher has lived the life of innocence.

Philosophy's questions: 'Being', 'Truth', etc. need to be hurled down from the ivory towers of the 'Idea' into the streets wherein dwells 'man' who is essentially political. Marx calls for the end of the "self-sufficient philosophy (*die selbständige Philosophie*)" with its "empty phrases" and also the end (*aufhört*) of the cruel world of speculation so as to herald the beginning of real life (*wirkliche Leben*), along with "real, positive science" (*wirkliche positive Wissenschaften*).[34] It is in this world of the 'Real' that both the mechanisms of society and thought can be understood. According to Marx, on the one hand, in the history of human civilizations we have the warring faction of the "estrangement of the human essence" (*Entfremdung des menschlichen Wesens*), whilst, on the other hand, is the great rebellion of the democratic multitude, which calls for the "transcendence of the estrangement" (*die Aufhebung der Entfremdung*), as also "the appropriation of the human essence" (*die Aneignung des menschlichen Wesens*).[35]

When Marx talked of the importance of understanding that we exist in the *Holzweg* of an imagined madness, he claimed that it was important to understand how a distorted-duplicated world produced by philosophy was so important to humanity. He thus asked: "Why does this inverted consciousness (*verkehrtes Weltbewusstsein*) of an inverted world (*verkehrte Welt*) take so much attention of society?"[36] Why has it taken such a dominant form? And Marx claims that if the emancipatory interests have to be the leitmotif of any cognitive science, then it is imperative to understand this bewildering world standing on its head (*auf den Kopf stellen*).[37] And this strange idealized upside-down world becomes "the general theory of this world", "its encyclopaedic compendium", "its logic in popular form", "its moral sanction" and "universal basis of consolation and justification".[38]

When philosophy is understood as the manifestation of the estranged mind and the reification of the life-world, then turning one's attention to it is of critical importance. For this, Hegel, the exemplary philosopher of estrangement, who both spoke the truth and lied, enters the scene of the Marxist repertoire:

> Hegel's *Enzyklopädie*, beginning as it is with logic, with *pure speculative thought*, and ending with *absolute knowledge*—with the self-conscious, self-comprehending philosophic or absolute (i.e., superhuman) abstract mind (*abstrakten Geist*)—is in its entirety nothing but the *display*, the self-objectification, of the *essence* of the philosophic mind, and the philosophical mind is nothing but the estranged mind (*entfremdete Geist*), of the world thinking within its self-estrangement—i.e., comprehending itself abstractly.
>
> *Logic*—mind's *coin of the realm*, the speculative or *mental value* of humanity and nature—its essence which has grown totally indifferent to all real determinateness, and hence unreal essence

> (*unwirkliches Wesen*)—is *alienated thinking*, and therefore thinking which abstracts from nature and from real humanity: *abstract* thinking (*das abstrakte Denken*).[39]

The question remains: "If Hegel is considered the essence of estranged thinking, why not totally reject him, as the positivists rejected Hegel with the entire continental tradition?" What is so profound about Hegel that Marx, a philosopher who stressed on observation, could claim to be a student of one who was totally oblivious to observation? It is well-known that Hegel's dissertation was on the planetary orbits; a problem that he thought could be solved by *a priori* pure reason. He thus tried to prove Plato's theory that there exist only seven planets. Specific mention should be made of Hegel's refusal to concede that any planet can exist between Mars and Jupiter. That he is wrong is evident, right from the date when Hegel published his thesis, when an asteroid named 'Ceres' was discovered, not to mention later discoveries of Neptune and Pluto.

So what is so important for Marx that one ought to read Hegel very carefully? Why did Marx talk of a double reading of Hegel—of being able to read a rational method that is engulfed in the phantasmagorical mist of mysticism?[40] Why did Marx talk of the discourse of "the complete domination of dead matter over humanity"[41] as metaphysical?

Note the phantoms that plagued Hegel's mind, and also note what Marx the exorcist and "pupil of that mighty thinker" did with Hegel, the master deceiver and truth teller. We take two texts: first, the 1873 'Afterword to the Second German Edition' of *Capital*, Vol. I, and second, the 1843 critique of Hegel's metaphysics of the state:

> My dialectical method is not only different from the Hegelian, but is its direct opposite (*direketes Gegenteil*). To Hegel, the life-process of the human brain, *i.e.*, the process of thinking, which under the name of "the Idea", he even transforms into an independent subject (*selbständiges Subjekt*), is the demiurgos of the real world, and the real world is only the external, phenomenal form of "the Idea". With me, on the contrary, the ideal is nothing else than the material world reflected by the human mind, and translated into forms of thought.

> The mystifying side of the Hegelian dialectic I criticised nearly thirty years ago, at a time when it was still the fashion. But just as I was working on the first volume of "Das Kapital", it was the good pleasure of the peevish, arrogant, mediocre *Epigonentum* who now talk large in cultured Germany, to treat Hegel in the same way as the brave Moses Mendelson in Lessing's time treated Spinoza, *i.e.*, as a "dead dog". I therefore openly avowed myself as the pupil of that mighty thinker, and even here and there, in the chapter on the theory of value, coquetted with the modes of expression peculiar to him. The mystification which dialectic suffers in Hegel's hands, by no means prevents him from being the first to present its general form of working in a comprehensive and conscious manner. With him it is standing on its head (*Sie steht bei ihm auf dem Kopf*). It must be turned right side up again (*umstülpen*), if you would discover (*entdecken*) the rational kernel within the mystical shell.
>
> In its mystical form, dialectic became the fashion in Germany, because it seemed to transfigure and to glorify the existing state of things. In its rational form it is a scandal and abomination to bourgeoisdom and its doctrinal professors, because it includes in its comprehension and affirmative recognition of the negation of that state, of its necessary downfall (*notwendigen Untergangs*); because it regards every historical developed social form as in fluid movement, and therefore takes to account its transient nature not less than its momentary existence; because it lets nothing impose upon it, and is in its essence critical and revolutionary.[42]

After a glimpse at the text of the 'old' Marx, a Marx infatuated with political economy, and trying to reason with Hegel by making him, if not think correctly, at least stand properly, and then let him hear the dirge that he (Marx) has written to capitalism that lies in ruins (*Untergangs*), let us look at the rather 'young' Marx, the Marx in his radical critique of Hegel's philosophy of schizoid textuality:

> The real relationship is described by speculative philosophy as *appearance* (*Ersheinung*), as *phenomenon* (*Phänomen*) ... (and real action) takes place behind the scenes. Reality is not deemed to be itself but another reality instead. The ordinary empirical world is not governed by its own mind but by a mind alien to it... (Consequently the) Idea is subjectivized and the real relationship ... is conceived as their *inner imaginary* activity ... (For) in speculative

> philosophy it is the reverse (*umgekehrt*). When the Idea is subjectivized the real subjects—civil society, the family, 'circumstances, caprice, etc.'—are all transformed into *unreal*, objective moments of the Idea ...
>
> (So we see that human beings) are indebted for their existence to a mind other than their own; they are not self-determining but are instead determined by another....
>
> (Thus) the condition is posited as the conditioned, the determinator as the determined, the producer as the product...
>
> (For Hegel) makes the Idea into the subject, whilst the genuine real subject ... is turned into the predicate....[43]

For Marx the quest for the 'genuine' is the essence of his philosophical endeavour. And so, becoming the "genuine real subject" implies the movement from the cocoon of life lived as a form of alienation (*Form der Entfremdung*): a strange, bizarre and estranged reality (*fremde Wirklichkeit*).[44] Criticism thus turns to this estranged reality. What Marx calls the *Bestimmung*, the determination, that joins the disjointed realms of the base and the superstructure, the body and the mind, becomes the bridge and the missing link in Marx's adventurous search for an authentic philosophy. *Bestimmung* becomes the bridge that joins the soulless body with the bodyless soul. To this great bridge of judgement we descend.

Subverting the Spectropoetics of Philosophy

Truth, submitted to this bridge of judgement has become monstrous. And in this monstrous realm philosophy is born. It is born at the very place where humanity is slaughtered. Philosophy constitutes the rites of wisdom. It claims to seek wisdom, but it lies. Why is this so? It is so because philosophy (like the flows of capital) speaks not the truth. And, like capital flows (the Ur-moment that is the foundational stone for all class societies), philosophy is the flight from the Real. Recalling the psychoanalytic metaphor: the Real is castrated to create the Imaginary and the Symbolic worlds of philosophy. Philosophy is the story of both castration anxiety and its very celebration.

That is why Marx says that philosophy is the speculative narrative of the "phantastic isolation and fixity" of 'man'.[45] So what does philosophical consciousness look like? This is what

Marx says:

> From this moment onwards consciousness *can* really flatter itself that it is something other than consciousness of existing practice, that it *really* represents something without representing something real, from now on consciousness is in a position to emancipate itself from the world and to proceed to the formation of "pure" theory, theology, philosophy, morality, etc.[46]

What then is wrong with philosophy? Engels had defined Kant as *impotence in action*.[47] Why is this so? Because philosophy (with its castration anxiety-celebration) falls down on its knees in front of the fetish found in the *Holzweg* of estrangement. "Philosophy and the study of the actual world", so Marx says, "have the same relation to one another as onanism and sexual love."[48] Instead of embracing the Real, philosophy refuses to do so. Instead it pays homage to the fetish of estrangement and in front of this monstrous idol slaughters humanity. Philosophy is the death of the human essence (*das menschliche Wesen*). The human essence dies so that philosophy is born. That is why philosophy is nothing more than a ghost. Thus we have to descend into the realm of spectres again.

To answer the question: "Why does philosophy as the estranged mind yet exist?" one must not analyse the 'mind' alone in abstraction but see the wild horse that the philosopher is riding. To borrow the metaphor from historical materialism: one must understand the base in order to understand the estranged superstructure that is erected on this base. Philosophy and economics become partners in this game of estrangement and are henceforth to be seen as concretely bound together. The metamorphosis of commodities is inexorably tied to the uncanny metamorphosis of 'man', and the consequent macabre dance involved in the production of the 'Idea'. This time the charges against communism (levelled by the Pope and other members of the ruling classes), that it is an evil anti-Christian spectre, are reversed, when Marx calls capitalism (along with all class societies) a society that is *essentially* spectral—that its Ur-base, the base of all bases is this uncanny "ghostly objectivity" (*gespenstige Gegenständlichkeit*)[49]—a society that has "only form without content".[50]

Let us have a look at the economic base from which emerges the estranged philosophical mind. Philosophical binaries—'Matter'/'Idea', 'body'/'soul', etc. have an uncanny double in the form of capitalism's principle binary—use value/value. Whilst theology negates the earth and the mortal body to create the spectacular soul and the heavens, philosophy negates the world of 'man' that is essentially political to posit the psychotic world of the 'Idea', and capitalism (like theology and philosophy) negates the bodily form (use values) to posit value (the 'soul' and the 'Idea' of capitalism). This 'soul' and 'Idea' are the Ur-substances of capitalism, theology and philosophy. They are the *gespenstige Gegenständlichkeit*.

Let us now have a look at the phenomenology of this *gespenstige Gegenständlichkeit* found in the dreaded capital flows. Now according to Marx, capitalism is a society that continuously sheds its concrete bodily forms (in the slaughter of 'man' and the politics of the human essence) in order to acquire the form of capital flows. It thus becomes a disembodied society (the negation of use values and the positing of values), where it develops a mind (value) without a body (use value). Now those who are aware of Marx's reading of capital flows know that it is decoded in the formula $M\text{-}C\text{-}M^1$, where M stands for money (the 'mind', 'soul' and the 'Idea') invested in the circuit of capital accumulation, whilst C is the commodity that comprises the means of production and labour power (the earthly basis), whilst M^1 is surplus value (the super mind) or value over and above the original investment (M). Marx claims this is fetishism or a specterology, an occult-like process where, as if by magic, a fruit called 'M^1' grows from a tree named 'M'. Marx also christens this a contentless form, a phantasmagorical form where all birth marks of its origin are erased. And this phantasmagorical erasure emerges because its very Ur-moment involves an abstracting from the "material elements and shapes" of the human life-world, where (as we noted in the previous chapter) we turn a blind eye to material existence.[51] Thus (in capitalism as in philosophy, or, to be precise, theology) we "put out of sight" the "concrete", and consequently, get not only the metaphysical and theological worlds of "idealization"

(*Idealisierung*), the "one" and the "abstract",[52] but we also succumb to this abstract and metaphysical world. These theological worlds of estrangement and capitalism are also the worlds of the "invisible", "imaginary", and "ideal".[53] It is the world of metempsychosis and transmigration[54]—the world of ghosts and, like Hamlet, the philosophers and the capitalists are chasing spectres. So we have this uncanny similarity between theology and capitalism, wherein we have not only the destruction of the body to create the spectral mind, but also the desire for this spectral mental-world. That is why, when Marx talks of a critique of the philosophical estranged mind, he insists on the critique of the alien base from which has sprouted the not-so-desirable tree of philosophy. So how should we sum up this entire process in one sentence? The summary goes this way: *The accumulation of capital—capital flows—produces the reified mind in this phantasmagorical process of disembodiment*.

That is why Marx says that one ought not to turn one's back to philosophy by muttering angry phrases, but by actively negating philosophy,[55] which is itself based on an active protracted war against the base itself. That is also why when Marx proceeds into the basis, not only the basis of an empirical ideological superstructure, but the Ur-Base, the ontological base of almost everything if not the base of class histories, then he says that this base is very slippery and deceptive. Marx, however, insists that he has found this grand Ur-base in the graveyard of humanity, this world of magical things endowed with life—this world of tremendous accumulation of commodities. Now this immense accumulation of magic creates the "automatic fetish",[56] this "automatic creating thing"[57] which is also a "queer thing abounding in metaphysical subtleties and theological niceties".[58] The philosophical mind is transplanted in this automatic fetish where we have this queer metaphysician and theologian (posing as philosopher and theoretician) giving us sermons on the mount.

For philosophy that grows from the soil of this automatic fetish, starts miming this terrible fetish. The philosopher now allies himself with estrangement and celebrates the *Holzweg* of estrangement—and in involving the forgetfulness of 'man' who is essentially political, who only remembers the psychotic 'Idea'—has become like the process of the metamorphosis of the commodity: the schizophrenic with the disjointed lost body and acquired psychotic mind—a "born leveller and cynic", a prostitute as well as a theologian, who as Marx informs us, "is always ready to exchange not only soul, but body, with any or every other commodity, be the same more repulsive than Maritornes ("the puppet". My insertion, M.J.) herself" (*Geborner Leveller und Zyniker, steht sie daher stets auf dem Sprung, mit jeder andren Ware, sei selbe auch ausgestattet mit mehr Unannehmlichkeiten als Maritorne, nicht nur die Selle, sondern den Leib zu wechseln*).[59] As a prostitute that has lost its body, philosophy, like the commodity, exists only to exchange itself with another prostituted commodity, preferably for the grand idealized sign: money (the "Idea"), that the young Marx says, "which confuses and confounds all things".[60] So this uncanny combination: prostitution and theology (in the celebration of the death of the body) forms the basis of our thinking. Our hegemonic ideology industry seems to say that critical and revolutionary thinking is nonsense, it belongs to the anti-Christ communist; whilst the prostitute-theologian—the schizophrenic with the reified mind and the disembodied body—is both the essence of society as well as the ideal we all must strive for.

Let us now see how the philosophic mind is based on the not-so-philosophic body. From this metaphor one may understand how the mind (*Geist*) emerges not from thinking, but money (*Geld*)—from the occultation of capital (M-C- M^1). When Marx says that the base determines consciousness, he means that M^1 signifies estranged consciousness. It is well known that Marx insisted that money and capital are the idealized essences of capitalism. They are the "common whore(s) of mankind", as well as "the real *brain(s)* of all things".[61] And as the terrible as well as the beautiful signs, they manifest themselves as the spectral philosophical consciousness. When Marx is talking of the metamorphosis of commodities, where humanity is lost to posit the 'thing', the 'thing' is lost to posit the pure sign; he is talking of the metamorphosis of humanity itself—from human to thing to spectre. Capitalism is the society of the magician and the alchemist—it "transform(s) paper into gold by the magic of its imprint" (*die Magie seines Stempels Papier in Gold zu verwandeln*).[62] Capitalism is thus the process of magic and reification as much as it is the process of horror and terror—the horror of the loss of the self and the creation of the estranged fetishes, especially the fetishized magic of creating gold from fraudulent paper. The ideology of capitalism is also its madness. And now we get this terrible transfigured capitalist kitsch: *reification is psychosis (recall Freud's definition of psychosis as "the withdrawal from reality"), ideology is madness, and capitalism is mental illness.* Philosophy is the summary, the last word and worldview of this psychosis-reification-capitalism. It is the mimesis of the spectre and the narrative of the process of disembodiment. Thus, when Marx claims that the proletariat as the democratic multitude needs to be the gravedigger of capitalism, he means that one needs to bury this madness once and for all.

When Marx is advocating an anti-specterolgy, he implies a force of abstraction,[63] that is able to pry into the estranged ghostly object and reveal its notorious essence. When Marx mentions the deep structure of class civilizations as the ghostly reality, he means that this spectre would be creating further illusions and deceptions, these being manifested as the ideological superstructure of the "society of the spectacle" (as Guy Debord calls it), whether as political and legal delusions, or as philosophical fantasies of "the falsest of false paths" (*der Holzweg der Holzwege*) littered as we saw with estranged fetishes. When we realize that the history of philosophy is written as the story of self-consciousness, apparitions, spectres, whimsies, etc.[64], we need to realize that the history of this shadowy-metaphysics is bound with a disembodied-metaphysical context of estranged society itself.

To free oneself from this phantom reality is the primary task to be undertaken. So Marx argues in front of the tribunal of the human essence for a "reform of consciousness".[65] And what does this philosophical reform have to do? It has to exorcise the spectres of God-Capital-State and to stop its awful marchpast on the globe. When it is claimed that Marxism is class struggle in the realm of theory constituted within the aetiology of estrangement-reification-fetishism, the rehabilitation of humanity is insisted upon. Marx's humanism (the principle of the realization of the human essence) implies the struggle with the world of the thing (*Sache, Ding*) and with it, the dual flows: capital and psychotic flows. Thus when we ask the philosophical question: "What is 'man'?", this question is raised in contrast to the other half of the question: "What is a thing?"

Once 'man' breaks free from the cocoon of the thing and the spectre of God-Capital-State, then alone is a reform of consciousness possible. In the 1843-44 critique of Hegel, when Marx wrote the obituary of traditional philosophy in the variations on a theme of the *Aufhebung* and *Verwirklichung* of philosophy, he implied a restoration of the human essence from the altar that God-Capital-State had stolen and imprisoned.

That is why the young Marx in his 1843-44 critique of Hegel talked of the double tasks to be undertaken—the tasks of philosophy and history. The task of philosophy is to unmask self-estrangement and the task of history is to establish the truth of this world.[66] Marxist philosophy has to deal with the problem of Ur-philosophy—the monstrous flight from the Real—which does not involve wisdom, but the rites of 'man', not the birth of humanity, democracy and liberty, but their very deaths, not the celebration of the human essence, but the exile of humanity because philosophy has been monopolised by *Entfremdung*.

We need to ask: "What constituted the essence of philosophical discourse and what forms the master text of philosophy?" Is it with Anaximander and Thales to Aristotle via Socrates and the foundation of the Greek *polis* or with the foundation of class civilizations and the birth of the Judaic account of creation? For does not philosophy (in its essential form) account for the story of the estranged guilt-ridden 'man' (contra the guiltless and faultless 'God'), and is not the history of philosophy nothing but the hegemony of the story of this guilt-ridden estrangement 'man'? In this case, the Judaic rendering of creation, found in the *Book of Moses*, does not apply only to the Judaic, Christian and Islamic civilizations, but is the crux of the hegemony of Western Reason and its account of 'fallen' men and women. This then forms the Ur-text of philosophy. What are its basic guidelines? Why have men and women fallen from grace and been condemned to wander around the globe, guilt ridden and in pain, suffering and death? Because they chose two things: (i) to rebel and (ii) to seek knowledge of good and evil. In this story (wherein is supposedly embodied not only the history of philosophy, but the history of men and women) the narcissistic egoist Lord God (the first capitalist and landlord) condemned humanity to labour, pain, guilt and death for daring to listen to Satan (the first rebel) and seizing a part of surplus value and the Ideological State Apparatus (the fruit from the tree of the knowledge of good and evil). Now, when one says that this forms the essence of philosophical discourse, that philosophy even after its secular revolutions (since the Greeks) has not been able to free itself from this *essence*, then one can say that we are yet living this 'fall' into the *Holzweg* where the philosophical Ur-fetish ('Being' [*Sein*] or God *against* 'beings' or humanity) like the "traditions of all the dead generations weighs like a nightmare on the brains of the living".[67] And this tradition-fetish, like the sandman-fetish and the commodity fetish, "stands on its head", as Marx says (almost imitating the great truth teller and deceiver Hegel) "and evolves out from its wooden brain grotesque ideas, far more wonderful than (the ghost evoking. [My insertion. M.J].) "table turning" ever was".[68]

The question remains: "What does philosophy now do riding on the wild horse of this phantomatic-ghostly objectivity (*gespenstige Gegenständlichkeit*)?" How would humanity react to these ghosts in this age of globalization? That this phantom-fetish of capital and psychotic flows would destroy all societies, and turn them in accordance with its own fetish-image, which even the Great Wall of China could not resist, is noted in the *Manifesto*. That a hundred and fifty years after the *Manifesto*, these same flows would tear open the iron curtain, making a mockery of Stalin's revisionist attempts on the taming of the capital flows.

The mind and the spirit of the revolution (*der Geist der Revolution*) are attacked again and again, the spectre (*das*

Gespenst) rises. That is why, when Marx says that "nursery tales" are manufactured, we should cease to believe them. And if those who oppose the original spectre (God, capital and the state) are declared spectres, then *one must meet the nursery tale with a Manifesto of its own*. Thus Marx says: exorcise the spectres, refuse to abide by their philosophy of spectropoetics, and thus deny the *nursery tale of the spectre of communism (dem Märchen vom Gespenst des Kommunismus)*. Consequently, one has to deny these "imaginary flowers", and insist that we throw them out in order that we "pluck the living flower".[69] The movement from capitalist civilization to the communist one is the movement from death to real life. Real life is always radical, always bending towards a humanizing process, ever ready to grip the masses.[70]

The question of 'man' emerges again, 'man', who is in direct confrontation with the 'thing', the *Sache* and the *Ding*, that is hostile and opposed to humanity. In this way, Marx lines up the human essence to wage a war in the *Holzweg* of estrangement where humanity rises against the government of these estrangement fetishes. When Marx talked of an *Aufhebung* of philosophy, he meant an insurrection against this estranged government.

Therefore, one needs to find out what *Entfremdung* means and how alienation-reification-fetishism forms the background of our not-so-civilized thinking. *Entfremdung* is like the Buddhist notion of *Dukha* and we, the children of both tradition and modernity, are living in the black hole of *Entfremdung-Dukha*. The solution is simple: remove *Entfremdung-Dukha* and philosophy as the authentic quest for wisdom is possible. Thus when one looks at the other side of *Entfremdung-Dukha*, one also sees the other side of capital and psychotic flows. For, if there are two dominant flows that we live and experience—capital + psychosis—which not only determine thinking but also terminate it, then there is also the great flush of history in which great futures await us, but only when the flush of history is able to wash away the *things* and *spectres* that have hitherto haunted us: "All that is solid melts into air, all that is holy is profaned, and humanity is at last compelled to face with sober senses, the real conditions of life, and the real relations with its kind".[71]

It is with this sober sense that Marx decided to re-write the history of philosophy.

REFERENCES

1. Karl Marx, *Das Kapital*, Erster Band (Dietz Verlag: Berlin, 1993), p. 52.
2. Ibid., pp. 85-98.
3. Karl Marx, *Capital*, Vol. I, trans. Samuel Moore and Edward Aveling (Moscow: Progress Publishers, 1983), pp. 64-5.
4. Iranian tradition holds Alexander responsible for the destruction of both Iran and its ideology as collected in the *Avesta*. The Zoroastrian text *Ardâ Viraz Nâmag* says how the evil spirit sent "the accursed Alexander, the Roman... to Eransahr" (*ān guzastag alaksandar ī hrōmāyig…ō ēreānšahr mad*).
5. Walter Benjamin, 'Eduard Fuchs. Collector and Historian', in *One-Way Street. And Other Writings*, trans. Edmund Jephcott and Kingsley Shorter (London: New Left Books, 1979), p. 359.
6. Karl Marx, *Economic and Philosophic Manuscripts of 1844* (Moscow: Progress Publishers, 1982), p. 127; 'Nationalökonomie und Philosophie (1844)', in *Karl Marx. Die Frühschriften* (Stuttgart: Alfred Kröner, 1964), p. 250-1.
7. Louis Althusser, *Lenin and Philosophy and Other Essays*, trans. Ben Brewster (New York and London, 19710, pp. 30-1, 26, 32.
8. Karl Marx, *Capital*, Vol. I, p. 29.
9. See Louis Althusser, 'Reply to John Louis', in *Essays on Ideology* (London: Verso, 1984), p. 67.
10. Karl Marx, *Capital*, Vol. I, p. 20.
11. Karl Marx, 'Theses on Feuerbach', in *Marx Engels. Selected Works* (Moscow: Progress Publishers, 1975), p. 28.
12. Karl Marx, *Economic and Philosophic Manuscripts of 1844*, pp. 63, 136.
13. Ibid, p. 63.
14. Ibid, p. 131.
15. Ibid, p. 132.
16. Karl Marx, 'Nationalökonomie und Philosophie (1844)', p. 248.
17. Karl Marx, *Economic and Philosophic Manuscripts of 1844*, pp. 93-4; 'Nationalökonomie und Philosophie (1844)', p. 239.
18. Karl Marx, 'A Contribution to the Critique of Hegel's Philosophy of Right. Introduction', trans. Rodney Livingstone, in *Karl Marx. Early Writings* (New York: Vintage Books, 1975), pp. 249-250; 'Zur Kritik der Hegelschen Rechtsphilosophie. Einleitung', in *Karl Marx. Die Frühschriften* (Stuttgart: Alfred Kröner, 1964), p. 251.

19. Karl Marx and Friedrich Engels, 'Manifesto of the Communist Party', in *Marx Engels. Selected Works*, p. 52.
20. Ibid.
21. Louis Althusser, *Lenin and Philosophy and Other Essays*, pp. 26, 32.
22. Ibid, pp. 15-17, 38-39, 42, 72, 92, 99; Louis Althusser, *Montesquieu, Rousseau, Marx*, trans. Ben Brewster (London : Verso, 1982), pp. 166-168.
23. Karl Marx, *Economic and Philosophic Manuscripts of 1844*, p. 129; 'Nationalökonomie und Philosophie (1844)', p. 253.
24. Ibid, p. 127; ibid, pp. 250-251.
25. Ibid.
26. Karl Marx, 'A Contribution to the Critique of Hegel's Philosophy of Right. Introduction', pp. 249-250; 'Zur Kritik der Hegelschen Rechtsphilosophie. Einleitung', in *Karl Marx. Die Frühschriften*, pp. 214-215.
27. Ibid, p. 257.
28. Karl Marx and Friedrich Engels, 'Manifesto of the Communist Party', p. 35; 'Manifest der kommunistischen Partei', in *Karl Marx. Die Frühschriften*, p. 525.
29. Ibid.
30. Sigmund Freud, 'The Uncanny', in *The Penguin Freud library. Vol. 14 Art and Literature* (London: Penguin, 1990), pp. 339- 376.
31. E.T. A. Hoffmann, 'The Sandman', in *Tales of Hoffmann* (London: Penguin, 1982).
32. Sigmund Freud, op. cit., p. 352, n. 1.
33. Karl Marx and Friedrich Engels, *The German Ideology*.
34. Ibid, p. 43.
35. Karl Marx, *Economic and Philosophic Manuscripts of 1844*, pp. 109, 127, 134; 'Nationalökonomie und Philosophie (1844)', pp. 251, 264, 271.
36. Karl Marx, 'A Contribution to the Critique of Hegel's Philosophy of Right. Introduction', p. 244.
37. Karl Marx and Friedrich Engels, *The German Ideology*, pp. 41, 101-2; Karl Marx, *Das Kapital*, p. 27.
38. Karl Marx, 'A Contribution to the Critique of Hegel's Philosophy of Right. Introduction', p. 244.
39. Karl Marx, *Economic and Philosophic Manuscripts of 1844*, p. 129; 'Nationalökonomie und Philosophie (1844)', p. 253.
40. Karl Marx, 'To Friedrich Engels in Manchester, January 14, 1858', in *Marx. Engels. Selected Correspondence* (Moscow: Progress Publishers, 1975), p. 93.

41. Karl Marx, *Economic and Philosophical Manuscripts of 1844*, p. 58.
42. Karl Marx, *Capital*, Vol. I, p. 29; *Das Kapital*, Erster Band (Berlin: Dietz Verlag, 1993), pp. 27-8. We have translated *notwendigen Untergangs* as "necessary downfall" and not "inevitable breaking up" as done by Moore and Aveling. The question is: what is the relation between "necessity" and "inevitability"? Why is the "inevitable" (*unvermeidlich*) inserted in revolutionary Marxism? In the *Manifesto* Marx does use the term *unvermeidlich*: "What the bourgeois, therefore produces, above all, is its own grave-diggers. Its fall and the victory of the proletariat are equally inevitable (*unvermeidlich*)". This rendering of the inevitable is loaded with revolutionary meanings, a use that Trotsky would exemplify. On the revolutionary messianic use one has to consider Walter Benjamin. In contrast is the un-dialectical use by Stalin who, like the right Mensheviks operated in the phantasmagorical and fatalistic view of history, in which events are said to happen "automatically". The view of history as an automaton is critiqued by Marx as fetishism.
43. Karl Marx, 'Critique of Hegel's Doctrine of the State', in *Karl Marx. Early Writings* (New York: Vintage Books, 1975), pp. 61-62, 65.
44. Karl Marx, *Economic and Philosophical Manuscripts of 1844*, pp. 93, 132; 'Nationalökonomie und Philosophie (1844)', pp. 239, 269.
45. Karl Marx and Friedrich Engels, *The German Ideology* (Moscow: Progress Publishers, 1976), p. 43.
46. Ibid, p. 50.
47. Friedrich Engels, 'Feuerbach and the End of Classical German Philosophy', in *Marx. Engels. Selected Works*, p. 600.
48. Karl Marx and Friedrich Engels, op. cit., pp. 253-4.
49. Karl Marx, *Das Kapital*, Erster Band, p. 52.
50. Karl Marx, *Capital*, Vol. III (Moscow: Progress Publishers, 1986), p. 392.
51. Karl Marx, *Capital*, Vol. I, p. 45.
52. Ibid, p. 46.
53. Ibid, pp. 98-9.
54. Ibid, p. 199.
55. Karl Marx, 'A Contribution to the Critique of Hegel's Philosophy of Right. Introduction', p. 249.
56. Karl Marx, *Capital*, Vol. III, p. 392.
57. Karl Marx, *Theories of Surplus Value*, part III, p. 507.
58. Karl Marx, *Capital*, Vol. I, p. 76.

59. Karl Marx, *Das Kapital*, Erster Band, p. 100.
60. Karl Marx, *Economic and Philosophic Manuscripts of 1844*, pp. 121-124.
61. Karl Marx, *Economic and Philosophic Manuscripts of 1844*, pp. 121-122.
62. Karl Marx, *A Contribution to the Critique of Political Economy* (Moscow: Progress Publishers, 1977), trans. S.W. Ryazanskaya, p. 119.
63. Karl Marx, *Capital*, Vol. I, p. 19.
64. Karl Marx and Friedrich Engels, *The German Ideology*, pp. 51, 61.
65. Karl Marx, 'To Arnold Ruge in Kreuznach, Sept., 1843', in *Marx. Engels. Collected Works*, Vol. 3, (Moscow: Progress Publishers, 1975), p. 144.
66. Karl Marx, 'A Contribution to the Critique of Hegel's Philosophy of Right. Introduction', p. 244.
67. Karl Marx, 'The Eighteenth Brumaire of Louis Bonaparte', in *Marx. Engels. Selected* Works, p. 96.
68. *Capital*, Vol. I., p. 76; *Das Kapital*, Erster Band, p. 85. What Moore and Aveling translate as "far more wonderful than 'table turning' ever was", is in the original German, *"viel wunderlicher, als wenn er aus freien Stücken zu tanzen begänne"*. The German edition has the following note by Marx, "One may recall that China and the tables began to dance when the rest of the world appeared to be standing still—*pour engourager les autres*". (*Man erinnert sich, das China und die Tische zu tanzen anfingen, als alle übrige Welt still zu stehn schien—pour encourager les autres*).
69. Karl Marx, 'A Contribution to the Critique of Hegel's Philosophy of Right Introduction', p. 244.
70. Ibid, p. 251.
71. Karl Marx and Friedrich Engels, 'The Manifesto of the Communist Party', p. 38.

CHAPTER 5

Georg Lukács and the Problem of Romantic Aesthetics

I cannot bear an inessential life.

—Georg Lukács, 30 Nov., 1911.

Estrangement as the House of Aesthetics

According to a certain line of thinking, it is not beauty and the sublime that form the leitmotif of the work of art but estrangement. Estrangement (*Entfremdung*) is the House of Aesthetics. Or, if one is to believe Hegel, estrangement is the House of Existence itself. One has to understand this estranged character of existence in order to understand both aesthetics and the world. The line of thought of theoretical aesthetics, which deliberates on the work of art from the variations on the Greco themes of *aisthēsis* ('perception'), *aisthanesthai* ('to perceive') and *aisthētikos* ('capable of perception') to A.G. Baumgarten's "the science of sensory knowledge" and "the science of sensory beauty" and culminating in Kant's analytics of the sublime and the beautiful falls in this purview of *Entfremdung*. Nothing escapes *Entfremdung*, not even beauty. In fact, beauty itself is estrangement. Or, to borrow a Sartrean metaphor, beauty is nausea because existence itself is nausea. One tries to run away from this nausea but one cannot. Each one of us is this nausea.

Whilst nausea formed the basis of Existentialist art, cultural alienation became a more definite form that got rooted in the Romantic genre of nineteenth and early twentieth-century art.

According to Hegel, the overcoming of alienation is an important overcoming that is possible in the domain of the Absolute Mind,[1] a domain that includes, besides art, revealed religion and philosophy. Aesthetics for the idealism of Hegel is not only the House of Estrangement; it is also the House of Utopia. This leitmotif that Hegel had stressed is the inspiring moment of philosophy—the longing for Utopia. To long for Utopia is not only the motif of Western art, it is the essence of human existence itself. So if one asks: what the essence of the work of art is, one may answer: estrangement and the longing for Utopia. One has to experience this estrangement (in fact suffer in this estrangement) as well as long for Utopia to produce a work of art.

There is a sharp conflict emerging in the history of humanity: the conflict between the void and fullness, estrangement and the longing for Utopia This conflict is not only applicable to Western art, but applies to the entire world. Nothing escapes this conflict. The history of art is the history of this conflict. Take the case of the art of the Romans, Greeks and the Indians. The Romans had power inscribed in their art form; the Indians had the grace of timeless Time as their leitmotif, whilst the Greeks who, of course, did not think that the Greco world stood at the level of estrangement, championed the epic form. The aesthetic life-world of the Greeks was the epic—that which understood life as fullness and not the void. Fullness is said to contradict estrangement. It is to this tension: fullness and the void, estrangement and Life that we will focus our attention in this chapter. We begin with our main proposition: the tension between estrangement and Utopia has been the driving force of the history of philosophical aesthetics. By the end of the nineteenth century, this storm and stress was reflected in European aesthetics with the Hungarian philosopher, Georg Lukács as the chief representative of this historical tension.

This chapter is on Lukács's theory of the art form, a reflection that he began in early twentieth century as a Romantic championing Nietzsche, Kierkegaard, Dostoevsky and the German mystics, to his Hegelian-Marxist notion (or probably the Leninist notion if one is to believe Slavoj Žižek)[2] of the proletariat as the identical subject-object of history in *History and Class Consciousness.* There are three distinct phases that Lukács underwent (here we are mentioning only the texts that pertain to the question of Romanticism and culture): (i) the Romantic phase which includes *The Soul and the Forms* (1910), *Aesthetic Culture* (1910), *The History of the Development of Modern Drama* (1911), *The Poverty of Spirit* (1912), *Philosophy of Art* (1912-14), *The Theory of the Novel* (1916) and the unfinished *Heidelberg Aesthetics* (1916-18), (ii) his magnum opus *History and Class Consciousness* (1919-1922), that is predated by his 1918 essay 'Bolshevism as a Moral Problem', 'Tactics and Ethics' (1919), 'Moral Mission of the Communist Party' (1919), and 'Old and New Culture' (1919), and his role as the Deputy Commissar of Public Education (1919) in the Hungarian Soviets, and (iii) the later Lukács who, after the attacks of Karl Kautsky in *Die Gesellschaft* (June 1924), Deborin in *Arbieterliteratur*, Ladislaus Rudas, a one-time supporter of Lukács, in the *Arbieterliteratur* (1924), followed by the criticism of Bukharin and Zinoviev in the Fifth World Congress of the Communist International (June-July, 1924) on *History and Class Consciousness* as bourgeois idealism and the consequent Stalinization of the Soviet Revolution) decided to keep silent on his magnum opus—*History and Class Consciousness.* The third phase includes *The Historical Novel* (1937), *The Young Hegel* (1938), *Literature and Democracy* (1949), *The Specificity of the Aesthetic* (1962), *Essays on Thomas Mann* (1964), *Realism in our Time* (1964), *Goethe and his Age* (1968) and *Studies in European Realism* (1972). Relating these three phases has been a problem. On whether there is a sharp epistemological break or continuity, István Mészáros and György Márkus (one-time students of Lukács) qualified these three phases in the Hegelian language of an *Aufhebung*, a dialectical supersession that is simultaneously a preservation of the previous stage at a higher level of complexity.[3] Whilst there is a distinct move from the first (Romantic) to the second stage (Hegelian-Marxist), the movement to the third stage (the dogma of Socialist-Realism and the capitulation to the Stalinist bureaucracy) cannot be termed as a move into a 'higher stage'. What concerns us here is the question of Romanticism based on the crisis of culture and the metaphysical tragedy of human existence in his early works and the synthesis of his earlier messianic concerns with Marx, coupled with Fichte and distinct echoes of the Young Hegelian Max Stirner and the consequent resignation in the face of Stalinism.

This brings us to the central question of this chapter: the question of Romanticism in the arts. It is quite often said that Romanticism, unlike other aesthetic genres, Classicism, Realism, Naturalism, Symbolism and Impressionism is a loose concept. In the words of Victor Hugo, it is a "vague and indefinable concept". Sometimes it is used in a pejorative sense. Yet it is Romanticism that is probably the most important of the aesthetic genres spanning a period from the French Revolution to the late nineteenth century. It includes the European composers, Haydn, Mozart, Beethoven and Wagner, and sometimes also includes the Baroque master, Johann Sebastian Bach. It also included the Russian composer Tchaikovsky, the French composers Bizet and Saint-Saëns, and it is quite possible that the period of Romanticism in European music terminates in early twentieth century with the rise of the Neo-Classical music of Igor Stravinsky and the two French Impressionists, Ravel and Claude Debussy. It is almost at this period that Lukács begins his career as a critic and essayist.

Aesthetically, whilst Romanticism emerged from Classicism (if not in opposition to it), the core of its philosophical ideology was its critique of industrial civilization. Tonality and chromaticism in music were its leitmotifs in its pastorale ode to pre-industrial cultures. Thus whether its' the works of the English poets, Keats, Byron and Shelley, or the music of Chopin and Schubert, the poetry and essays of Charles Baudelaire, or the short stories and works on music of E.T.A. Hoffmann, it is this critique of the age of the machine that defines the Romantic genre. Whilst Classicism was based on rigorous discipline and the seeking of harmony in form, Romanticism sought to destabilize this discipline. Classicism sought the great cities; Romanticism depicted the peasant. Classicism sought reason; Romanticism (if not celebrating irrationality as found in the works of Baudelaire and Hoffmann) would not be a slave to reason. Or, if there was to be a 'reason', it had to be subservient to the model of aesthetics. For the Romantics it is art that can make people act according to the principle of reason. And since reason itself has betrayed reason, then it is left to the arts to rescue both reason and humanity. For early German Romanticism (*Frühromantic*), especially the thinkers surrounding August William Schlegel, his brother Friedrich Schlegel, Friedrich Schelling, Ernst Schleirmacher and Friedrich von Hardenberg or Novalis (as the world would know him) this relation between art and reason took place where art was given a privileged place. The arts, henceforth, were understood as the highest value bestowers in life. Cultural education as the re-valuation of all values takes place in this aesthetic life-world.

From this Romantic idealization of the arts, there develop four central ideas: (i) the autonomy of the arts, where art represents human freedom, (ii) the grand synthesis of art, religion and politics, (iii) the privileging of organic community (*Gemeinschaft)* against modern, individualist society (*Gesellschaft*), and (iv) the moral mission of cultural *Bildung* according to the principle of the beautiful. For Lukács this cultural-aesthetic model was of great importance. And since the influence of early Romanticism was strong on him, a contradictory theme developed in his early works—the tendency of a 'high' art coupled with a spontaneous anarchist movement from below which would not only be involved in the cultural *Bildung* but which would dissolve all societal reifications. This is the central theme of Lukács as the cultural educationist. In a certain way he would be carrying on the traditions laid down by Fichte's *Lectures on the Vocation of a Scholar* (1793) and Schiller's *Lectures on the Aesthetic Education of Man* (1795). For Lukács, art is cultural education, and revolution is the realization of this aesthetic education. And this aesthetics would ponder over the questions: "Why is there no more the world of Classicism which had found the 'full man', full of beauty and rationality?" and "Why are we engulfed in the modern age's dilemma of 'transcendental homelessness'?"

Though Romanticism in the arts, in the beginning of the twentieth century, was giving way to the Modernist avant-garde, this transcendental homelessness would strike at the heart of Europe. It also struck the young Lukács. But with this striking the longing for Utopia would also begin. Utopia manages to create an important task: to create the 'hero' who destabilizes the reification of the mundane life-world. Utopia in the works of Lukács is the seeking of a humanist homeland, similar to the Utopia of Goethe. What was prominent in the works of Lukács till 1928 was his refusal to compromise with reality. Though passionate about Hegel, the Hegelian theme of 'the reconciliation with reality' remained foreign to him. Now this theme of absolute unreconciliation was also a dominant trend in the ideology of Romanticism. It is the deed (the 'radical act') that comprises this irreconcilability of Romanticism. So, if there has to be a philosophy it has to be a philosophy of the deed. Whilst the Young Hegelians (Marx included, in his own way) were gripped with this philosophy of the deed, it was Goethe who, as the Romantic par excellence, gave poetic form to this question of the deed:

> 'Tis writ, 'In the beginning was the Word'
> I pause, to wonder what is here inferred.
> The Word I cannot set supremely high:
> A new translation I will try.
> I read, if by the spirit I am taught,
> This sense: 'In the beginning was the Thought',
> This opening I need to weigh again,
> Or sense may suffer from a hasty pen.
> Does Thought create, and work, and rule the hour?
> T'were best: 'In the beginning was the Power.'
> Yet while the pen is urged with willing fingers,
> A sense of doubt and hesitancy lingers.
> The spirit comes to guide me in my need,
> I write: 'In the beginning was the Deed.'[4]

But if the deed took central place in Romanticism, it could not escape Marx's hermeneutics of suspicion. In *Capital*, Vol. I, he says that this Faustian deed is the same as the deed of the commodity owners—they act before they think: "In their difficulties our commodity-owners think like Faust: "*Im Anfang war die Tat*" (In the beginning was the deed). They therefore acted and transacted before they thought. Instinctively they conform to the laws imposed by the nature of commodities."[5] Though the young Lukács concentrated on this question of the deed, the question of the commodity did not escape him. In *History and Class Consciousness* he stated that the question of the commodity takes central place not only in economics, but in *every aspect of society*.[6] By 1919 the dialectics between the commodity and the deed took central place in his system. It was probably Theodor Adorno who took this Lukácsean concern of relating commodity production with culture (especially in his analysis of music). But unlike Lukács, who stressed on the novel form, Adorno concentrated on the total work of art (*Gesamtkuntswerk*).

This chapter is a consequent inquiry into two distinct sites: (i) the makings of the aesthetics of Romanticism, which focuses on the 'hero' of European art, and (ii) the notion of the reification of consciousness. For Lukács the sketching of the hero is simultaneously a search for the revolutionary subject of history. The hero subverts all reifications. For Lukács (like the entire repertoire of what is known in Marxism as historicism and humanism, and unlike the structuralist "history as a process without a subject") to constitute the subject is central to his philosophy. The subject is the hero of history. Decentring the subject (following the fashion of the French structuralists—most notably Louis Althusser and following this pattern of thinking, the post-structuralists and deconstructionists) is not only an epistemological error; it is reactionary metaphysics, which not only the bourgeoisie but also revolutionaries of the calibre of Engels succumbed to.[7]

An important point to understand Lukács's aesthetics, is to note culture and aesthetics (like history itself) as *a process with a subject*. Now this aesthetics of the hero-subject becomes at the same time political (critiquing the high Romantic [*Hochromantic*] trend of "art for the sake of art" [*l'art pour l'art*]). Now this theme of political art—or art as political and cultural education manifested as revolution formed the core structure of twentieth century avant-garde art. It is this subject-based philosophy of aesthetics that becomes the epistemic basis for other seminal Marxist philosophers of art and culture, Walter Benjamin,

Theodor Adorno, Bertolt Brecht, Herbert Marcuse, and Ernst Bloc. Reflection on Lukács's concept of the 'reification of consciousness' (*Verdinglichung des Bewusstsein*) is not only a reflection on the 'dialectical image' (Benjamin), 'phantasmagoria' (Adorno), the 'one-dimensional man' (Marcuse) and the 'culture industry' (Horkheimer and Adorno), but also a reflection on the problems of our contemporary age. Three important themes follow: (i) the notion of estrangement in Lukács, (ii) the search for the revolutionary subject and Lukács's reflection on the mystics, the anarchists and Marxism, and (iii) the relation between the reification of consciousness and the spectacle of the culture industry which the Frankfurt School consequently developed. It is at this epistemic site that Lukács (and later Adorno) had posed: can art be possible in the age of capitalism that is determined by the culture of the mechanical mode of production? What is the relation between a genuine work of art and this mechanics of the culture industry? And finally: does art have the possibility to destabilize this reified life-world? But most important, if art is possible, then is 'Life' possible?

According to this line of thinking, which does not understand art for the sake of art, but links aesthetics to ethics and politics: we live in the age of late capitalism, or in the age of the empire—to be precise, empire-ism or the Americanization of the world—where the globalization of capital postulates the cultures of not only 'post-politics' and 'post-ideology', but also produces the culture industry and the Ideological State Apparatus which attempt to colonize almost every sector of cultural and political resistance. They have literally rendered unnecessary the process of thinking. Attention thus must turn to the estranged mind (*entfremdete Geist*) and the traumatic dream worlds opened up with the colonization of the life-world.[8] Whilst for the early Lukács this colonization is brought forth by Western civilization, in *History and Class Consciousness* it is the reification inherent in the capitalist mode of production that brings forth the practice of instrumental reason—the reason not to know, but to conquer. And it is this instrumental reason to the will to conquest that was soon to bring forth the entire globe in the jaws of the World War. And it is in the midst of the war that Lukács asked the most pertinent question: "*Who will save us from Western civilization?*"[9] Yet Lukács did not appeal to existentialism, as did other German thinkers like Karl Jaspers, Heidegger and Karl Löwith. For the young Lukács—the hero of history—the proletariat would humble the nihilism of Western civilization.

The importance of Lukács is that by articulating the idea of the reification of consciousness based on the fetishism of the phantom commodity as the essence of Marxism, he could pose the question of the primacy of aesthetics, culture and politics that was in rigorous contrast to the hegemonic versions of Marxism of the Second International. According to this dogma, consciousness was to be understood as an 'emanation' of 'matter' and 'copies' (sometimes 'reflections') of economic situations. In this case, art becomes a mimesis of an underlying economy, and as such, has no validity of its own. Of course, Marx never said anything like this. Engels in his 1890 letter to Josef Bloc protested against this vulgarization of Marxism and its transfiguration into economism,[10] and in response to the economist view of history, said to Conrad Schmidt in 1890 that the economists wanted an "excuse for not studying history". As Marx used to say, commenting on the French 'Marxists' of the late 1870s: "All I know is that I am not a 'Marxist'".[11]

According to Marx's historical materialism, when it is said that the economic base determines (*bestimmte*) the ideological superstructure, then this statement has to be read in a humanist discourse where: (i) the economy comprises the idea of the human essence (*das menschliche Wesen*), and (ii) where determination (*Bestimmung*) is not to be understood as determinism but as formation (*Gestaltung*). Thus the economic base determining the superstructure is read in the passion of the historical class struggles combined with the dread of estrangement and the longing for Utopia.

Lukács's contribution is that he was the first of the post-Marx-Marxists to combine the theory of class struggle with estrangement. Remember that Marx's Paris *Economic and Philosophic Manuscripts of 1844*, which dealt explicitly with the human condition as the being-in-the-world-of-alienation, would be known to the world only after *History and Class Consciousness* had already entered the scene of history. Till the late 1920s, *Capital* would be misread as a positivist predetermination, a misreading that did not spare the young Gramsci.[12]

In contrast to the positivist dogma of Kautsky and Plekhanov that reified Marxism into the doctrine of the marchpast of objective laws independent of humanity, Lukács (like Gramsci and Karl Korsch) kept humanity (in the form of the proletariat as the identical subject-object) at the basis of history. In a Gramscian sense, one had to "put the "will" (which in the last analysis, equals practical or political activity) at the base of philosophy".[13] Gramsci continues: "But it must be a rational, not an arbitrary, will, which is realized in so far as it corresponds to objective historical necessities, or in so far it is universal history itself in the moment of its progressive actualization".[14]

When the First Imperialist World War broke out in 1914, the representatives of the Second International under the leadership of Plekhanov and Kautsky supported the respective bourgeois governments for the war. Lenin broke with the Second International and continued his radical view of Marxism as the seizure of power that he had laid down in *What is to be Done?* (Remember, Plekhanov, the dogmatic and doctrinal Marxist, called Lenin a Nietzschean).[15] This breaking of the hegemony of bourgeois thinking meant a concrete study of dislodging class hegemony. The 'mind' that a certain form of ignorant Marxism had exiled as a reflection of 'matter' was brought in the forefront of revolutionary discourse. What Lukács (like Gramsci and Korsch) did was to lay the philosophical foundations of the study of the 'mind'. His study would be seminal in the Marxist theory of the mind and culture that would not only inspire the inner circle of the Frankfurt School, but also Wilhelm Reich, Eric Fromm, Lucien Goldmann, Jean Hyppolite, Fredric Jameson, etc. Derrida's *Spectres of Marx* would also show traces of Lukács, though Derrida did not explicitly demonstrate it.

By 1917 (primarily due to the Bolshevik Revolution, an act that Herbert Marcuse would soon qualify as a "radical act"[16])

Lukács moved away from Kantianism into a messianic form of left-wing politics and thus moved beyond the problems of the soul and tragedy and embraced revolutionary Marxism. What Lukács gave to the world was *History and Class Consciousness*, a text, if we are to believe Merleau-Ponty that formed the basis of a certain "Western Marxism".[17] Marxism, at least from the peripheries, could be emancipated from the *cunning of (bourgeois) reason*. And with *History and Class Consciousness* Lukács would break from not only neo-Kantianism but also with the mysticism of Meister Eckhart, Kierkegaard and Dostoevsky, the thinkers that he had dabbled with in the time of his youth. The journey with Kant and Kierkegaard would end with Hegel's dialectic in full flow, bursting with the thunder of the 1917 Bolshevik Revolution. The problem of the "metaphysics of tragedy" (a problem that haunted him in his 1910 *The Soul and the Forms*)[18] would be overcome in the dialectics of revolution. Revolution (for Lukács) would be the solution to tragedy.

Estrangement in the Iron Cage of Objectivity

To understand Lukács, one has to understand both the originality of this thinker as well as the diverse (sometimes even contradictory) influences. Whilst his immediate peers were Max Weber, Dilthey, Windelband, Rickert and Simmel, he did not stop at the neo-Kantianism of the Heidelberg Circle. The radicalism of Ervin Szabo (who would be the first Hungarian translator of Marx and Engels) as well as Endre Ady, the *energia* of Henri Bergson, the irony of Thomas Mann, the anarcho-syndicalism of Georg Sorrel and the mystical revolutionarism of Dostoevsky would form the core structure of his thought.

According to Lukács, capitalism is unliveable and inauthentic. It does not produce according to the laws of beauty, but essentially, according to the dictates of the distasteful. *Entfremdung* is itself this distastefulness. It is the black hole from which the 'intellectualized cultures' of modern, rationalized, industrialized civilizations (as against the 'aesthetic culture' of authenticity) have emerged.

To this nature of *Entfremdung* one must turn, for it influenced not only Hegel and Marx (in their radically different ways), but also the entire generation of the Romantics and Existentialists. So what is this *Entfremdung*, and how is one to understand the Romantic, Existentialist, Modernist and Marxist versions of it? Is it an Existential emptiness, or the Buddhist notion of *Dukha*? Is it the void from which sorrow emerges? Is this sorrow linked to the history of tragedy from the Greeks to Goethe's *The Sorrows of the Young Werther* and *Faust*? This is one part of the idea of estrangement and the work of art—an idea that the German poets of the eighteenth and nineteenth centuries perfected. But there is another idea of *Entfremdung*—frightening terror that Freud called "the uncanny" (*das Unheimlich*). According to Freud, the work of art emerges from this *Unheimlich.*[19] So if *Entfremdung* is the House of Aesthetics, then *das Unheimlich* comes marching into this house. But it does not break down this House; it cohabits with *Entfremdung.*

To understand the young Lukács's aesthetics and the crisis of culture, let us highlight three distinct sites of his operation: (i) the alienation of the human condition, (ii) the equation of objectivity with estranged objectivity, and (iii) the crisis of culture that is constituted within a Fichtean "age of absolute sinfulness"[20] coupled with the Marxist genre of the decadence of class societies. In order to understand this crisis of culture, let us slightly shift from Lukács to Marx's analysis of the regression of thinking and feeling that is based on the theory of the accumulation of capital. Accumulation of capital (for Marx as was later for Lukács) is simultaneously the accumulation of regressive thinking and feeling. According to the Frankfurt School's writings on aesthetics and culture (which would be developing from Lukács's idea of the reification of consciousness), the Ideological State Apparatus of late capitalism in the form of the culture industry "pacifies rebellious desire",[21] as also cherishes as art "shining white teeth and freedom from body odour and emotions".[22] Why does this happen? It happens (for Marx), not only because the culture industry wants to control human desire, but more important, because the accumulation of capital is also the accumulation of the crisis of culture and also the accumulation of insanity. The notorious Monsieur Capital who with Madame Rent, as Marx exclaims in *Capital*, Vol. III, does his *ghost walking as a social character and also as a mere thing*[23] is inherently insane—and, contrary to the discourses of modernity, seeks not so much science and technology as it seeks magic and necromancy.[24] In *The Increase of Lunacy in Great Britain* Marx said that increase of wealth is accompanied by an increase in lunacy.[25] Marx's *Capital* is not only the critique of capital accumulation, but also the critique of the culture industry and insanity. Why do we say so? We say so because the great capitalist referent and sign—surplus value (M^1) has lost totally its human and material content—it is "only form without content".[26] It is an estrangement, which is simultaneously a disembodiment—a mind that is produced that is split from the body. It is thus the estranged mind, or what Lukács called "the reification of consciousness". Freud called this "psychosis"—a withdrawal from reality. Lukács, one must remember, never took Freud seriously, and unlike the surrealists, did not experiment with the politics of the unconscious.

For the young Lukács, to deal with modern industrial society is mainly to deal with a sense of the *Unheimlich*, a condition that is overcome sometimes in mythology, sometimes in revolution. Mythos for Lukács in the *The Soul and the Forms* is the world where the individual gets sense of the *heimlich*—a theme that he developed from Novalis. For Lukács, following Novalis philosophy is read as nostalgia where the "impulse is to be everywhere at home in the world",[27] whilst the estranged individual as the stranger (*Fremdling*) is not totally lost in the world, but (as in Novalis's poem *Der Fremdling* as in his philosophical work *Faith and Love*) one who carries the memories of a past golden age which he believes will return again. One has thus found a home in mythos. And for Lukács the pre-novel form of narrative (i.e. pre-capitalist narrative form) had developed a form of aesthetical perfection. The epic form (especially the Greek epic form) was an exemplar of this perfection. Marx did appreciate the Greek epics—in the Introduction to the *Grundrisse*, Marx talked of how in the age of modernity one could experience the "artistic pleasure" in the epic form of beauty that also becomes a "norm" as well as an "unattainable model" of artistic excellence.[28] Yet, there is a sharp difference in Lukács's (both the young and the Sovietized Lukács) and in Marx's rendering of the variation on the theme of aesthetics. For Marx, there can never be nostalgia for pre-capitalist worlds, whilst Lukács, following Novalis, indulges in Romantic nostalgia.

On the contrary, for Marx capitalism as the last of the great class systems is inherently an insane, psychotic system (Eric Fromm develops this Marxist thesis) involved, not in the process of rationality but in *metempsychosis* and *transmigration*.[29] This question of Marx's idea of the necessary insanity of (capitalist) culture is based on three of his observations of the death-wish of estrangement in *Capital*, Vol. I: (i) where, as we noted in the previous chapter, one puts out of sight material existence[30] thus involving a 'judicial blindness'—to fail to see what lies in front of one's nose,[31] (ii) erasing the concrete life-world,[32] and (iii) putting 'out of sight' the useful character of the life-world.[33] Thus what we get is: (i) ontological blindness and the production of the commodity conceived as the *idealized and ghostly thing-in-itself*, both of which forming the basis of the crisis of culture, (ii) the dominance of this abstract and spectral life-world, and (iii) the useless life-world. Life is thus inauthentic. But it is not merely inauthentic. It also functions as the ideological apparatus of concealment predicted on the economic base whose essence has become "ideal" and "invisible".[34] The crisis of culture, for Marx, is based on these three points.

To understand Lukács's emphasis on the cultural realm in concrete combination with the economic epoch, it is necessary to point out briefly Marx's examination of culture and the problem of capital accumulation. In *Capital* Marx claims that the economic base of capitalism is a disembodied, psychotic base grounded on the accumulation of capital. Here Monsieur Capital appears in "a form quite distinct from his palpable bodily form"[35] and then marches into the political economy of the metempsychotic and transmigrated M-C-M^1 circuit where: (i) 'M' as the *primal idealized sign* is the original self of Monsieur Capital, (ii) 'C' as *crypto-matter about to be idealized* is actually Monsieur Capital transfigured as means of production and labour power whilst (iii) 'M^1' is the expanded self of Monsieur Capital, but now appearing as *the neurotic return of the pure idealized sign devoid of matter,* i.e. returning in this great spiritual form, which is "quite distinct from his palpable bodily form". Now this rather strange voyage of Monsieur Capital necessitates an augmentation of himself as this disembodied and thingified fetish. Monsieur Capital now appearing as surplus value keeps on recurring in this disembodied form. For Marx this Monsieur is both neurotic as well as psychotic. Now Lukács, in both his early as well as late periods, like Benjamin's analysis of the *flâeneur,* grasped this point. In *History and Class Consciousness,* he says that the problem of the thing-in-itself that cannot be changed, yet has to be, is the fundamental problem of bourgeois thought.[36] But what he grasps is that drama, as bourgeois drama, is the perfect realization of the fetishization of the capitalist life-world.

When the First Imperialist World War broke out, it was a kind of "the final stage", to borrow Adorno's phrase, "of the dialectic of culture and barbarism".[37] Rosa Luxemburg had demonstrated the unsurpassable antinomy of capitalism as the conflict between socialism and barbarism. For Marxism, unlike the metaphysicians of estrangement, we are not *condemned* to live this barbarism. Estrangement is not a state of permanence. Nor is it a Heideggerean *Da-sein,* where humanity is "thrown into the world". Nor is it what the *History of the Development of Modern Drama* called *Bestehn*—the "being-there" which is "naked existence as force". Instead, for Marx, the traumatic dream images of commodity fetishism are socially and historically constituted and have to be torn down along with its entire world-outlook. With Marx's revolution in thinking, "modern materialism" (to borrow Andre Breton's and Walter Benjamin's term) was born.[38]

Lukács would be ambivalent on this stand on modern materialism. In *History and Class Consciousness* he affirms Rickert's claim that materialism is an "inverted Platonism".[39] Yet he agrees with modern materialism's proposition that one cannot theorize in the castles of speculative abstractions, but in the anthropology of the life-world, what Marx called "the ontological essence of human passion coming into being".[40] To perceive, feel, hear and suffer is to wake up from the traumatic dream state. It is the overcoming of reification.

What is important in Lukács's aesthetics is that he tears the works of art from the decorum of the bourgeois spectacle and centres it on the central problem of the modern epoch—that of ethics.[41] That is why Dostoevsky's characterization of Stavrogin (based on the portrayal of the nineteenth century anarchist Sergi Nacheav) in *The Possessed* remained important for him. The radical act, for Lukács, had to be located in the problematic of ethics.[42] The communist revolution is the moral response of the proletariat to the amoralism and immorality of the capitalists. *History and Class Consciousness* too continues this trajectory of thinking. Revolution does not happen due to some innate telos within history (the official Marxist line), but is the creation of the revolutionary will. The proletariat in 1919 became the embodiment of this will.

The revolution as will and idea would now form the foundation of his ultra left-wing communism. In this case, the narrative of 'objective conditions' (a point that has always been stressed in all kinds of Marxism, following Marx himself) could be nothing but a myth. Objectification, so Lukács would claim (following not only Hegel, but also the ultra-idealist Fichte and the Young Hegelian Max Stirner), is alienation. Of course Marx never said it, whilst Hegel did. For Marx *a non-objective being is a non-being (Ein ungegenständliches Wesen ist ein Unwesen)*.[43] That is because for Marx, contra-Hegel:

> A being (*Wesen*) which does not have its nature outside (*ausser*) itself is not a *natural* being (*natürlichen Wesen*), and plays no part in the system of nature. A being which has no object is not an objective being (*gegenständliches Wesen*). A being which is not itself an object for some other third being has no being for its object (*Gegenstand*); i.e., it is not objectively related. Its being is not objective.[44]

Whilst Marx makes a rigorous distinction between objectivity (*Gegenständlichkeit*) and alienation (*Entfremdung*), Lukács collapses objectivity into alienation, and, to borrow Adorno's phrase, makes "any objectivity ... a matter of indifference".[45]

The world (for the idealists) as revolution is then not a real revolution but a phantom revolution. That is why Lenin chided "left-wing" communism (the group of the ultra-leftists, Lukács included) as "infantile disorder".[46] Lukács becomes the Hamlet of the international proletariat revolution, and he was to know it.

Pseudo-rebellion: *Gemeinschaft* and the Return of Primal Consciousness

The idea of pseudo-rebellion is Wilhelm Reich's. In the *Mass Psychology of Fascism* Reich talked of how fascism used emotions to arouse the popular masses. Since Reich, the idea of pseudo-rebellion is used to analyse popular reactionary movements. Pseudo-rebellion has Romantic anti-capitalism as its ideological basis. It mobilizes an anti-capitalist tradition, however of the reactionary, authoritarian type. What is important in Lukács, is that almost a century after he began his career as a neo-Kantian and eighty years after *History and Class Consciousness*, (that one may say that he is almost a landmark in the history of philosophy) is that even at the time of the "crises in the European sciences" (to borrow a phrase from Husserl), if not the crisis of capitalist civilization, Lukács could articulate the question of the primacy of culture in Marxist theory (a fact till then highly ignored), as well as the necessity of comprehending *philosophy as philosophy* (especially the importance in the understanding of Hegel, in particular, and Classical German Philosophy, in general), thus avoiding both the positivism of Soviet Marxism as well as the later postmodern post-philosophical thinking. The importance (in a reverse way) is also to understand the philosophy not of Marxism, but of anarcho-syndicalism, a philosophy shared by the anti-colonial Gandhi, to the anti-American and anti-Russian Heidegger, the contemporary Heideggereans in Iran as also the late Michel Foucault. Lukács is the classical romantic revolutionary in a hurry—in Lenin's words an "infantile disorder"—but a disorder that recognizes the fallacies of not only the Marxism of Kautsky and Plekhanov, but also the fallacy of onto-theology. It is said that Lukács's revolution (like the entire anarchist tradition) is not only against the capitalists—like Dostoevsky it is against existence, i.e. existence as Existence itself.

Let us sum up Lukács's Romantic motifs: Lukács's fatal error is based on his attempt to 'out-Hegel Hegel', by equating objectivity per se, i.e. trans-historical objectivity with alienation The second error is retreating into the neo-Kantianism of the *Geisteswissenschaften* (human sciences) / *Naturwissenschaften* (natural sciences) opposition (which he learnt from the Heidelberg Circle), resulting in the condemnation of the natural sciences (and nature itself) as eternally alienating. What Lukács rejected was objectivity (recall how he emphasizes the Fichtean "so much the worse for facts") and nature. Real history then cannot be predicted on the "dialectics of nature", but on the "phenomenology of the *Geist*". And, like the entire neo-Platonic and Romantic tradition, nature had to be condemned. Lukács was not only moving into the romanticism of the *Gemeinschaft* school, where he would share his aesthetics and politics with Coomaraswamy and Gandhi, but where the heroic proletariat as identical subject-object would move away from nature (in fact, declare war on nature), and march into the site of the interiors of the soul.

One knows how his pre-*History and Class Consciousness* works, like the *History of the Development of Modern Drama, The Soul and the Forms* and *The Theory of the Novel* were concretely rooted in the site of the Romantic *Gemeinschaft* tradition. So, did Lukács involve a rupture with his *gemeinscahftlicht* past? Or would this *Gemeinschaft* tradition continue to haunt him? One knows that the German Romantics' aesthetics of feeling and emotion criticized the rationalization and mechanization of modern society. Yet there can be two main critiques of rationalization and the reification of the life-world, the one that Marx involved in his critique of capitalism, and the ideology of Romanticism that Marx rubbished as "reactionary socialism". Both these are rigorously distinct. Romanticism, as distinct from Cubism and Surrealism, besides being based on the Nietzschean aristocratic ethics, would be uncompromising about its critique of modernity. Though they would write apocalyptic critiques of industrial civilization, it would involve merely the act of:

> half lamentation, half lampoon; half echo of the past, half menace of the future; at times by its bitter, witty and incisive criticism, striking the bourgeoisie to the very heart's core; but always ludicrous in its effect, through total incapacity to comprehend the march of modern history ...Nothing is easier than to give Christian asceticism a Socialist tinge. Has not Christianity declaimed against private property, against marriage, against the State? Has it not preached in the place of these, charity and poverty, celibacy and mortification of the flesh, monastic life and Mother Church? Christian Socialism is nothing but the holy water with which the priest consecrates the heart-burnings of the aristocrat.[47]

The Romantics upbraided capitalism for producing the proletariat, but forgot that the proletariat is not the subject that suffers and pleads for charity. On the contrary, it is the subject of history that demands the revolution.[48] What the essential difference between Romanticism and the Modernist avant-garde was the difference in their respective ideas of history—German Romanticism stressed mythology as redemption (the operas of Richard Wagner are a case in point) in contradistinction to the French ideologies of progress and development. Bertolt Brecht in his *Die Essays von Georg Lukács* said: "There is no going back. It's not the matter of the good old, but the bad new. Not the dismantling of technology, but its build-up. We will not be human again by leaving the masses, but only through going into them ...but not in the sense that we were human earlier".[49]

The Romantics, unlike the Modernists (especially the Saint-Simon type of Utopian Modernity) refused to embrace the idea of an immanent telos of progress and development in history. Lukács too echoed this theme and in *History and Class Consciousness* said that the greater the productive forces, the greater the reification experienced. Now Romanticism (especially that of Edmund Burke, Adam Muller and Nietzsche) tended to have ultra conservative ideas especially in relation to the French Revolution and its ideas of equality and fraternity. According to Nietzsche: history is determined by genealogy and the forces of origin (*Ursprung*) and descent (*Herkunft*). The forces of earlier descent (according to him) are noble as against the later descents that are reactive and of a lower order. Lukács's Romanticism, however, combined both Nietzsche's reading as well as the ethics of Dostoevsky and the historical idealism of Hegel. Yet, it must be mentioned, Lukács has at least one text of extreme retrograde morality, but like Nietzsche, he is able to combine this absence of morality with an alleged 'higher morality'. In the *Poverty of Spirit,* he claimed that a sort of perfection of the moral order was achieved by the ancient caste system, whereby duty and morality were synthesized. This, sort of ethical perspective was shared not only by Novalis, who, in *Christianity and Europe* talked of the "beautiful, magnificent times, when Europe was a Christian land...(and a) vast spiritual empire",[50] but also with Coomaraswamy who, in *Sati: A Defence of Eastern Woman,* supported the archaic practice of widow immolation as a higher ideal where man and woman were synthesized. Yet Romanticism, though retreating to a mediaeval pastoral ideal, did not opt for naturalism in the arts, but sought the 'Idea' that lay behind nature. If city life was condemned to hell, so too was nature.

So where does the problem arise with Lukács? It is with not being 'concrete'. It lies with the idealist view of history. According to Marx, communism is not "an ideal to which reality will have to adjust itself".[51] But for the early Lukács the subjective situation (the Kierkegaardean "truth is subjective") formed the corpus of his thought. In *Aesthetic Culture* he recalls the Dostoevskyean theme; *anything is permissible.* According to Dostoevsky, the complete principle went thus: "If God does not exist, then anything is permissible". For Lukács:

> Anything is permissible when everybody is living in expectation of a great final accounting, which however never arrives; for on the day of the last judgement all things will in any case be found to be easy, and the communal feeling of tragedy will grant absolution for every frivolity.[52]

Anything is permissible, ontologically and politically speaking, yet why is not anything (the "radical act") possible? It is because one is living in the living hell called "second nature"—"a charnel house of long-dead interiorities" which can only be brought to life by a "metaphysical awakening of the soul".[53] According to

Lukács:

> Estranged from nature (the first nature), the modern sentimental attitude to nature is only a projection of man's experience of his self-created environment as a prison instead of a parental home.
>
> When the structures made by man for man are really adequate for man, they are his necessary and native home; and he does not know the nostalgia that posits and experiences nature as the object of its own seeking and finding. The first nature, nature as a set of laws of pure cognition, nature as the bringer of comfort to pure feeling, is nothing other than historico-philosophical objectification of man's alienation from his own constructs.[54]

But this realm of living death does not propel him to seek the priest who sprinkles holy water to pacify rebellious desire. On the contrary, the subjective spirit (the soul) is in war with the objective spirit (Church, State, Nature). Lukács has two models in his aesthetics: that of Stavrogin (Dostoevsky's analysis of the radical act) and the Hegelian *Geist* in its overcoming of nature itself. Romanticism is thus caught in this double bind: to seek the radical act and the possibilities of the principle, anything is permissible; also, to search for the medieval solution of the Catholic Church's representation of the 'Idea' that lies behind 'Nature'. These are the two souls dwelling in the breast of Romanticism, each, as Goethe remarked, "going apart from the other". The dominant trend is that of the world abandoned by God himself and left to the mechanics of the alienated world-view to take care of itself. In this sense, the second double binding of the Romantic tradition is like the biblical conflict (best represented by Žižek)—where, on the one hand, God is shown as an omnipotent, but perverse subject, who desires to see humanity suffer and then at the appropriate moment intervenes to claim that he is the 'hero' of history. On the other hand, God is not an omnipotent subject, but more like the hero of Greek tragedy who is also subordinated to a higher destiny.[55]

Now Lukács carried this metaphysical and existentialist conflict with him and strangely also seemed to share a particular motif of anti-Naturalism (i.e. seeking the "Idea" behind "Nature") with Indian aesthetics (Coomaraswamy especially) who had said that one should not even use the term "aesthetics" since it signifies sensuality.[56] This type of Romantic anti-Naturalism does not even accept the art form of the "body". The body, as Coomaraswamy had said, is illusory.[57] One has to move into the realm of what Lukács in *The Soul and the Forms* called (after the German mystics) "imagelessness of all images".[58] But this going into a mystical, supra-Hegelian 'Idea' becomes not only phantasmagorical, where (as we said before) Monsieur Capital has left his 'palpable bodily form' and become 'ideal' and 'invisible'; but also where there is the operation of psychosis at work—*the compulsive desire to withdraw from reality.*

So how does the early Lukács understand the radical act? Lukács states that humanity has to transcend "laws" (i.e. "laws" of nature) because laws hold people in chains.[59] Unfortunately, Lukács would tend to hold this same ontological position even in *History and Class Consciousness.* Nature and objectivity (as we noted) are condemned as alienation. Nature is itself said to be deterministic and manipulable, in contrast to the 'inner' spiritual domain of 'man'. What does not involve 'man' is condemned to hell. Nature has forgotten 'man'. The revolution is thus against nature itself. Nature is then understood (not only in the Kantian but also in the structuralist sense) as a *process without the subject.* Seems strange how two contrasting episteme, structuralism and historicism-humanism, and two conflicting philosophers, Althusser and Lukács, meet in this site of estrangement. So if 'nature' is considered as deterministic and manipulable that does not involve 'man', then there can be no praxis, no freedom. Nature thus excludes freedom. The paintings at Lukács's exhibition, which are supposed to be about the story of 'man', are actually about the souls and forms of 'man', 'man' that has actually died with the birth of urban civilizations.

And if nature is manipulative, so too are the natural sciences. We thus descend into the Kantian dualisms of pure reason/ practical reason, science/ethics, nature/culture . We live in these almost eternally defined dualisms, somewhat akin to the biblical conflict of God with Satan. But Lukács does not believe in the eternal, for the subject as pure praxis has to rebel. But this rebellion is against "nature" and thus, in a way, against God himself. If Benjamin had talked of "shattering the continuum of history",[60] then Lukács wants to shatter History itself.

The 'hero' thus enters the scene of aesthetic history. In a peculiar way Lukács combines the hero of classical antiquity, reminding one of the ancient Iranian epic warrior-heroes Rustum and Sohrab, as depicted in the eleventh-century Persian epic the *Sháhnáma*, with the Dostoevskyean hero. Just as the Iranian hero has the glory (*Khavernah*) bestowed on him, so too Dostoevsky's hero has the aura sketched around his character. The hero is the mystic, pure, honest and full of goodness (*Güte*). Goodness is grace, the aura bestowed by God himself. Michael Löwy in his excellent study of Lukács has said that one cannot help comparing Lukács's dualism of grace and ordinary life with Weber's counter-position of "charisma" (a Greek word implying "gift of grace") and "routine".[61] In Iranian legend grace is robbed and the "fall" of humanity begins. In Russian literature of the nineteenth century, the hero is sketched both in the heroic Iranian-warrior form as well as the Christian form of love-seeking hero, as found in Dostoevsky's *The Idiot*. So it is Christian love as well as the Iranian form of smiting all evil that Lukács incorporates in his aesthetics.

The Russian novel of the nineteenth century incorporates both these aspects. In fact, the combination of these seemingly contradictory aspects forms the core structure of the Slavic personality. The Soviet State, after Stalin's counter-revolutionary takeover after 1928, also incorporated this antinomy: smiting evil (i.e. the revolutionaries) as well as bestowing goodness and charity with the public distribution system. This urge towards a grand Slavic-socialism combined with the mystical love of God remained a core of nineteenth and twentieth-century East European literature. There seemed to be no resolution to this aporia—in which terror and/or love is caught in the abyss between ordinary life and the radical act. Löwy notes (quoting Dostoevsky) how the ethical-literary gospel influenced Lukács:

> The moment he thought seriously about it, he was overcome by the conviction of the existence and immortality of God, and he quite naturally said to himself: "I want to live for immortality, and I won't accept any compromise." Similarly if he had decided

> that there was no immortality and no God, he would at once have become an atheist and a Socialist, for Socialism is not only the labour question, or the question of the so-called fourth estate, but above all an atheistic question, the question of the modern integration of atheism, the question of the Tower of Babel which is deliberately being created without God, not for the sake of reaching heaven from earth, but for the sake of bringing heaven down to earth.[62]

If not the idealization effect of classical idealism, then at least the Hegelian activist idealism of the pro-active *Geist* combined with the mysticism of the pre-Marxist militant bent towards heroic sacrifice to gain the great idealist end would return to haunt Lukács. The heroic subject is not the rational and pragmatic Lenin, but the mystic Jesus, the anointed one, tormented by the slings and arrows of the sufferings of mankind. After all, one knows that it is the estrangement from God that forms the motor force of the metaphysical dialectics of the mystic's alleged radical act. And it is this radical act that has so fascinated the history of world literature. In *Crime and Punishment* Raskolnikov's alleged radicalism is said to lie in the murder of a frail old woman, a murder that has to be committed because with the money robbed from the moneylender woman, humanity could be saved. After all, so Dostoevsky's character claims, all world saviours shed rivers of blood.[63] Till *History and Class Consciousness* the strong influence of Dostoevsky is evident. But then the proletariat changes the course of action of the 'hero'. Or does it?

In *History and Class Consciousness* the proletariat as *identical subject-object* enters the scene of world history to take on the role of the divine mystic and the messiah that saves the world soul from tragedy. Though revolutionaries in late antiquity and later (Jesus, Mazdak-I-Bambad and Mohammed) emphasised the will of the mystic and the sacrifices that they claimed to form the core of the radical act,[64] it ought to be remembered that for the Heidelberg Circle it was Russian mysticism and Russian literature that wielded them together and which provided a mode of rejecting Western capitalist civilization.[65]

But Lukács also knew that the dangerous zone that divides

materialism from idealism had to be breached. If for idealism the mystic is the subject of history, materialism needs to find an empirical subject that is located in the concrete moment of the historical conjuncture of class struggles. The proletariat (for Marx) becomes the class that has reached the vantage moment in history because of its historical antagonism to the bourgeoisie, to the accumulation of capital and to class societies in general. The moralistic version of the pre-Marxist revolutionary corresponds to Christian suffering and charity in contrast to the militant proletariat. For Marx, in contrast to the Romantics:

> The proletariat, on the contrary (*umgekehrt*), is compelled as proletariat to abolish (*aufzuheben*) itself and thereby its opposite (*Gegensatz*), private property, which determines its existence, and which makes it proletariat. It is the negative side (*negative Seite*) of the anti-thesis (*Gegensatzes*), its restlessness (*Unruhe*) within its very self, dissolved (*aufgelöste*) and self-dissolving private property.
>
> The propertied class and the class of the proletariat present the same human self-estrangement (*menschliche Selbstentfremdung*). But the former class feels at ease and strengthened in this self-estrangement, it recognizes estrangement (*Entfremdung*) as its own power and has in it the *semblance* (*Schein*) of a human existence. The latter feels annihilated (*vernichtet*) in estrangement; it sees in its own powerlessness and the reality of an inhuman existence (*unmenschlichen Existenz*). It is, to use an expression of Hegel, in its abasement the *indignation* at the abasement, an indignation to which it is necessarily driven by the contradiction (*Widerspruch*) between its human nature (*menschlichen Natur*) and its condition of life, which is the outright, resolute and comprehensive negation of that nature (*Verneinung dieser Natur*).[66]

But in contrast to Marx, it is not only the "comprehensive negation of that nature (*Verneinung dieser Natur*)", but principally the negation of Nature itself that the Romantic seeks. The Romantic does not want to negate contradictions that comprise reality. He wants to negate 'Reality' itself. The Romantic is the mystic who is necessarily bound to the idea of pure identity—what the Sufis call *Fana* and the Iranians once remembered as *Khshnoom*. Lukács's hero (at least till 1918) was this mystic and the saviour—but the saviour that never comes. Like Goethe's Faust, the young Lukácsean hero is then dragged into hell. In that case one will then have to wait for the absent saviour, whether the Zoroastrian *Soashant*, the return of Jesus, the Shiite imam, or even the tyrant and false prophet Generalissimo Stalin. Though the saviour never came, it is the spectres of the revolution and counter-revolution that now haunt us.

By 1928 one episode of the Romantic Utopia came to an end. The Slavic Utopia in war with Western civilization was realized not in the worker's paradise, but in the Stalinist bureaucracy. The Soviet Union became the graveyard of international communism. Even Trotsky, the 'hero' who chided Romanticism's child 'fate' (saying, following Proudhon: "Destiny—I laugh at it; and as for men, they are too ignorant, too enslaved for me to feel annoyed at them"[67]) would be disarmed and sent to his grave. We now stand at the memorial of the Bolsheviks. Besides the names of Trotsky, Bukharin, Zinoviev, Kamanev, Radek and the entire 1917 central committee of the Bolsheviks, along with countless revolutionaries, is also etched the name of a certain Georg Lukács, who remained silent. And along with the cacophony of this silence is also heard the voices of Hamlet and his spectral father:

> *Ghost*. Revenge his foul and most unnatural murder.
> *Hamlet*. Murder!
> *Ghost*. Murder most foul, as in the best it is;
> But this most foul, strange, and unnatural.
> *Hamlet*. Haste me to know't, that I, with
> wings as swift
> As meditation or the thoughts of love,
> May sweep to my revenge....

REFERENCES

1. G.W.F. Hegel, *Philosophy of Mind. Part Three of the Encyclopaedia of the Philosophical Sciences (1830)*, trans. William Wallace, (Oxford: Clarendon Press, 1990), pp. 293-7.
2. For the Leninism of Lukács, see Slavoj Žižek, 'Georg Lukács as the Philosopher of Leninism', Postface to Georg Lukács, *A Defence of History and Class Consciousness'*, trans. Esther Leslie (London: Verso, 2000).
3. István Mészáros, *Lukács's Concept of Dialectic* (London: Merlin

Press, 1972), p. 18; György Márkus, 'Life and Soul: the Young Lukács and the Problem of Culture', in *Lukács Revalued*, ed. Agnes Heller (Oxford: Basil Blackwell, 1983).

4. Johann Wolfgang Goethe, *Faust*, Part One, trans. Philip Wayne (London: Penguin Books, 1949), p. 71.
5. Karl Marx, *Capital*, Vol. I, trans. Samuel Moore and Edward Aveling (Moscow: Progress Publishers, 1983), p. 90.
6. Georg Lukács, *History and Class Consciousness. Studies in Marxist Dialectics*, trans. Rodney Livingstone (London: Merlin Press, 1983), p. 83.
7. Ibid, p. 3.
8. When Lukács talked of the reification of consciousness, he anticipated the young Marx's notion of estrangement, a concept known to the world in the early twentieth century more in Hegelian and biblical forms The idea taken over by Georg Simmel, Lukács's one-time teacher was more in the temper of this idealism of ontological and metaphysical alienation. The rigour of the political economy of estrangement that Marx emphasized, was till the late 1920s, buried in the silence of orthodoxy. David Ryazanov, the great Marxologist (incidentally eliminated by Stalin), would reveal the *Economic and Philosophic Manuscripts of 1844* and the *Contribution to the Critique of Hegel's Philosophy of Right* (both which centralized the notion of estrangement in the theories of capitalism and the modern state) only in the late 1920s and early 1930s. Between 1929-31, Lukács worked with Ryazanov at the Marx-Engels-Lenin Institute, where the latter showed him the drafts of the 1844 manuscripts before they were published.
9. Georg Lukács, *The Theory of the Novel*, trans. Anna Bostock (Cambridge, Massachusetts: The MIT Press, 1994), p. 11.
10. Friedrich Engels, 'Letter to Josef Bloc in Königsberg, London, Sept. 21, 1890' in *Marx. Engels. Selected Works* (Moscow: Progress Publishers, 1975), p. 682.
11. Friedrich Engels, 'Letter to Conrad Schmidt in Berlin, London, August 5, 1890', in Ibid, p. 679.
12. Antonio Gramsci, 'The Revolution against "Capital"', in *Selections from Political Writings, 1910-1920*, trans. John Mathews, selected and edited by Quintin Hoare (London: Lawrence and Wishart, 1977), pp. 34-7.
13. Antonio Gramsci, *Selection from the Prison Notebooks*, trans. Quintin Hoare and Geoffrey Nowell Smith (New York: International Publishers, 1971), p. 345.

14. Ibid.
15. Georgi Plekhanov, 'Notes to Engels's Book *Ludwig Feuerbach*', in *Georgi Flekhanov'. Selected Philosophical Works,* Vol. I (Moscow: Progress Publishers, 1977), p. 455.
16. Herbert Marcuse, 'Phenomenology of Historical Materialism' in *Telos*, 4, Fall, 1969.
17. Maurice Merlau-Ponty, *Adventures of the Dialectic*, trans. Josef Bien (Evanston, Ill: Northwestern University Press, 1973), pp. 30-58 See also Jürgen Habermas, *Theory of Communicate Action. Vol. 1. Reason and the Rationalization of Society*, trans. Thomas McCarthy (London: Heinemann, 1984) and Andrew Arato and Paul Breines, *The Young Lukács and the origins of Western Marxism* (New York: The Seabury Press, 1979).
18. Georg Lukács, *The Soul and the Forms* (London: Merlin Press, 1971), pp. 152-174. Michael Löwy in *Georg Lukács —From Romanticism to Bolshevism* trans. Patrick Camiller (London: New Left Books, 1979), p. 103, relates tragedy to the "trenchant dualism of two forms of life—living (*lebendige*) or 'true' (*wahre*) life, and 'unliving', 'impure', or 'ordinary' life. These two worlds should be 'kept rigorously distinct' (*streng voneinander zu scheiden*), and the main character of the dialogue proclaims his deep aversion to the lower world: 'I can no longer bear the unclarity and dishonesty of the everyday life.'"
19. Sigmund Freud, 'The Uncanny' in *The Penguin Freud Library. Vol. 14. Art and Literature*, trans. James Strachey (London: Penguin, 1990), pp. 335-376.
20. Georg Lukács, *The Theory of the Novel*, p. 18.
21. Herbert Marcuse, 'Affirmative Culture', in *Negations. Essays in Critical Theory* (Boston: Beacon, 1968), p. 121.
22. Max Horkheimer and Theodor Adorno, *Dialectic of Enlightenment*, trans. John Cumming (New York: Herder & Herder, 1972), p. 167.
23. Karl Marx, *Capital*, Vol. III (Moscow: Progress Publishers, 1986), p. 830.
24. Karl Marx, *Capital*, Vol. I (Moscow: Progress Publishers, 1983), p. 80.
25. Karl Marx, 'The Increase of Lunacy in Great Britain' in *Marx. Engels. Collected Works, Vol. 15* (Moscow: Progress Publishers, 1986), pp. 602-6.
26. Karl Marx, *Capital*, Vol. III, p. 392.
27. Georg Lukács, *The Theory of the Novel.*
28. Karl Marx, *Grundrisse*, trans. Martin Nicholas (London: Penguin Books, 1974), p. 111.

29. Karl Marx, *Capital*, Vol. I, p. 199.
30. Ibid, p. 45.
31. Karl Marx, 'To Friedrich Engels in Manchester, London, 25 March, 1868', in *Marx. Engels. Selected Works* (Moscow: Progress Publishers, 1975), p. 189.
32. Karl Marx, *Capital*, Vol. I, p. 46.
33. Ibid.
34. Ibid, pp. 98-9.
35. Ibid, p. 98.
36. Georg Lukács, *History and Class Consciousness*, p. 150.
37. Theodor Adorno, *Prisms* trans. S. Weber (London, 1955), p. 34.
38. According to Erwin Szabo as noted in Andrew Arato and Paul Brienes in *The Young Lukacs and the Origins of Western Marxism* (New York: The Seabury Press, 1979), p. 9, Marx was not a philosophical materialist but a revolutionary materialist.
39. Georg Lukács, *History and Class Consciousness*, p. 202.
40. Karl Marx, *Economic and Philosophic Manuscripts of 1844*, p. 120.
41. Yet this breaking of the work of art as spectacle is different from the type exercised by the Marxist poet and playwright Bertolt Brecht.
42. Georg Lukács, 'The Moral Mission of the Communist Party', in *Political Writings 1919-1929* (London: New Left Books, 1972).
43. Karl Marx, *Economic and Philosophic Manuscripts of 1844*, p. 137.
44. Ibid.
45. Theodor Adorno, *Negative Dialectics* trans. E. B. Ashton (London: Routledge & Kegan Paul, 1973), p. 50.
46. V.I. Lenin, *Left-Wing Communism an Infantile Disorder* (Moscow: Progress Publishers, 1977).
47. Karl Marx and Friedrich Engels, 'The Manifesto of the Communist Party', in *Marx. Engels. Selected Works* (Moscow: Progress Publishers, 1975), pp. 54-5.
48. Ibid, p. 54.
49. See Eugene Lunn, *Marxism and Modernism: a historical study of Lukács, Brecht, Benjamin and Adorno* (Berkeley: University of California Press, 1984), p. 145.
50. Novalis, 'Christianity and Europe. A Fragment', in *The Early Political Writings of the German Romantics*, ed. Fredrick C. Beiser (Cambridge: Cambridge University Press, 1996), p. 61.
51. Karl Marx and Friedrich Engels, *The German Ideology*, (Moscow: Progress Publishers, 1976), p. 57.
52. See György Márkus, op. cit., p. 5.
53. Georg Lukács, *The Theory of the Novel*, p. 64.

54. Ibid.
55. Slavoj Žižek, *The Fragile Absolute—or why is the Christian legacy worth fighting for?* (London: Verso, 2000), pp. 157-8.
56. Ananda K Coomaraswamy, *Christian and Oriental View of Art* (New Delhi: Munshiram Manoharlal, 1994), p. 46.
57. Ananda K Coomaraswamy, *Essays in Indian Nationalism* (New Delhi: Munshiram Manoharlal, 1981), p. 22.
58. Georg Lukács, *The Soul and the Forms*, p. 5.
59. Georg Lukács, *The Theory of the Novel*, p. 65.
60. Walter Benjamin, 'Edward Fuchs, Collector and Historian', in *One-Way Street and other Writings*, trans. Edmund Jephcott & Kingsley Shorter (London: New Left Books, 1979), p. 352.
61. Georg Lukács, 'On Poverty of Spirit. *A Conversation and a Letter*', in *The Lukacs Reader*, ed. Arpad Kadarkay (Oxford: Blackwell, 1995), pp. 45-7. Also see Michael Löwy, *Georg Lukács —From Romanticism to Bolshevism*, p. 104.
62. Fyodor Dostoevsky, *The Brothers Karamazov.* See Michael Löwy, p. 114.
63. Fyodor Dostoevsky, *Crime and Punishment* (Moscow: Ruduga Publishers, 1985), p. 280.
64. As the "identical subject-object" the Lukácsian proletariat becomes a type of a mystic Sufi (the same for his once friend and colleague of the Heidelberg Circle, Ernst Bloc's *Principle of Hope* where the proletariat appears as the prophet) who has realized that the revolution-divine is not something objective, or some sort of an "estranged other", but is to be found within the self's radical praxis—the praxis of revolution. Bloc saw the Russian Revolution as the installation of Christ as Emperor. See Michael Löwy, *Georg Lukács —From Romanticism to Bolshevism*, p. 53.
65. Ibid, p. 38. See also Georg Lukács, 'Stavrogin's Confession' and 'Dostoevsky: Novellas', in *Reviews and Articles from Die rote Fahne*, trans. Peter Palmer (London: Merlin Press, 1983), pp. 44-51.
66. Karl Marx and Friedrich Engels, *The Holy Family* (Moscow: Progress Publishers, 1980), p. 46.
67. Leon Trotsky, *My Life* (London: Penguin Books, 1975), p. 606.

CHAPTER 6

Psychosis and Phantasmagoria

READING JUSTICE AND EQUALITY IN THE TEXT OF MARX'S SUSPICION

If God did not exist everything would be possible.
—Fyodor Dostoevsky, *The Brothers Karamazov.*

We recall two concrete strands in Marx's repertoire: historical materialism and the genealogy of estrangement. This chapter submits the ideas of justice and equality to Marx's genealogy of estrangement. It proceeds primarily to the critique of the dominant ideas of justice and equality, now re-written in liberal and neo-conservative form, which largely frames the political constitutions of the West European and North American nation states, and now, who in their missionary zeal, are thrusting their empire of instrumental rationality on the entire world. As the genealogy of estrangement forms the methodological texture of this chapter, it submits the entire globe of Western hegemony to scientific analysis, from the *Book of Genesis* and contemporary American foreign policy, to the critique of the onto-theological idea of justice: i.e. the critique of the territorialization of the world and the consequent imperialist will to power. In contrast to this type of thinking, Marx argues for a system of justice that ought to be framed in the dialectics of *Gattungswesen* (species being) and *das menschlichen Wesen* (the human essence).

To think is to be suspicious. To think radically is to be doubly suspicious. Human history has to be questioned at its deepest roots. Not only philosophical and scientific answers, but also the very questions have to undergo a hermeneutical questioning. The ideas of justice and equality which are being repeatedly posed today in the age of late imperialism seem sometimes to be directionless and meaningless because they are posed by the perpetuators of injustice, 'the empire' itself. Our questions are posed not only in this age of the empire but the very questions of justice, ethics, the state and judicial systems are posed in both the age of the empire as also under its bullying shadow.

It has already been mentioned that the empire was conceived as a hegemonic project by the American Ideological State Apparatus after the defeats of Japanese expansionism in the East, the rout of Nazi Germany in 1945 and the withdrawal from this project by the British. Its second and more lethal stage started in the last decade of the twentieth century after the collapse of the Warsaw Pact-East European nations led by the Slavophil Soviet Union. Its ideology is alleged 'freedom' in contrast to the 'unfree' world of communism and the newer incarnations of anti-Americanism: the Serbians, the North Koreans, the Cubans, radical Islam and other spectres. The 'free' world of the empire (or in the language of Samuel Huntington, "the West") had to speak against the 'unfree' world of "the rest".[1] Justice, equality and the rest of the paraphernalia of the French Revolution are resurrected in the most bizarre way to resurrect the empire. But this is what psychoanalysis calls "strange"; a reality that appears in distorted (sometimes even in glorified) form. Its language is what Marx calls "borrowed language",[2] language borrowed not only from the past, but disguised language:[3] the language of the psychotic. If in the state of psychosis, "the subject receives the message in inverted form" (to borrow Lacan's phrase),[4] in the political discourse of the empire what we have is the psychotic speaking in this inverted form. We shall start with the first functional understanding of psychosis where the ego in the service of the id "withdraws from a piece of reality", in contrast to the neurotic who represses a part of the id in its dependence on reality.[5] Now in the world of international relations, the relation between the developed 'North' and the developing 'South' takes patterns similar to those of the psychotic and the neurotic. The chapter in Hegel's *Phenomenology of Mind* titled 'Lordship and Bondage' (popularised as the master-slave dialectic) could be re-titled as 'The Psychotic and the Neurotic'. Now what we are doing is reading the questions of justice and equality in the texts of psychosis and neurosis, but before a warning: that Marx, the master in the hermeneutics of suspicion, is passionate about classless society. One could call justice and equality, to be understood, what one knows from French radical thought, as *equaliberty*, as the '*Passions of Marx*'.

The irony of this idea of equaliberty—the non-antagonist community of equality and liberty—is that this idea is posed in history, yet it is an idea that continuously slips away.

We move from the site of slippages, Freud and psychoanalysis to Marx himself, specifically the problems of capitalist politics, in fact capitalism itself, and the problem of the phantasmagoria. Phantasmagoria is a term used quite often by Marx. Capitalism is called a horrendous society wherein relations between people appear as "the phantasmagorical form (*phantasmagorische Form*) of a relation between things".[6] Phantasmagoria as psychosis now enters the scene of justice. It is from this prelude on psychosis and the phantasmagoria that we move into the reading of justice in the text of Marx's suspicion. At a very surface level, Marxism is brought within the theory of distributive justice, where not only are the distribution of duties, rights and responsibilities brought to the forefront of justice theory, but the political economy of the distribution of goods (in fact, the entire mode of production and the structure of class-stratified society) is brought to the forefront of the understanding of justice. But for Marx, if justice is not to be confused with retribution, most certainly not an onto-theologically defined nationalist or communitarian retribution, then also the liberal democratic and the utopian socialist usage come under Marx's hermeneutics of suspicion. The state, as the liberal democratic state that emerged in Europe and North America after the anti-feudal revolutions, carries as its banners the ideologies of liberty, equality and fraternity, but as Marx states, has behind it infantry, artillery and cavalry.[7] So Marx, the passionate humanist, is continuously suspicious about the terminology of politics and the politics of terminology.

Before venturing into the hermeneutics of suspicion, let us have a glimpse at the brief history of equaliberty that Marx himself was heir to. This is the revolutionary usage, where *the Rights of Man and the Citizen* form a type of a nodal text. This type of equality, synthesized with liberty, is understood as a moral universalism in history and politics. The French Revolution has this revolutionary constitutional usage where insurrection forms the basis of democracy and the rule of the subaltern masses. Marxism becomes the perfection of this insurrectionist form of the politics of equaliberty.

There is a second idea of equality—the reified idea of equality—equality as measurement. This is in contrast to the heroic utopian idea of equality and the universal idea of humanity. This idea is located within the genealogy of the commodity. Marx reads Aristotle and the problems of equality and value in this terrain. It is in this terrain that the heroic utopian idea loses its battle with the genealogy of the commodity. Questions posed in this terrain appear in estranged form (*entfremdete Gestalt*).[8] They are questions bound to an alien reality (*fremde Wirklichkeit*).[9] One thus descends into the realms of alienation in the underworld.

In 1875 Marx responds to the Lassallean left in the German working class movement in the pamphlet known as *Critique of the Gotha Programme.* Consider the Lasallean utopian language now embodied in this estranged format:

> The emancipation of labour demands the promotion of the instruments of labour to the common property of society and the co-operative regulation of the total labour with a fair distribution of the proceeds of labour.[10]

Now Marx is very serious about this idea of justice as fairness. To this notion of "fair distribution" Marx questions this idea itself, and asks whether the bourgeois does not state that its society is "fair"? The problem is that when one talks of fairness and justice, then one has not made the crucial distinction between the legal understanding and the standpoint of the critique of political economy.[11] When one has not understood the latter standpoint, when one misses out the dynamics of society, then one uses the language of the phantasmagoria, and the ideas of "justice", "fair distribution" and "equal right" become "meaningless phrases".[12] It is what Marx calls "the language of commodities"[13]—*estranged language*. Further, Marx states that in posing the idea of equality, one can in no way work according to the principle of the "calculable by equity".[14] The ideas of justice and equality seem to be tied down to the genealogy of the commodity and its ideologies of rational calculations. So how should one understand the problem?

Critical theory locates this in the act of measuring itself, in Marcuse's term, in the "art of measuring" (*Messkunst*)[15] and the will to calculate and control. Critical theory would claim, especially Horkheimer and Adorno, that Western Reason is founded on this very will. Thus the idea of equality as calculation and control falls within this ambit. But it is not only the West that has invented measuring. Ancient Iranian mythology talks of Jamshîd, the Iranian Yima/Yama, as extracting the valuable commodity, the *paymân*, the Right Measure, from the realm of Ahreman, the devil.[16] The Zoroastrian text *Dēnkard* III, 297 says:

> Thus indeed is it said by the Early Teachers from the instructions of the Good Religion: the religion of Ohrmazd is (but) one word, the Measure; that of Ahreman is two words, excess and deficiency.[17]

But this Iranian idea of measure, like the Aristotelean idea of the "Mean" in *Nicomachean Ethics*, does, in no way, signify equality in the modern understanding of equality, or the revolutionary usage in revolutions in late antiquity and early medievalism. One knows that Khausru I (531-579 A.D.), the Sasanian monarch, disagreed with the very idea of equality from the perspective of the ruling class. For Khausru, contra Mazdak-I-Bambad, the leader of the peasantry, fighting against the Iranian nobles, landlords and the priests (also known ironically as 'the first communist'), the very idea of equality is abominable. Thus spake the Ideological State Apparatus of Khausru:

> O seeker after wisdom! thou hast framed
> A new religion in the world and made
> Community of women and of goods.

How will a father recognise his son,
The son in like recognise his father?
When every man is equal in the world,
And great and little are no more discerned,
Who then will serve and how can any rule?
Who then will labour for us, thee and me
And how shall good men be discerned from bad?
When one shall die to who will appertain
His house and goods when toiling slave and Shah
Are equal? This will desolate the world;
Such evil must not come upon Iran.
When all are masters who will be servant?
When all have treasures who will be treasurer?
None of the leaders of the Faith spake thus,
And thou art mad although thou hidest it,
Thou leadest all mankind to Hell, and thou
Accountest not all evil-doing wrong.[18]

So the ideology of equality was brushed away in Iran in the sixth century A.D. But not only was the idea of equality brushed aside—the massacre of the Mazdakites followed, the Sasanian state became more authoritarian and absolutist leading to its own collapse in 651 A.D. For Marxism, this brushing aside of the ideology of equality in Sasanian Iran was tied up with the Asiatic mode of production and the emerging feudal relations in Iran.

In another sense, Marx suggests that Aristotle was epistemologically prevented in understanding the value of commodities, because the "equal something" or the "common substance" of commodities could not simply be fathomed in ancient Greek society that was based on inequality.[19] "Exchange" so Marx quotes Aristotle, "cannot take place without equality, and equality without commensurability."[20] Further, Marx notes Aristotle's remarks on value and equality: ""It is however, in reality, impossible, that such unlike things can be commensurable"—i.e. qualitatively equal. Such an equalization can only be something foreign to their real nature, consequently, only "a makeshift for practical purposes"".[21] Marx summarizes the question of the problem of understanding the political economy of value and raising the question of equality in a society founded on slave labour:

> There was, however, an important fact which prevented Aristotle from seeing that, to attribute value to commodities, is merely a mode of expressing all labour as equal human labour, and consequently as labour of equal quality. Greek society was founded upon slavery, and had, therefore, for its natural basis, the inequality of men and their labour-powers. The secret of the expression of value, namely, that all kinds of labour are equal and equivalent, because, and so far as they are human labour in general, cannot be deciphered, until the notion of human equality has already acquired the fixity of a popular prejudice. This, however, is possible only in a society in which the great mass of the produce of labour takes the form of commodities, in which, consequently, the dominant relation between man and man, is that of owners of commodities. The brilliancy of Aristotle's genius is shown by this alone, that he discovered, in the expression of the value of commodities, a relation of equality. The peculiar conditions of the society in which he lived, alone prevented him from discovering what "in truth", was at the bottom of this equality.[22]

And to go to the bottom of this type of equality is the mission that Marx seeks to accomplish. Getting to the bottom, one will be able to find out what this notion of equality signifies: not human equality, but reified equality, equality in the abstract, equality between things, the rationalized equalizer that seeks commensurability and equivalence—thus phantasmagorical equality. Now Marx says that the method of differentiating the ideas of human equaliberty from the reified equality between things is dialectical and historical materialism, now understood as the genealogy of the estranged thing.

So Marx insists on going to the bottom to uncover this radical difference. And Marx says that this equality as measure that lies at the bottom of the commodity also lies at the bottom of all class civilizations. It claims that equality is its essence, yet it practises inequality. Marx thus thinks it extremely necessary to go to the bottom of class civilizations to uncover the ruse: why equality and inequality are so inexorably bound together. Marx thus begins his quest.

What he finds is a tremendous accumulation of commodities—actually an accumulation of dead things, of *stored up dead labour*. He follows this trail that leads to the bottom. He wants to know what the *common something* is between two commodities. What he discovers is that there is no concrete material reality that forms the essence of commodities, but on the contrary, abstract labour, now taken the form of abstract idealized non-reality—the value form that lies at the bottom of class histories. Marx notes—as we have already pointed out in this book—this as a *phantom reality.*[23] And it is this phantom that lies at the bottom of class civilizations that continuously deludes us: the latest delusion is about the liberal idea of equality and the judicial notions emanating thereon (i.e. the delusory idea of liberty and equality before the fraternity of capital) which is as speculative as the theological equality before the God that is simply not there.

Now this *phantom reality* has escaped from the bottom. It has left the underworld like the gods that have escaped the netherworld to haunt our human life-world. What one can say is that the idea of equality—equality as equality between things, hence phantasmagorical equality—existed only in "germ form",[24] hence undetected form, in ancient Greek society. This germ form has now taken global form. But this notion of equality between things (in the language of the critique of political economy: equal values are exchanged) actually signifies real human inequality (the law of unequal exchange: whilst equal values are exchanged between two commodities, when it comes to the exchange of capital and labour power unequal exchange takes place). Now every government of the world—whether the government is the government of the Holy Roman Empire, or the Sasanian state, the Caliphate, or modern liberal, neo-conservative, fascist or Stalinist-Maoist—this notion of the "bottom of this equality", commodified-fictitious equality, if not altogether open racist inequality, is inscribed on its governmental bottom. A spectre is now haunting the world, the spectre of the phantasmagoria. Presently, it is nestled within the empire.

Now what Marx does is relate philosophical and judicial notions to the economic structure of society such that his theorem: *reified existence determines the estranged mind*, allows a broadening of Marx's critique of political economy where the economic base will be dominated from now on by the genealogy of the *alien object* and the *estranged mind.* Capitalist societies will always be haunted by the estranged mind.

We shall thus direct the ideas of justice and equality (as well as injustice and inequality) to two of Marx's ideas, the first very well-known, the idea of class struggle; and the second, repressed within the Marxist oeuvre, estrangement and its relation to philosophical questioning. So, if history is known as the history of class struggles, then it can also be known as the history of the struggle between estrangement and anti-estrangement. *The posing of the questions of justice and equality are posed in the fault lines of estrangement and anti-estrangement.*

The idea of justice and equality are now to be tempered in these two epistemic terrains: class histories and the aetiology of estrangement. We saw how the hegemonic idea of equality is deconstructed in the genealogy of the commodity. Let us now see how the idea of justice is related to the question of estrangement. For Marx, hitherto known human history is not qualified as conscious history, but an unconscious history, in fact a "pre-history"[25]—a history dominated by the repressed unconscious. The state, law, morality, etc. are actually products of repression.[26] In this type of history humanity does not act directly, it does not appear as itself, but as another reality.[27] For Marx:

> In capitalist society however where social reason appears only *post-festum* great disturbances may and must constantly occur.[28]

It is a type of a schizophrenic history—a history that appears in duplicated form, nay, in fact, appears as an imaginary world.[29] Humanity now speaks through its double. So the very questions—justice and equality—as well as injustice and inequality are spoken through this double. Because for Marx, as with Freud, one "traces mental life back to an interplay between forces that favour or inhibit one another".[30] This forms the core structure in which philosophical and political questions ought to be dissolved. The coalition with Freud becomes evident. Our modern civilization is a discontented civilization—

it is both estranged as well as mentally ill—a point that later Eric Fromm would work on. Marx and Freud now form a concrete alliance: what we are dealing with is not a normal state of affairs—nay, in fact, it is the most abnormal situation known, abnormal because the greatest perpetuators of injustice are sculpting a global model of governance.

In this case, how can there be any possible idea of justice and equality? Yet there is textual evidence that for the past three thousand three hundred years the question of justice has been continuously posed, and textually speaking, we may start possibly with Moses and Zarathustra. Let us call it the prophetic notion of justice, emerging from the Judaic and the Iranian traditions, though it must be noted that both Moses and Zarathustra have radically different perspectives. Whilst Zarathustra's idea undergoes a historical repression (possibly with the post-Zarathustra Magis, who concocted the later parts of the *Avesta,* and then with the regression of Zoroastrianism from the scene of world history since 651 A.D.), the tradition of Moses's notion of justice is alive—alive not only in the Judaic faith, but also embodied as the foreign policy of the empire as also the ideology of Wahabi Islam and the Heidegger-inspired Iranian Shiite imams. This one could call the onto-theological idea of justice. It is also a strange idea of justice since arch enemies in the contemporary global scenario share this same tradition.

But contra to this onto-theology are a number of contrasting ideas of justice tempered by the secular revolutions as found in the social contract theory of Locke, Rousseau and Kant. Then we have the great liberal and utilitarian traditions, John Rawls being one prominent example. And there is the great hermeneutical master of suspicion: Marx himself, sometimes said to carry on in the prophetic tradition (Ernst Bloc's rendering qualifies for such a reading) and more often than not, to be understood as anti-prophetic and deeply humanist. For Marx, justice can only be human justice and if there can be anything called communist justice, it can only be defined as *the appropriation of the human essence* (*die Aneignung des menschlichen Wesens*).[31] Contrary to the transcendent rendering of justice,

Marx applies the anthropological principles of justice (i.e. justice as fairness) which is bound to historical political economy and the dismantling of class societies. Thus 'justice' theory is directed to the forms of ownership of means of production, the distribution system arising and the historical conjuncture of class struggles. A distributive theory of justice may now *possibly* be applied to Marx. But this distributive theory is not only focused on distribution of duties and rights or the socialist distribution of goods, but to the very mode of production itself. It inquires into this very question of ownership, monopoly and privileges. It thus directs itself to private property.

But Marx warns that there is a deeper structure to private property—estrangement (*Entfremdung*) and that *Entfremdung* and private property are intrinsically bound not only to the question of justice (i.e. not only to the juridical system or justice as an ethical imperative) but that *Entfremdung* and private property are intertwined to all known class civilizations themselves.[32] Thus, consciousness emerging from class civilizations is a form of estranged consciousness. The estranged mind (*entfremdete Geist*)[33] has returned. So, if consciousness is dominated by the estranged mind, then so is the juridical system hegemonized by this form of alienation. In this sense, not only would Roman law, or the Sasanian legal system under Khausru I, or the Islamic Shariat law, be forms of alienation and dominated by the interests of private property and the political elites (and hidden within is the terrible scream of the *Entfremdung*) but even contemporary secularized legal systems of modern societies.

What Marx seems to suggest is to submit the very idea of justice and the judicial system to the architectural model of explanation where justice is seen standing on the bodies of alienation, private property, class struggle and the interests of the ruling classes. If the justice system stands on these bodies, then real justice (the possibility of fairness, etc.) can emerge only with their deaths. It is with the death of the alienation-private property combine that justice as fairness can be born. Marx thus offers a hermeneutics of translations whereby the surface system of law and morality is submitted to a deep structure analysis.

Thus the triumvirate of alienation, private property and class hegemony, which is hidden by the ruling classes in the closet of pure-practical reason, is torn from safe abodes by Marx and brought into the stage of reasoning world history. They are shown not to be rational and moral but terror-ridden systems themselves. For Marx, *Entfremdung* implies a feeling of loss and hostility, it is related to Freud's notion of *das Unheimlich* (the uncanny) where *das Unheimlich* suggests the loss of the home and the consequent feeling of dread and psychotic terror emerging thereon.[34]

And why does this feeling of dread and terror emerge as the estranged mind? Because humanity is faced directly against the "alien object"[35] and this form of estrangement, this form of anti-humanism, becomes the ruling motif of class societies. The very idea of justice itself as well as the system of justice are now dragged into this black hole of alienation. And into this black hole we descend.

The Empire

From this notion of alienation let us move into more familiar territories—the territory of Occidental Reason that the empire is thrusting all over the globe. Martin Heidegger's question in *On the Way to Language* returns again this time in the form of the question of the Americanization of the globe. And so, behind this idea of globalization stand the ideologies and practices of the empire. One can call this process of globalization the act of the empire—thus empire-ism—but one needs to understand this process of empire-ism and the legal and political codes that it enforces on the world.

Now, if we saw that behind class civilizations stands the estranged mind and that the very idea of justice is estranged justice, let us look into the deep structures of Occidental Reason and the political economy of empire-ism. Two concrete terrains are bound to this project of empire-ism: (i) the Judeo-Christian tradition—or rather a certain type of a Judeo-Christian tradition, for there are subversive histories within this tradition and as Žižek says "the authentic Christian tradition is much too precious to be left to the fundamentalist freaks"[36] (and this hegemonic form of the Judeo-Christian tradition followed, as we saw, by the American empire as well as by its antagonists, Wahabi Islam and the Iranian Shiites) and (ii) the spirit of capitalism. So now when one talks through the international community on justice and equality one is speaking in this estranged language of Occidental Reason.

First, let us see the core structure of Occidental Reason and then go into their idea of justice. For Occidental Reason (both in its theological and secularized forms) the world is divided into two basic domains: that of the centre (i.e. the West European and North American centre) which is essentially 'good', 'wise' as well as 'just' and governed by Christianity (or according to the Islamists, by Islam, or *their* rendering of Islam) and free trade; and the confused world (the netherworld that blends and blurs good and evil. In the pre-Islamic Iranian tradition it is the world of the "Mixture" (*Gumēzishn*)) of the periphery, which is tempted by Satan and eternal rebellions. Now the good centre tries (with its theologically inspired privileges taking the form of 'rights') to conquer the peripheries usually with consent and governed by the culture industry and its Ideological State Apparatuses. What it can conquer without brutal force becomes a part of the 'good' centre. What resists the occupation of the empire is deemed evil, whereby the war on this 'Axis of Evil' is deemed just. Now this type of justice, in fact unparallel violent pretensions of justice, is deep-rooted in the essential expansionist mode of Occidental Reason. Like the psychotic who is struck by what Freud calls "hysterical blindness",[37] the 'good' centre 'sees' terror in the lands of the periphery, a terror that would engulf itself and its Holy Lands.

This type of territorialization of the world forms the second part of the core structure of Occidental Reason. It is expansionist because it believes that it has innate theologically inspired wisdom, thus making the transcendence of its dominion of geo-political goodness in the lands of the periphery necessary in order to liberalize, reform, privatize and globalize them. In the language of classical Marxism, the forces of production of the developed capitalist world have transcended their national boundaries, thus making their movement into the Third and

Fourth Worlds of Asia, Africa and South America an imperative.

Now this conflict between the former and the latter, besides the conflicts within both these geo-political sites, becomes the driving force of contemporary world politics. But knowing that the conflict could lead to its own annihilation, the former makes a judicial pact with the latter. What we know as the United Nations is the body that is supposed to uphold this modern-day pact. It is the modern covenant, yet seeming to be the repetition of the original Judaic covenant between God and sinning humanity. In order to understand the contemporary judicial pact, one will have go into the deep interiors of Western civilizations and into the *Book of Genesis* itself.

"Be fruitful and multiply"[38] is the dictum that Lord God, the first capitalist and landlord, tells his chosen children, after his first children, the proto-proletariat, Eve and Adam, break the prohibition of not eating the forbidden fruit from the tree of the knowledge of good and evil. The forbidden fruit (a part of surplus value and the Ideological State Apparatus) is seized by Eve and Adam, inspired by Satan, the first revolutionary. God condemns them to the 'Fall', the world of labour, pain and death. The world of the here and the now is the cursed world of the 'Fall'. We live in this *throwness into the 'Fall'.* The crime was partaking in the forbidden share of surplus value, the punishment would be incurred from the transcendent 'outside'—Lord God, the first capitalist himself who condemns the proletariat to the eternal panoptic system of capitalism.

So Lord God finds out about the act of rebellion and curses Satan (the first rebel), Eve (the first woman) and Adam (the first man). The judgement from the 'outside' is that the woman shall suffer pain whilst "bringing forth" children and the libidinal desire for the husband shall rule over her.[39] And because Adam listened to the *voice* of his wife contra Lord God's restrictions and prohibitions in the Garden of Eden, the *ground* is *cursed* by God and only in *toil* and *labour* shall Adam be able to eat.[40] Mankind is cursed into the regimes of libidinal and political economies. The first man becomes the first proletariat for joining in the first rebellion. The original pact is broken: *man and woman are thrown in the being of toil and pain.* And in this phenomenal world of wickedness, sins, corruption and curses and punishment, God tells his chosen ones to be fruitful and multiply.

Being fruitful and multiplying is, according to Marx, the essence of the capitalist mode of production. Now, in order to understand this link between capitalism and imperialism on the one hand and the deep structures of Occidental Reason on the other, and also in order to understand the genesis of modern capital accumulation and its expansionist mode, one proceeds into the very question of Occidental genesis itself.

It is in this deep structure that one may be able to fathom the ideas of justice and the ideal society proclaimed by Western democracies (as well as its uncanny Islamic counterparts). The prohibition of the knowledge of good and evil, the sense of curbing rebellion, the curse of Lord God on the rebels, the consequent 'Fall' of humanity from the primal grace, and violence emanating from the original sin forms the background of the onto-theological idea of justice that has been guiding Western Reason.

Paradise is lost because the proto-proletariat, Eve and Adam, broke the totem and taboo of the first capitalist and landlord, tempted by the first rebel, Satan himself. Death is proclaimed, and since the 'Fall', the history of humanity is nothing but the history of corruption, violence and wickedness. But Lord God is also now the original judge besides being also the original curser and murderer for it is 'He' who sends the flood to "blot out man"[41] and to "make an end of all flesh" and destroy mankind "with the earth"[42] and "to bring a flood of waters upon the earth, to destroy all flesh ...(whereby) everything on earth shall die".[43]

But God, the wrathful one, also seems to have a heart and finds Noah, the righteous and the blameless and creates a covenant with him.[44] Now this establishing of the covenant with Noah and the chosen ones becomes a sure sign that "never again shall all flesh be cut off by the waters of a flood, and never again there be flood to destroy the earth".[45] This metaphysics of the covenant forms the basis of the idea of justice in the age of the empire.

It is well known that Hegel, the master metaphysician

glorified the state as the phenomenon of 'the Idea': the rather not-too-pleasant march of God on earth. The true world, for Hegel, is this world of 'the Idea', and the West (with its state apparatus) sits at the top of it. If Hegel thought the 'the Idea' was on top of the pyramid of life, with the state and the bureaucrats as 'the universal class' as being the vanguard, then what he implied was that the Prussian state be the vanguard of international relations and a precursor to the shadowy international community. Now this glorification of the state as 'the Idea' was actually the glorification of the Prussian state as the bearer of hegemonic Western Reason The Prussian state is dead, empire-ism and its manifold bodies take its place: the World Bank, the International Monetary Fund, and the United Nations, besides the lethal American state itself with its Repressive State Apparatus.

Those who desire to resist the empire will have to resist this idea of justice as well as the postmodern vehicles of justice. How is this possible? What is to be done? How should we, living in the lands of the periphery and being dragged into the centre of global capital accumulation, pose the question of justice and the international system of legal bodies that carry with it its own military apparatuses that devour entire nations and civilizations? Should the question of justice be posed in the same regime of imperial righteous onto-theology, or can one move into an entire new zone where one can pose the question of justice in an entirely different way? Did Marx, who heralded his gaze of suspicion on the world of classes, have a system of reading justice? Should one talk of emancipatory projects within the regime of rights and justice, and thus talk of justice as fairness, or are these questions moralistic and 'false' and that there is a deeper mechanism to history other than the talk of justice and equality?

'Political' liberty, which is detached from the dialectics of *Gattungswesen* and *das menchliche Wesen* and which takes the form of a government that proclaims and assures these estranged notions of 'justice' and 'liberty' (as we see from the experiences from the Balkans to Afghanistan and Iraq), have become postmodern spectacles that the world is now compelled to worship. As a fetish it takes the form of a *projected lack* and thus what it lacks in the real world (justice, equality, liberty and fraternity) it projects on to this duplicated world. And these duplicated worlds, we know after Freud, are "dangerous substitutes for the repressed" and "burdensome reactions on the part of the ego".[46] Justice and equality are the surface structures and expressions of that which is actually repressed: injustice, oppression and the entire class structure of society. They are as good as the theological notion of the netherworld.

For the state itself, in appropriating the metaphysics of justice and equality, has taken the form of estranged reason and poses as an alleged "general interest" of society. This "general interest" of society is a modern-postmodern myth, like the myth of "the elimination of all social and political inequality",[47] and, like the Judaic myth of creation, puts the burden and responsibilities on the subaltern classes whilst shifting the privileges and gains to the ruling classes. Socialism is not a bettering of the bourgeois state, or any state. One does not perfect the state machine, to borrow Marx's phrase: *one has to smash it.*[48]

One must stress that though the project of socialism is itself a moral act and that ethics forms the groundwork of Marx's critique of political economy, socialism is not about moralizing sermons. For Marx, the categorical imperative is unlike Kant's heralding a Kingdom of Ends; on the contrary, the categorical imperative is to revolt against dehumanized conditions[49] and dismantle the entire class mechanism. The solution for Marx is not political emancipation but human emancipation,[50] not the recreation of a state but the transcendence of the state (*Aufhebung des Staates*) itself. For it is in this transcendence of the state, along with it the transcendence of private property and alienation, that humanity as humanity would at last be able to speak with its own voice. To speak with one's own voice is also the death of psychosis. One has to think beyond the given (under) worlds of class societies.

REFERENCES

1. Samuel P. Huntington, *The Clash of Civilizations and the Remaking of the World Order* (New Delhi: Penguin, 1996).
2. Karl Marx, 'The Eighteenth Brumaire of Louis Bonaparte' in *Marx. Engels. Selected Works* (Moscow: Progress Publishers, 1975), pp. 96-7.
3. Ibid, p. 96.
4. Jacques Lacan, *The Psychoses. The Seminar of Jacques Lacan. Book III 1955-1956*, edited by Jacques-Allain Miller, trans. With notes by Russell Grigg (London: Routledge, 1993), p. 49.
5. Sigmund Freud, 'Neurosis and Psychosis', and 'The Loss of Reality in Neurosis and Psychosis', in *The Penguin Freud Library. Vol. 10. On Psycho-pathology.* (London: Penguin, 1993), pp. 213, 221.
6. Karl Marx, *Capital* Vol. I (Moscow: Progress Publishers, 1983), p. 77.
7. Karl Marx, 'The Eighteenth Brumaire of Louis Bonaparte', p. 126.
8. Karl Marx, *Economic and Philosophic Manuscripts of 1844* (Moscow: Progress Publishers, 1982), pp. 98, 131, 132.
9. Ibid, pp. 93-4.
10. Karl Marx, 'Critique of the Gotha Programme', in *Marx. Engels. Selected Works* (Moscow: Progress Publishers, 1975), p. 317.
11. Ibid, pp. 317-8.
12. Ibid, p. 318.
13. Karl Marx, *Capital* Vol. I, p. 59.
14. Ibid.
15. Herbert Marcuse, 'On Science and Phenomenology', in *The Essential Frankfurt School Reader,* ed. Andrew Arato and Eike Gebhardt (New York: Continuum, 1985), p. 471.
16. See Shaul Shaked, 'First Man, First King: Notes on Semitic-Iranian Syncretism and Iranian Mythological Transformations', in *From Zoroastrian Iran to Islam* (Hampshire: Ashgate Publishing Ltd., 1995), p. 243.
17. See Shaul Shaked, 'Paymân: An Iranian Idea in Contact with Greek Thought and Islam', in Ibid, p. 218.
18. Firdausi, *The Sháhnáma of Firdausi*, trans. A.G. Warner and E. Warner (London: Kegan Paul, Trench, Trüber and Co. Ltd., 1925), Vol. VII, pp.207-208..
19. Karl Marx, *Capital,* Vol. I, p. 65.
20. Ibid.
21. Ibid.

22. Ibid, pp. 65-6.
23. Ibid, p. 46.
24. Ibid, p. 67.
25. Karl Marx, 'Preface', *A Contribution to the Critique of Political Economy*, trans. S.W. Ryazanskaya (Moscow: Progress Publishers, 1977), p. 22.
26. Karl Marx and Friedrich Engels, *The German Ideology* (Moscow: Progress Publishers, 1976), p. 101.
27. Karl Marx, 'Contribution to the Critique of Hegel's Philosophy of State', in *Karl Marx. Early Writings* trans. Rodney Livingstone and Gregor Benton (New York: Vintage Books, 1975), p. 62.
28. Karl Marx, *Capital,* Vol. II (Moscow: Progress Publishers, 1974), p. 319.
29. Karl Marx, 'Theses on Feuerbach', in *Marx. Engels. Selected Works* (Moscow: Progress Publishers, 1975), p. 29.
30. Sigmund Freud, 'The Psychoanalytic View of Psychogenic Disturbance of Vision', in *The Penguin Freud Library,* Vol. 10, *On Psychopathology* (London: Penguin, 1990), p. 109.
31. Karl Marx, *Economic and Philosophic Manuscripts of 1844*, pp. 94, 109.
32. Ibid, p. 72.
33. Ibid, p. 129.
34. Sigmund Freud, 'The Uncanny' in *The Penguin Freud Library,* Vol. 14, *Art and Literature* (London: Penguin, 1990), pp. 339-376.
35. Karl Marx, *Economic and Philosophic Manuscripts of 1844*, p. 136.
36. Slavoj Žižek, *The Fragile Absolute or, Why is the Christian Legacy worth fighting for?* (London: Verso, 2000), p. 2.
37. Sigmund Freud, 'The Psychoanalytic View of Psychogenic Disturbance of Vision', p. 108.
38. 'Genesis', in *The Holy Bible* (New York: Wm. Collins, 1952).
39. Ibid, p. 3: 3. 16.
40. Ibid, p. 3: 3. 17.
41. Ibid, p. 5: 5. 7.
42. Ibid, p. 5: 5. 17.
43. Ibid, p. 5: 11. 17.
44. Ibid, p. 7: 9. 8.
45. Ibid, p. 7: 9. 8., 11.
46. Sigmund Freud, 'The Psychoanalytic View of Psychogenic Disturbance of Vision', p. 111.
47. Friedrich Engels, 'Engels to Bebel in Zwickau, London, March 18-28, 1875', in *Marx. Engels. Selected Correspondence* (Moscow: Progress Publishers, 1975), p. 276.

48. Karl Marx, 'Marx to L. Kugelmann in Hanover, London, April 12, 1871', in *Marx. Engels. Selected Works* (Moscow: Progress Publishers, 1975), p. 670.
49. Karl Marx, 'Contribution to the Critique of Hegel's Philosophy of Right. Introduction', p. 251.
50. Karl Marx, 'On the Jewish Question', in *Marx. Engels. Collected Works,* Vol. 3 (Moscow: Progress Publishers, 1975).

CHAPTER 7

Human Rites
The Death and the Birth of the Subject

Our epoch is a birth-time, and a period of transition. The spirit of man has broken with the old order of things hitherto prevailing, and with the old ways of thinking, and is in the mind to let them all sink into the depths of the past and to set about its own transformation. It is indeed never at rest, but carried along the stream of progress ever forward.

—G.W.F. Hegel, *The Phenomenology of Mind.*

In the same way atheism being the supersession (Aufhebung) of God, is the advent of theoretical humanism, and communism as the supersession (Aufhebung) of private property, is the vindication of real human life (wirklichen menschlichen Lebens) as man's possession and thus the advent of practical humanism, or atheism is humanism mediated with itself through the supersession of religion, whilst communism is humanism mediated with itself through the supersession of private property. Only through the supersession of this mediation (Aufhebung dieser Vermittlung)—which is itself, however, a necessary premise—does positively self-deriving humanism, positive humanism come into being.

—Karl Marx, *Economic and Philosophic Manuscripts of 1844.*

Metamorphosis

Marxism has very often talked of the international proletariat as the heir of Classical German Philosophy. The forgetfulness of Hegel has led not only to the disarming of the proletariat but history itself. History returns as mythology. The 'new' returns as the *repressed archaic.* It is in this context that we raise the statement of the blindness to Hegel, which turns to a strange form of non-Marxist Marxism—to be precise, the return to pre-dialectical modes of thinking, at best a return to Kant. Lenin's deep insight itself returns to haunt us again. Why do we say so? We say so because without the understanding of the dialectic of the abstract and the concrete, and the mystical and the rational in Hegel, one cannot understand modern civilization (especially class histories and their ideologies of subjugation), leave alone the first section of Marx's *Capital*: the problem of the metamorphosis of commodities. It is known since Lukács and Adorno (but more specifically with Freudo-Marxism) that the metamorphosis of commodities is directly linked with the problem of the distorted and criminal mind. It is also known that this criminal mind appears as bourgeois ideology, or as we mentioned in the first chapter (in Marx's own words), as "ideology in general".[1] The fallacy with ideological thinking is that "it by no means examines its general philosophic premises..."[2]

The idea of human rights—"the very Eden of the innate rights of man...(where) alone rule Freedom, Equality, Property and Bentham"[3]—is the most recent of these fictions. In fact, the discourse of 'rights as such', as rights in the abstract, is thinking of humanity in the abstract. That the discourse of human rights now has become a part of imperialist America's slogan for the conquest of the globe ought not to be surprising because this idea itself has gone through a process of metamorphosis. Our engagement with human rights is situated in the context of this metamorphosis in class-stratified societies and the nature of consciousness emanating therefrom.

When Marx said situate the notion of human rights in the double contexts of the economic base and the prevailing culture, he meant that the question of rights have to be understood in the context of the historical conjuncture of class struggles. Rights and their violation are found in these double regimes of class struggles and social estrangements. To understand the dialectics of the rights question, one has to descend into the realms of class histories as well as the black hole of estrangement.

In the previous chapter we went into the interiors of Western Reason and stated that in both the Platonic and the biblical forms, Western Reason is built on the solid foundations of domination and the conquest of the entire globe. For Marx this principle is itself built on the deep structure of reification. We call this deep structure: *the black hole of alienation*. And so, if anti-humanism stands at the basis of both biblical and Platonic philosophies, so too it stands at the basis of imperialism. Consequently, to understand the deep structure of human rights (its metamorphosis and manipulation) one needs to go into the unconscious of Western Reason and imperialism. After all, why does the United States of America, the biggest abuser of the rights of the peoples of the Third and Fourth World nations, repeatedly talk of 'human rights'? One thus asks: why have human rights been transfigured into human rites? Why has humanity been slaughtered, and why have contemporary philosophies in the slaughter-house of humanity and the death of 'man', not inscribed the epitaph of imperialism, but on the contrary, inscribed its very glories? In plain words: why and how does imperialist ideology operate its main mechanism of alienation and castration anxiety?

Now this realm of the black hole of estrangement is double-edged: (i) the social-history of estrangement which studies modern-day estrangement (i.e. subjugation to bourgeois ideology), and (ii) the ontology of estrangement which analyses primal estrangement—the *Entfremdung* which gave birth to global class societies. Wilhelm Reich had a term for this: orgone.[4] The orgone is what Marx calls the cell[5] of both capitalist societies as well as the primal cause of the breakdown of previous (or primitive) communist societies. It is this cell, orgone, that contains not only the violation of human rights but also the very violation of humanity itself.

It with this understanding of the cell form of estrangement that one critiques not only the contemporary hierarchical structures of society, but also the 'origins' of these stratifications and the violence emanating therefrom. The critique is dual-fold: the critique of the concrete, empirical structures of violence and the deep interiors of class civilizations that have given rise to these violent structures. Critique thus turns towards both the present as well as the past. The past, unfortunately, is not dead. Modern capitalism loves the past. To borrow Marx's statement: *in capitalism, the past dominates the present;*[6] *where the dead have seized and gripped the living;*[7] *the dead which weigh like a nightmare on the brains on the living.*[8] Plato's 'Idea' as well as Monsieur God and Madame Rent are not dead, but continue doing their ghost walk.

This theme of being haunted by the past pertains to both capitalism and also to neurosis, a neurosis that appears as the repetition of the self-same tormenting event.[9] It becomes even more pertinent to the India of the Asiatic mode of production that boasts of the myth of a 'splendid' past of a non-existing 'Golden Age'. How 'Golden Ages' appear as both splendid and neurotic is something that scientific analysis must turn its attention to. And that is why Marx said that one must not be obsessed by the 'body' of capitalism, or be fooled by its alleged innocent 'mind'. On the contrary, Marx insists on analyzing the anatomy of capitalism, and thus looking through his microscope to expose its grotesque cell form.

And so, in order to understand the two souls of modern capitalism, liberalism and fascism, one needs to look into the cell form of capitalism. The cell form will contain all the contradictions of capitalism within it, including its own downfall.[10] But most important, the analysis of this cell exposes the anti-humanist character of capitalism. Second, one has to understand that the totalitarian free market economy is built on a *permanent crisis* whose response should not be reform but *permanent revolution.* Whilst fascism, starting in the early 1920s, was one terroristic form of totalitarian management of this permanent crisis, it failed in its gendarme role of the manager of this crisis and post-1945 Anglo-American liberalism took up this role of global policeman. Washington now holds not only this secret and dreaded cell, but also the entire body of the Frankenstein-like permanent crisis. The question of rights that Marx had directed against the state and the ruling classes is now necessarily driven against this new embodiment of permanent crisis and violence: the empire with Washington as its headquarters.

Capitalism and the Theological Unconscious

It is quite possible that there are four texts that were written in the nineteenth century but which are extremely futurist texts—the *Economic and Philosophic Manuscripts of 1844, The Manifesto of the Communist Party, Grundrisse* and *Capital.* They are posthumous texts, texts that did not belong to the nineteenth century, maybe not even to the twentieth century. Maybe the twenty-first century is the time for them to be realized. Just as it was remarked about the impact of the French Revolution with the profound answer, it is too early to judge, so too, it is too early to judge Marx. Probably the twenty-first century will serve better to understand Marx and ourselves.

We live in troubled times. Yet we live in joyful times. Wordsworth's words: "It was bliss in that dawn to be alive, but to be young was very heaven" pertains to these times as well. For these are the times of revolutions, a million rebellions and a million festivals to celebrate these insurrections. If it is said that the times of globalization are the times of the empire, then it is also the time for the barbarians to raid this empire. Empire always signifies its collapse. The borderless multitude has come. And so have modernity and the death of all identities. We must celebrate some births and some deaths. With the coming of the borderless multitude also come great expectations. The 'citizen' and the 'man' who arrived in 1789 have returned again. Shall we let them go?

"Since the commencement of the eighteenth century", so Marx once said, "there has been no serious revolution in Europe that has not been preceded by a commercial and financial crisis".[11] One needs to flow with these capital flows in order to understand crises and revolutions. Unlike the petty-bourgeoisie that cries in front of each crisis, the proletariat, the futurist borderless subject, revels in it.

In the *Critique of the Gotha Programme* Marx said, stop looking at the world from the looking glasses of the bourgeois conception of right.[12] Stop looking at the bourgeois idea of equality and its ideology of equal right.[13] For, this form of equality is fiction. It signifies inequality, but like the psychotic, talks of equality. This type of equality is like the promised netherworld of the theologians—the world that never comes. Instead talk of the right to insurrection. This forms the basic right for Marx—the right to revolt. So was Marx understood? Maybe yes, maybe no. Maybe Marx would ponder and say: "Some people are born posthumously. Maybe the day after tomorrow belongs to me." And thus to this morrow we need to turn.

So where do we stand? The ministers will say: "We stand in the land of the great hoary past and with the help of globalization we shall return to an even more hoary past." But do these people living in the past tense not understand that history itself is the great storm of progress? Yet we are like Walter Benjamin's angel of history looking backwards and being hurled forward by the storm of progress.[14] And what great revealing things do we see? We see two narratives embedded together—that of the primitive accumulation of capital (the origins of capitalism) and that of the primitive accumulation of myths as found in the Judaic book of creation, also known as the *Genesis* or the *Book of Moses*. In this double binding we see how the rights of 'man' have become the rites of 'man', and how political anti-humanism becomes the dominant discourse of the ideology of the state (a view shared by the neo-conservatives in America, the Wahabi Islamists, the Iranian Shiites and our own nationalist Hindutvavadis). First, let us see what Marx has found:

> This primitive accumulation plays in Political Economy about the same part as original sin in theology. Adam bit the apple, and thereupon sin fell on the human race. Its origin is supposed to be explained when it is told as an anecdote of the past. In times long gone by there were two types of people; one, the diligent, intelligent, and above all, frugal elite; the other, lazy rascals, spending their substance and more, in riotous living. The legend of theological original sin tells us certainly how man came to be condemned to eat his bread in the sweat of his brow; but the history of economic original sin reveals to us that there are people to whom this is by no means essential. Never mind! Thus it came to pass that the former sort accumulated wealth, and the latter sort had at last nothing to sell except their own skins. And from this original sin dates the poverty of the great majority that, despite all its labour, has up to now nothing to sell but itself, and the wealth of the few that increases constantly although they have ceased to work. Such insipid childishness is every day preached to us in the

> defence of property. M. Theirs, *e.g.*, had the assurance to repeat it with all the solemnity of a statesman, to the French people, once so *spirituel*. But as soon as the question of property comes up, it becomes the sacred duty to proclaim the intellectual food of the infant as the one thing fit for all the ages and for all stages of development. In actual history it is notorious that conquest, enslavement, robbery, murder, briefly force, play the great part. In the tender annals of Political Economy, the idyllic reigns from time immemorial. Right and "labour" were from all time the sole means of enrichment, the present year always excepted. As a matter of fact, the methods of primitive accumulation are anything but idyllic.[15]

In this double binding of theology and political economy, the rites of 'man' are performed. Let us have a look at the onto-theological and anti-humanist rendering of the problematic of rights, which remain the essential aspect of the Ideological State Apparatus of the bourgeoisie in the period of late imperialism. For understanding this, one has to go to the deep interiors of the formation of class societies, the state, patriarchy, the idea of the territorialization of the earth, the formation of organized violence and the will to power. Horkheimer and Adorno in the *Dialectic of the Enlightenment* traced the formation of this violent will to power to Homer's *Odyssey* and despite the enlightenment (which they claim is now turned into myth), Western Reason (due to this violent telos) necessarily realizes itself in fascism and American imperialism. Whilst the practice of human rights violation by both the global and local imperialists is located in concrete capital accumulation, this telos of Western Reason does not play a passive part. For the Occidental imperialist point of view, one sees how the narcissistic "Lord God" (to borrow the terminology from the good book) performs the rites of 'man' and 'woman'. First, there is an estrangement and repression performed where the monopoly of the phallus signifier castrates the feminine principle. Thenceforth, the story of humanity is written down as the story of 'man'. Mother Right is given way to Father Right: patriarchy is born along with private property, the division of labour, privatization of sexuality, the birth of the monogamic family, and the formation of the first sign of armies to organize in a 'rational' way the formation of organized violence. The *Old Testament* is a testament to these tremendous counter-revolutionary changes taking place in society. Here the distinct picture of the authoritarian personality, the blind worship of the estranged personality cult, duties of the slave (or the proto-proletariat children of the male-centric estranged 'Lord God') and the erasure of human rights are all drawn out. Comparative mythology brings out the issue how pre-patriarchal societies were organized according to the feminine principle where the creator is woman (or the woman and man in a democratic sexual act), and not the male-phallic 'Lord God' who creates the world out of some estrangement onanism. "God said, let there be light and there was light"—is the most anti-democratic statement, and class civilization has this estrangement statement embodied within it as an onto-theological fetish to be blindly obeyed. In the *Old Testament* "Lord God" has expelled all other gods. God has become a monopolist God. Monotheism, in fact, symbolizes onto-theological monopolism. In the Western framework, monism implies dictatorship. This is evident in the foreign policy of the twenty-first century: the way in which the American state bullies the 'other' states.

Though the Judaic *Book of Moses* gives us this narrative of the formation of the dictatorship of the first capitalist and landlord, it continues in the Christian and Islamic traditions with critical reservations. We are talking of critical reservations because both Christianity and Islam (as in Judaism too) have had histories of subversions and revolutions. This brings to mind Žižek again, who insists on rescuing the Christian legacy from the Christian fundamentalists,[16] just as Walter Benjamin and Ernst Bloc, who insisted on reading Judaism from a perspective of subversive anti-authoritarianism. One knows how a thousand years back Islam saved the world from mediaeval superstition. Not only was Greek philosophy 'saved' and 'resurrected', but also knowledge was given the secular-humanist privilege wherein prospered the sciences, arts and morality. One knows how Jalal-u-Din Rumi, Hafiz, and the Sufis kept the human as the subject of history at the centre of philosophical and poetical discourse. One also knows that *'Ilm'* or knowledge is given the second highest status in the Koranic hermeneutic after Allah, and we also know that Allah need not be the wrathful first capitalist, but passionate love. Recall Fakhrud-Din Irâqî's dictum: *La-ilaha-illa-al-ishq* ("there is no God but love"). Recall also Rumi's 'Moses and the Shepherd' from his *Mathnavi.* Not only passionate love but also the struggle for rights finds the central place in Islam. Yet after every revolution appears the counter-revolution. The neurotic archaic estrangement returns again.

What happens in this counter-revolution is that an ideology in dominance is born that will work actively with class histories—for the monopolist, onto-theological idea of estranged God as capitalist-landlord as well as the curser and punisher just refuses to go. God is not only the first capitalist and landlord, but also the first judge and executioner. Let us have a look at this essentially patriarchal and anti-humanist narrative and thus let us once again go into the deep interiors of Western Reason.

Lord God (the first capitalist and landlord) creates the heavens and the earth. This is the original paradise (or at least the American version of it). In this original paradise (read: American liberal democracy) Adam was created to celebrate liberal democracy. Since celebrations cannot be enjoyed in solitary confinement, Eve is produced from Adam's rib. In this liberal democracy of paradise there is no work or any idea of toil. As if by magic, fruits grow from trees and one could eat from any tree except from a certain tree that Lord God forbade his proto-proletariat children from eating. This totemic tree is the tree of the knowledge of good and evil. One cannot eat its fruits (just as in capitalism, in fact even in the capitalism of conspicuous consumption one cannot consume, but only have illusions of consumption). Risking eating implies death. Now in Marxist terms, this totemic tree, wherein the taboo of not transgressing its private property, is surplus value. One ought not to touch surplus value, for it is the monopoly of the capitalists. In Freudian terms, the fruits are Adam and Eve's invisible mother's breasts. *Touch not thy mother's breast, or else fear castration. Touch not surplus value, or else fear war against terror.* This is the original picture of the rites-rights problematic in the

Judaic tradition that would also be realized in full-blown form as the mythos of Western Reason. There is the double fear of castration and execution created by the first capitalist and landlord. The rites of collective humanity are born when the rights are seized.

Then comes along Satan (the first revolutionary). He insists on humanity's claiming its rights. He tells Eve to seize surplus value. He tells her that the threat of dying is a myth and a lie created by the capitalist to perpetuate its unjust rule. The fruit must be eaten! Eve eats it and she and Adam are struck with shame. The monopolist Lord God, when strolling in the garden of paradise, finds both of them in shame and finding that the totem has been seized and the taboo violated, curses the revolutionary Satan to eternal creeping, Eve to the lust of man's flesh and the consequent pain suffered in libidinal economy, and Adam cursed to the suffering and toil of political economy. Adam becomes the first proletariat and Eve the first housewife. Because the first rights-rites are violated humanity is cursed to the 'Fall'. Human history is a continuous history of this fall.

Now turn this picture to contemporary times. Lord God is the United States of America. Satan is communism. Adam, Eve and all their descendants are the mortal proletariat and peasantry, inhabiting especially the Third and Fourth World nations. The righteous ones, like Noah, are the elites of the world who toe the American line. The original covenant that Lord God unilaterally signed with Noah is replayed as the modern-day pacts as embodied in the United Nations, the World Bank, the International Monetary Fund, etc. Those who break the covenants shall be condemned either to the biblical floods where Lord God wants 'to blot out man', or to the more modern methods of occupation and annihilation—the American style.

But where lies the biggest problem? That even the adversary follows the same ideological line. Not only the Wahabi fundamentalist Al Qaeda and the Iranian Shiites (who basically share the same biblical narrative of human rights) but even the world that does not share the same onto-theological framework follows the same line. Why is this so? How has the eternal repetition of the primal sacrifice to stop? Why should we obey these covenants when they are not in our favour? Why should we fear the biblical floods and modern-day wars?

Modern India's tryst with destiny, which began in 1947, did not start with a confrontationist view. When would India learn to smite the imperialist aggressor? Coomaraswamy had most graphically sketched out the 'Indian' imagination. India, we are told, is not like Greece and Rome. Greece and Rome are masculine and aggressive. India is feminine and coy. Now this imaginary and symbolic reading of a 'feminine' India was not only Coomaraswamy's idealist point of view. This ideology was mobilized in the middle of the nineteenth century. It not only formed the crux of Gandhi's politics but a large part of the Indian imagination. The fascist RSS, from its inception under Hegdewar, and the Hindi Mahasabha under Savarkar, held the same view. The only difference is that the Indian fascists want to 'militarize Hinduism'. The Indian feminine character has to be protected by a male-centric fascist party. After all, why should India not be armed, the fascists ask? Doesn't one see the Hindu deities, the fascists continue, armed to the teeth? So let us militarize Hinduism and India, for are they not exactly the same, the fascists ask? And because India has always been threatened (by the Muslims, we are told) what matters is not rights but duties.

So what happened in concrete politics? India, because of the prominence of the secular democrats (especially Ambedkar), got a secular democratic constitution with rights at its core. And this is what the fascist RSS condemns. For them the essential discourse is not of citizenship but the fiction of warring races. M.S. Golwalkar, the second fuehrer of the RSS, talked of celebrating the 'Race Spirit' of India. We are told that: those who are not members of the "Hindu Race" do not fit into the idea of the Indian nation.[17]

There have been at least three prominent sets of binaries unleashed since the 1920s and which remain important today: race vs. citizen, archaism vs. modernity, and fascism vs. democracy. The point is to choose which half of the political barricade one belongs to. Which side should one choose—the totalitarian conservative type of political mobilization, which essentially erases rights and which claims that the communitarian imaginary (Hinduism, Islam, America) that is seeming threatened by hostile forces, or the democratic politics of universal citizenship?

Let us take an example from the contemporary Iranian Shiite politics. Davari-Ardakani, a prominent Iranian philosopher reared on the uncanny combination of the *Koran* and the philosophy of Heidegger, claims that contemporary problems lie with humanism, secularism and the forgetfulness of primordial Being. Since this primordial Being is forgotten, 'man' and subjectivity are born. Now what does 'man' do? 'Man' plays the same tricks that the father of 'man' Adam played. He obeys the woman and rebels against the capitalists and landlords. 'Man' has forgotten his tryst with God and primordial Being. One is suffering, as Davari-Ardakani, like the rest of the Iranian Shiite Heideggereans, claims, from Westoxication that is born with the Renaissance and the Enlightenment. Consider how anti-secularism and anti-humanism work in the Iranian Heideggerean framework:

> Notwithstanding the roots of Westoxication in Greek philosophy with its 2500 years of history, its specific and predominant form has emerged with the Renaissance. With the appearance of Westoxication, the old form of history is abolished and a new man is born who is no longer submissive to the *Haqq* (Truth, right, authentic). He forgets the *Haqq* so that he can replace Him to expropriate the earth and the heavens...
>
> The freedom of religious beliefs in the Declaration of Human Rights means alienation from religion; it means leaving the individuals to their own devices so that they may do whatever they want with religion in their lives and have any religion they want ... (M)odern man sees his own image in the mirror of *Haqq*, has entered into a covenant with himself. Therefore it is inevitable and natural that such a man would turn his back to religion and cover up his act with claims to nationalism, internationalism, liberalism, collectivism and individualism.[18]

Now what happens is that we have a very strong anti-Enlightenment shared code between the RSS, the Iranian Shiites, the Taliban and the American neo-cons. In contrast to this anti-humanism one posits the discourse of what the young Marx called the philosophy of "the human essence" (*das menschliche Wesen*). This *das menschliche Wesen* defines the real possibilities of human rights because it postulates not anything but the human essence as its fundamental ontological core. Authentic human rights can be possible only when *das menschliche Wesen* is sighted. We see from the above quote of Davari that primordial Being (the "Him" that is wrathful, the one who curses and punishes) necessarily extinguishes the human essence. In another work, *What is Philosophy?* Davari-Ardakani, in true Heideggerean style says: "Human essence lies in his *nobodyness* and nothingness. He has no real existence and essence. His essence lies in annihilation."[19] So who has the essence, the somethingness? Who can be the 'somebody'? The answer is simple: not 'man', but primordial Being. We know that this nativist primordiality can work in manifold reactionary ways. It works not only with the RSS (the 'Him' is the 'Hindu Race and Nation'), but also right-wing Christianity and the Islamists ('Him' is the return of the estranged first capitalist and landlord). We also know how the most violent form of this primordial Being worked with the Nazis.

Now in contrast to this discourse of Being and the annihilation of humanism is Marxist philosophy. In 1844, Marx wrote to Ludwig Feuerbach:

> In these writings (*Philosophie der Zukunft* and *Wesen des Glaubens*) you have provided—I don't know whether intentionally—a philosophical basis for socialism and the Communists have immediately understood them in that way. The unity of man with man, which is based on the real differences between men, the concept of the human species brought from the heaven of abstraction to the real earth—what is this but the concept of *society*![20]

Since this human sensuality in the forms of *das menschliche Wesen* and *Gattungswesen* (species being) forms the essence of the social and historical discourse, one gets a real subject of history, not a theological and Heideggerean annihilation of humaneness and the human essence. Now for Marx there is indeed an active negation of this human essence. What is it? It is the construction of a "pseudo-essence" which is "the self-estranged essence in its denial", also known as the "objective being dwelling outside man and independent of him, and its transformation into the subject".[21] Now this transformation of the pseudo-character into a real character, and the negation of the humanness is one part of the very frightening problem.

Humanity is lost as the Judaic ideology (with its uncanny Christian and Islamic partners) claims: that the sinning and rebellious 'man' broke the covenant with God. So now we have the fallen 'man' along with the disgraceful fallen woman. To talk of humanism is an error for all conservatives as it implies fallenness from primal grace. Meanwhile, as if to compete in the global world of eternal free trade, the Indian framework, dominated by the paganism of the purity and pollution fetish, enters the scene of world history, claiming that 'mankind ' can never be equal. And here, on the stage of history, came Jyotirao Phule and Ambedkar, to challenge this fetish of inequality. Pagan *Rg Veda* would form an ontology of inequality where its tenth mandala states the division of labour on the fetish of the *varna* principle. This tenth mandala is the ideological fetish whereby the Brahmins have maintained their unjust hegemony for over three thousand years. The Brahmins, like their global conservative partners, would laugh heartily at humanism and secularism. Both would be global partners in the rites of humanity.

So when one says that one is living in the age of globalization and conceptualizing a politics of human rights, then one must be aware that one is doing this in the shadows of the empire of capital, where anti-humanism plays the double roles of the Western imperialist type as also the local Brahmanical imperialism. Little imperialism and big imperialism are here marching hand-in-hand. Both grumble when it comes to the rights question. They say better to sing the ode to the end of history, the death of the subject and the birth of the empire. And here the state of the state of this empire, which lies in the developed 'North' zone of capital accumulation, carries within the scope of its phenomenal mind almost all the states of the globe. Though it dislikes the rights question, it yet teaches the entire globe about human rights. The entire globe, through what

Max Horkheimer in the *Eclipse of Reason,* called, a "repressed mimetic impulse", learns the discourse of human rights from the esteemed master. And so the United States of America, the only state to be convicted of terrorist charges at the Hague, becomes the biggest teacher of human rights. Maybe this is what Hegel wanted to call "the cunning of Reason" (*die List der Vernunft*).

And so the father and son enter the scene of world history once again. When one is reflecting on human rights and its relevance to India, one is reflecting not only on the empire, but also the problem of the father and the son as found in Western Reason. The lesser states or, if one may call them, the 'son states' are told to mime the 'father state'. In this sense the spirit of the empire is rewriting the myth of Western Reason—the marchpast of Lord God and Abraham's sacrifice. (We are bracketing here the myth of Oedipus and the Oedipus complex.) The desiring son in this newly sketched out global mythology does not kill the father, but the father (Lord God) seeks to capture and kill the son. The son can live only in the thrall of the father, only if the son mimes the father principle—the spirit of globalization. This is the return of the primeval sacrifice. And in the hands of either Lord God and Abraham lay not a duplicated son, but in reality, the entire globe.

So what should the son states do, or at least the fighters for human rights in these states? One is confronted with two sites: the world of the past—the past of India, that of caste and the cult of tradition; and the world of modernity—the Hegelian "birth-time", which is also the "period of transition" to the radically new.[22] India that is living with modernity is also the India that is living (or dying, or at least, choking as the Indian subalterns would claim) with the ghost of the past. The struggle for rights is being fought not only in the battlefronts of modernity and tradition, but also in the battles fought within modernity itself.

The spirit of the modern struggle for rights is sketched in the inter-contextuality of the French Revolution. *The Rights of Man and the Citizen* forms the necessary epistemic and historical core of the rights question along with it the philosophies of the

Enlightenment. When Marx had parodied European schism, where France was said to be the nation of revolutions just as Germany was the nation of mythology, one may ask: where stands India—in the world of mythology or revolutions? Second, should one operate with nationalist concepts and thus work within the framework of an 'India', or should one make a terrain shift and talk instead of a Popular Front for the Liberation of Asia? Should this Popular Front be a New International of the popular masses? Why should one talk of 'India', 'Pakistan', 'Bangladesh', etc., for do they all not signify the geo-politics of a divided and re-divided imperialist world? After all, are not 'India', 'Pakistan', etc. all internally colonized spaces governed by a comprador elite? Does not 'India' itself signify a heterogenous space of great multiplicities, unified and yet divided by a caste elite which refuses to relinquish power, and insists on human rights violation on national and religious minorities, workers, tribals, women and dalits? Why imitate the oppressor?

At least a certain form of an Orientalist rendering of India has been bequeathed to us. We, the children of a secular India, are also the children of the nineteenth-century Romantic tradition. It is well-known that the latter half of the nineteenth century was the churning moment that produced this long line of fictitious nationalisms. The main model of this fiction is a continuous redrafting of the *pursa sukta* model of caste hegemony from the *Rg Veda.* This redrafting has not only taken casteist forms but also the forms of secular democracy. This organic, naturalist, biologist model with Brahimins as the 'head'—the self-appointed ideologists— and the Sudra as the feet, with the other mediating castes as other organic parts, not only stayed as the societal model but also remained (and remains) an archetype for the Indian nation state. It remained dominant at least till Phule arrived on the scene of history. It would again be redrafted after Phule is made to exit from the scene of history. Phule would not perform a Marxist inversion of Hegelian idealism, (in his reinterpretation of Indian history) but literally, in the style of the French Revolution, chop off the head. Unlike Marx, who thought that idealism could be inverted to create materialism, for Phule there seems to be no such possibility. It seems that Phule would at least agree with the following statement by Heidegger: *the reversal of metaphysics remains a metaphysical principle.* For Phule and the subaltern dalits it seems one is very wary of the 'head' and the Brahmanical phenomenology of this 'mind'. So it is best to shift out from this phenomenological site. Remove the head, so one section of the radical dalit subalterns claim, and one removes the entire ideological problematic. For the Phulean discourse, to talk of human rights, this head of Brahmanical onto-theology has to go. Brahmanism is non-negotiable for a 'real' democratic India. Human rights and the caste principle are diametrically opposite. Whilst human rights are based on the ontology and politics of equality, the caste signifier implies unconditional inequality. For Marxism, especially for the Indian Marxists, one does not have to go as far as Phule's methodology. For them, on the one hand one can treat the Brahmanical 'mind' as the narcissistic subject of psychoanalytic discourse, and on the other hand, conceive of the process of industrialization and secularization as 'inevitably' deconstructing caste hegemony. Human rights though, to be actively fought out, are caught up in this logic of an Indian Marxist 'inevitability'. The problem that radical secular democracy bequeathes is this wide abyss between Marxism and the indigenous radical subalterns.

In contrast to Phule's radical reading of Indian history, modern India (now a liberal India) was born from the marriage of English constitutionalism and Indian idealism. In fact, the whole edifice of the Indian ideological system stands on this matrimonial alliance. But then, who would be able to deconstruct this alliance, an alliance that is now in alliance also with the Abrahamanical father-figure of the empire? For Marxism it is the proletariat that would be the vanguard class in the struggle for democracy, the proletariat that are the real actors of history conceived as the real subaltern masses. And to conceive of viable human rights of practical reason one has to descend into the realm of the masses.

And it is to this world of the subaltern masses and the subaltern rendering of history that we turn. For the understanding of the struggle for rights one needs to turn away from the romantic renderings of history, this rendering hegemonized since James Mill's *History of British India*, which gave the unfortunate communal classifications: 'Hindu', 'Muslim', etc. and which the Indian imagination readily internalized. Now what happens is that both the Indian political, as well as the social repertoire are constituted on the basis of this *estranged communitarianism*. One needs, on the other hand, to actively turn away from the idealist and communal hermeneutic tradition, in a Nietzschean way, to involve an *active forgetfulness of this history* in order to understand the real history of the struggle of the subaltern masses. And for that, one has to (contra colonialism) postulate a theoretical humanism. The regime of rights can only be understood in the space of a theoretical and political humanism.

To conceive of the possibilities of human rights one has first to conceive, in active opposition to communalism and casteism, of *humanity as humanity*. So one recalls two themes: (i) the very Hegelian theme of no going back in history, and (ii) Ludwig Feuerbach's philosophical anthropology in order to understand the idea of theoretical humanism. It is with this theme that one goes deep into the interiors of philosophical humanism and conceives of a modern democracy. The very conception of human rights can only be possible when one has articulated a rigorous philosophical humanism. The young Marx had used two terms to articulate this rigour: *das menschliche Wesen* (the human essence) and *Gattungswesen* (species being). History for Marx, the grandmaster of historical humanism is constituted within this storm and stress of the alienated human essence and the *Aufhebung* (transcendence) of estrangement. To think of a programme of human rights is to think out this conflict. Behind the thinking of human rights is a thinking of this *menschliche Wesen.*

Otherwise, we have an uncanny collapse of an emancipatory project into a project of the ruling classes. Marxist secularism as the philosophy of the human essence is also about the politics of human rights. Secularism is mainly about the struggle for rights. What the liberal project of rights does is to transfigure rights into a fiction—the fiction of law and the state. In the *Critique of the Gotha Programme*, as we just saw, Marx mentions that rights can never be above the economic structure of society and the cultural development prevailing.[23] Now what does this mean? For one thing, it implies that we look below the regime of rights into the realm of political economy and secondly to see the "cultural development contained thereby".[24] His celebrated historical materialist reading of rights is seen in the perspective of looking against the view of seeing legal relations and political forms as "comprehended by themselves" or "on the so-called general development of the human mind", but on the contrary, to read them as being tied within the concrete context of the "material conditions of life", which is the master text of civil society: and thus to do an anatomy of this civil society in the laboratory of political economy.[25] Marx says that rights originate or are literally rooted (*wurzeln*) in the soil of political economy.[26] Marx thus claims that he has a found a radically new text to understand rights: the discipline called the critique of political economy. And it is in this radically different text—the text as the *differend*—whereby one contextualizes rights.

In this radical difference, the human essence would be able to speak with its own tongue. Hitherto the language that humanity spoke was considered as slippages. Humanity has tried speaking something, and quite something else—a contrary—emerged. Two sites of these slippages come up: the political language of authoritarianism (which includes classical feudal monarchies that were overthrown by the bourgeois revolutions, as also contemporary right-wing dictatorships that grew from the inspirations from the fascist movements of the 1920s and 1930s, caste movements, apartheid and the Stalinist dictatorships. What they have in common is that they usurp the autonomy and the rights of the individual and transfigure them into state power). The second site of slippage is that of the politics of liberalism. Now taking both these in the background we attempt to understand them in the historical materialist critique of political economy. The question posed is: what language ought the human essence speak?

And how does this human essence destabilize the politics of the authoritarian personality? How does liberalism unleash the myth of surplus rights just as it unleashes its economic surpluses on the entire globe? How does one intervene in the speech-acts of Western democracies which insist on global parliamentary democracies and highlight 'human rights' violation, especially in the Third and Fourth World nations of South America, Asia, Africa and the East European nations? What strange game does liberalism play: being allegedly liberal at home and despotic abroad? Why does liberalism talk of human rights in the abstract and never of the rights of the proletarian masses, and very feebly about the rights of women and minorities? How does liberalism splinter the regimes of liberty, equality and fraternity, such that if there is freedom there can be no equality, and if there is equality there is no freedom, and that if there are the rights of 'man', then the rights of the citizen are repressed? Why is it that 'man' and the citizen, the egoistical individual and the collective being, are in hostile opposition?

Now what Marxism claims is that the problem lies not only with liberalism but also with the narcissistic capitalist mode of production. The ideological superstructure is the speech-act of the repressed unconscious. In this case, both the authoritarian denial of rights as well as the liberal affirmation of rights find themselves in the realm of the superstructural unconscious. Liberalism says the opposite of what it represses. Why is it so? Because it is tied with two illiberal forces: private property and estrangement.

And if, Marx said, that the base of the history of class societies is private property, he meant and explicitly said that behind private property lies the hellhole of human alienation with the estranged mind attached to it. When Marx talked of an ideological superstructure being determined by an economic base, he did not mean that the superstructure is to be taken in value neutral form, but one has to see the estranged and uncanny character of this 'mind'. The 'mind' is a terrible psychotic mind that is deeply embodied in the body of class histories. This time, the organic metaphor of society is much more archaic and violent than the subaltern depiction of the *pursa sukta* metaphor. But then, as pointed out: there is no going back into history.

So Marx, it seems, claims that one ought to engage the question of rights in the culture of class histories, which are themselves determined by human estrangement. Marx says, stop looking through the estranged superstructural gaze, especially understanding human rights as a legalized fetish. In the language of classical Marxism one may say, stop looking through the discourses of autonomy, stop looking through the eyes of the superstructure, instead engage the base itself or else the problem becomes spectral-ideological.

To rethink in terms of real possibilities one needs to go into this uncanny base of class civilizations. Lacan's Real, Imaginary and Symbolic are redrafted into Marx's *Capital*. The concluding moments on the rethinking of human rights and the constant slippages are thought out in this Lacanian triad read now in Marx's *Capital*. Now for Marx it is not merely the case that because one sits in the towers of the juridical superstructure one cannot see what remains at the ground level. Marx says that at the very ground level, existence "as a material thing" is ideologically castrated and blinded.[27] The blinding of the sensuous-material conditions (*sinnlichen Beschaffenheiten*)[28] returns again. We are simply refusing to see these *sinnlichen Beschaffenheiten*. This central site is the site where the Real, Imaginary and the Symbolic fuse and confuse. What pertains to us here: the subject of human rights lies on this site of fusion and confusion. To understand this let us move into the domains of the Real, Imaginary and the Symbolic in *Capital*.

So when Marx said look at the base of the juridical superstructure, he finds that the base is not some rational economy, but an irrationality (like a religious hallucination) where the dominant aspect of reality becomes the invisible, imaginary and ideal fetish.[29] This disembodied and schizophrenic character of class civilizations is because the world of reality is the world of accumulated dead labour—the accumulation of death itself. And if Marx says that he has seen the core structure that can be explained in one or two words, he says that the base of everything is nothingness—*gespenstige Gegeständlichkeit*[30]—ghostly or phantomatic reality, the world that has no 'stuff' at all. For in the world that has no stuff, a psychotic world, there can be no humanity. To mention human rights is thus a fallacy.

We thus bid adieu to the transcendent, transmigrated and metempsychotic worlds of magic and necromancy. Modernity as capitalist modernity is nothing but the return of the primeval sacrifice and the death of humanity. It is here that the last rites of humanity are performed. And from these last rites, and the last ashes emerges not the death of 'man', but real humanity. When Marx performed the anatomy of civil society he found the bourgeois and the death wish. But besides the bourgeois, Marx saw also the proletariat and its will to live and revolt. It is in this discourse of the critique of political economy, the death wish and the primeval sacrifice that Marx wished to constitute his reading of the regime of rights.

The Death of God and Capitalism

So what is to be done? How should one constitute an authentic discourse of human rights? How should one operate at a base level such that uprooting class societies lock, stock and barrel solves the problem once and for all?

Let us then go to "the real ground of history".[31] Let us abolish classes and thus abolish the cell form of these classes—commodity production from which grows money, capital and class domination. Let us then abolish commodity production and the state which is nothing but the managing committee of commodities. As commodities and the state are forms of estrangement and perpetuators of terror, let us wage a just war on these terrorist institutions. So let us realize that capital accumulation is the ground from which grows the horrible tree of wars and starvation. Once this tree is removed, there shall be neither temptations nor the monopolist to create war on humanity.

In removing this tree, let us also remove all known human estrangements. Let us remove all barriers. Let us then transcend national boundaries and the entire violent discourse of nationalism. Let us go to all occupied territories and smash all rusty iron curtains. Let us remove all veils and let us look at ourselves not with shame but with pride. Or let us have shame, for shame can be nothing but another kind of revolution.[32] Let us not be angels but humans. Let us remain on this real ground of history and breathe its fresh air than being caught in the polluted fog of the phantasmagoria. Just shake this real ground and 'man' and 'woman' who have fallen (or condemned to the 'fall') will rise again. Rise up humanity, this is your inalienable human right.

The sacrifice has at last ended. Satan can at last smile and God (along with all the spectres of anti-humanism) will retreat into the collective imagination of human pre-history.

And just ponder: what if God himself is Satan? Thus Marx laughed and along with him laughed the whole world.

REFERENCES

1. Karl Marx and Friedrich Engels, *The German Ideology* (Moscow: Progress Publishers, 1976), pp. 34-6.
2. Ibid, p. 34.
3. Karl Marx, *Capital*, Vol. I, p. 172.
4. Wilhelm Reich, *The Mass Psychology of Fascism*, trans. Vincent R. Carfagno (New York: Farrar, Straus & Giroux, 1971).
5. Karl Marx, *Capital*, Vol. I (Moscow: Progress Publishers, 1984), p. 19.
6. Karl Marx and Friedrich Engels, 'The Manifesto of the Communist Party' in *Marx. Engels. Selected Works*, p. 48.
7. Karl Marx, *Capital*, Vol. I, p. 20.
8. Karl Marx, 'The Eighteenth Brumaire of Louis Bonaparte' in *Marx. Engels. Selected Works*, p. 96.
9. Sigmund Freud, 'Neurosis and Psychosis' and 'Loss Of Reality in Neurosis and Psychosis' in *On Psycho-pathology. The Penguin Freud Library* (London: Penguin, 1993), pp. 215, 218, 221, 226. .
10. Lenin, *Collected Works*, Vol. 38, *Philosophical Notebooks* (Moscow: Progress Publishers, 1980), pp. 358-360.
11. Karl Marx, 'Revolution in China and Europe' in *Karl Marx. Friedrich Engels. Collected Works*, Vol. 12, *1853-1854* (Moscow: Progress Publishers, 1975), p. 99.
12. Karl Marx, 'Critique of the Gotha Programme', p. 320.
13. Ibid.

14. Walter Benjamin, 'Theses on the Philosophy of History', in *Illuminations,* trans. Harry Zohn (Glasgow: Fontana / Collins, 1979), pp. 259-60
15. Karl Marx, *Capital*, Vol. I, pp. 667-8.
16. Slavoj Žižek, *The Fragile Absolute, —or, why is the Christian legacy worth fighting for?* (London, New York: Verso, 2000).
17. M.S. Golwalkar, *We, or Our Nation Defined* (Nagpur, 1947).
18. Riza Davari-Ardakani, *Inqilab-i Islami va Vaz'-I Kununi 'Alam* [*The Islamic Revolution and the Current Conditions of the World*] (Tehran: Markaz-e Farhangi-I 'Alame Tabatabai, 1982), Quoted in Farzin Vahadat, 'Post-revolutionary Islamic Discourses on Modernity in Iran: Expansion and Contraction of Human Subjectivity', in *International Journal of Middle East Studies,* Vol. 35, Nov. 2003, No. 4, pp. 605, 610.
19. Riza Davari-Ardakani, *Falsafih Chist?* [*What is Philosophy?*] (Tehran: Anjuman-i Islami-i Hikmat va Falsafih-i Iran, 1980), quoted in Farzin Vahadat, ibid, p. 607.
20. Karl Marx, 'To Ludwig Feuerbach in Bruckberg, Paris, August, 1844', in *Marx. Engels. Collected Works,* Vol. 3 (Moscow: Progress Publishers, 1975), p. 354.
21. Karl Marx, *Economic and Philosophic Manuscripts of 1844* (Moscow: Progress Publishers, 1982), p. 140.
22. G.W.F. Hegel, *The Phenomenology of Mind,* trans. J.B. Baille (London: George Allen & Unwin Ltd., 1966), p. 75.
23. Karl Marx. 'Critique of the Gotha Programme', in *Marx. Engels. Selected Works*, p. 320.
24. Ibid.
25. Karl Marx, 'Preface', *A Contribution to the Critique of Political Economy* (Moscow: Progress Publishers, 1977), p. 21.
26. Ibid.
27. Karl Marx, *Capital*, Vol. I, p. 45.
28. Karl Marx, *Das Kapital,* Erster Band, (Berlin: Dietz Verlag, 1981), p. 52.
29. Karl Marx, *Capital*, Vol. I, pp. 98-9.
30. Karl Marx, *Das Kapital,* Erster Band, p. 52.
31. Karl Marx and Friedrich Engels, *The German Ideology* (Moscow: Progress Publishers, 1976), p. 61.
32. Karl Marx, 'To Arnold Ruge, March 1843', in *Marx. Engels. Collected Works*, Vol. 3 (Moscow: Progress Publishers, 1975), p. 133.

Index